A Voice UnDefeated

COLLIN RAYE

A Voice UnDefeated

With a Foreword by Governor Mike Huckabee

IGNATIUS PRESS   SAN FRANCISCO

Cover photograph **[to come]**

Cover design by Enrique Aguilar

© 2014 by Ignatius Press, San Francisco
All rights reserved
ISBN 978-1-58617-817-8
Library of Congress Control Number 2013950844
Printed in the United States of America ∞

To our precious little child in heaven, Haley,
who knows Jesus Christ face-to-face.
May her constant intercession help us get to where she is.

Contents

Foreword

In January of 2012 I was privileged to be a speaker on the same stage with Collin Raye at the March for Life in our nation's capital, and I was reminded of the first time I met him. It was in the mid-nineties, when I was governor of Arkansas, and I got to play with him a number of times at the Collinfest, which takes place in his hometown of De Queen every summer. This illustrious son of Arkansas has a whole music festival named after him, an honor accorded to few musicians (and to even fewer governors)! I couldn't help but be impressed by the enthusiasm with which Collin performed on stage: his energy was boundless, and his voice was pure. I had loved his music since I first heard his incomparable "Love, Me" hit the charts in the early nineties; yet seeing him perform *in person* was a true gift.

Generally when we look at a star like Collin, we see a life lived under the lights: an outwardly perfect and shining personality that has taken years to cultivate; yet the polished image of the performer on stage is actually just an outline of the real person who lives most of his life behind the curtain. That private person has a history and a whole realm of "real life" stories and circumstances that have contributed to making him the star that he is. These reveal the fuller picture of the man with all the limitations, heartaches, and sufferings that each of us struggles with daily—and maybe even a few more. I can certainly attest to the fact that public life has its own set of difficulties, which men who live purely private lives are spared. Collin's autobiography, *A Voice Undefeated*, offers us a fuller picture of a true American artist.

Because I am a musician, I particularly enjoyed reading an insider's view of what went into the making of his albums during his time in Nashville, but the number of hardships that Collin has had to overcome to get where he is today was a total revelation to me. Of particular note are the extraordinary—actually calamitous—health incidents that have afflicted members of his family through the years: from watching both his brother and his son languish in hospitals after terrible car accidents; to keeping vigil at the bedside of his comatose wife who almost died during childbirth; to the death of his nine-year-old granddaughter, Haley, in 2010 from a neurological disease that even the best minds in the medical field could not figure out. In between those two incidents, the tale of countless, perhaps thousands of, hours he spent looking after his loved ones in hospitals is nothing short of amazing. I won't spoil the story for you by giving too much detail here, but suffice it to say that Collin has often picked himself (and his family) up from catastrophe while continuing to walk forward on the journey of life to the place of peace and wholeness where he stands today. Lesser men would have crumbled in the face of it all and given up, but Collin has met all the challenges with great honesty and, above all, with faith.

There is a "river of grace", as he calls it, that has flowed through his life from the beginning. That, undoubtedly, is the real story that Collin wants to tell. His perception of God's guiding hand throughout his life is the foundation of any success he has had, and he very appropriately gives credit for his successes to the One who gave him his talents and sustained him through all his trials. The story is not just pious history, though; Collin is not shy about recounting his faults and owning up to the way they have contributed to some of his own defeats. Yet this personal honesty has a way of playing the true Light of his life, Jesus Christ, against the darkness of the human condition and of humanizing the life of a star who many think can do no wrong. His story is at times heartrending and at other times heartwarming, but it is essentially a witness to how the goodness of God can work miracles in anyone's life, especially for those who are humble enough to accept correction and guidance from a loving Father in heaven.

I am blessed to call Collin Raye my friend and to have accompanied him, for a few steps anyway, on his family's difficult journey in the last few years with the decline and loss of his beautiful granddaughter. Collin is a man who has known both the heights of popularity and the depths of suffering, and to this day I marvel at his resolve to continue fighting the good fight and performing for the good of others. He is a self-made man with no sense of entitlement; he is a man of faith and optimism despite many crushing defeats; he has always given the world wholesome things (such as his music) and has never hesitated to stand behind the most important causes, such as the rights of the handicapped and the unborn.

Collin's autobiography is well named after his hit "Undefeated", and I imagine that his many devoted fans will find it to be a treasury of information about a fascinating man who has already captured their hearts with his music and charisma. I am also sure that his story will be a burst of inspiration to many thousands more who will read it looking for some measure of encouragement from a public figure who has never let them down—and who, by God's grace, never will.

Mike Huckabee
Former Governor of the State of Arkansas
April 3, 2013

Introduction

May angels lead you into paradise; may the martyrs come to welcome you and take you to the holy city, the new and eternal Jerusalem. May choirs of angels welcome you and lead you to the bosom of Abraham; and where Lazarus is poor no longer may you have eternal rest.

—Funeral Prayer

The stirring and poetic words that end every Catholic funeral are always so consoling, and I truly needed the prayer of the Church on the day we laid to rest my nine-year-old granddaughter. The grief I had felt at Haley's death was indescribable, and now we had arrived at the final good-bye.

After Deacon Lee Davis had finished the closing prayer, those who could not join us at the cemetery for the burial paid their final respects there at the funeral home. I remained standing in the front, and Haley's mother, my daughter, Britanny, stayed seated with Haley's younger sister, Mattie, while the guests followed the customary ritual of filing by the casket. Some knelt at the prie-dieu, some stood, before coming over to wish us their best. The meeting and greeting was difficult, but it was over quickly. The well-wishers finished their condolences and slowly filed out of the room, milling about the reception area and talking in the whispered tones appropriate to a funeral parlor until all their conversations had run their course. The sound of their voices gradually dissipated as they left one by one.

Britanny and I hovered around the open casket, dismayed by the thought that soon we would be unable to see Haley's precious body again. We knew by faith—without the slightest doubt at all—that her soul was with God, but we were still attached to the little body that represented the baby girl we loved so very much.

When Britanny and Mattie were ushered to the car that was waiting to take us to the cemetery, I stayed behind, near the casket, unwilling to let Haley go. I kissed her again, once, twice, three times and stroked her hair,

which had been braided so carefully and lovingly the day before. Her innocent body lay in the beautiful white casket with gold trim and gold handles
that was half the size of an adult's. The funeral home had done a good job
of making her lovely face look as lifelike as possible while covering the
signs of the horrible suffering she had heroically endured for more than
five years. At that point, however, I really wasn't thinking about how she
looked; my immediate concern was that, once they closed the casket, I
would never see her again.

In the solitude of that last moment with her, the funeral director looked
at me with sympathy and sensed my deep anguish over the departure. After
delaying as long as he could, he leaned over to me and gently whispered,
"Are you ready for me to close it?"

I kissed Haley's precious little head again, and as I had done a few days
before in the hospital, when it was clear that she was no longer coming
back to us, I gathered all the willpower that was in me, stood up, turned
on my heel, and said with the deepest sorrow I have ever felt in my heart,
"Yes, go ahead and close it." At that point I was beyond crying.

The funeral-home men did their work quickly and professionally.
Watching them secure the bolts tightly, one by one, at the four corners of
the casket, I knew that a big part of me would go into that casket when it
was finally sealed. I realized that my family and I would never see our baby
again in this life. It was like looking at the great Continental Divide from
above: one era of our lives came to an abrupt end with the closing of the
lid, and another era began with a river of grace flowing out of the casket.

1

A Constant Hand on the Back of My Neck

One Man's Struggle for Integrity

(1960–1972)

You then, my son, be strong in the grace that is in Christ Jesus....
Take your share of suffering as a good soldier of Christ Jesus.

—2 Tim 2:1, 3

To me, the most inspirational character in modern American literature is Atticus Finch, the upright small-town Southern lawyer in *To Kill a Mockingbird*—my favorite novel of all time. Author Harper Lee won a Pulitzer Prize for her effort, and I still find it hard to believe that it was the only novel she ever wrote. Her story of one man's struggle against society in the face of the severe moral challenges of his times has helped to form my character and my view of the world from the age of twelve, when I first discovered the book, until today. It is a quintessentially American story about the power of enduring values over human weakness and wickedness.

At the core of Atticus' appeal is the way he models the struggle for manly integrity. He lived and practiced law in a society marred by poverty, prejudice, and hatred, largely like the one in which I was raised, and brought to it the nobility of a man willing to act according to his ideals in the face of public opposition. Atticus was protector, teacher, and moral compass for his two children; he was their steadfast Rock of Gibraltar when it came to the deep questions of life. His moral discipline and unusual habits seemed a regular source of embarrassment to his children until they discovered, in his defense of a black man falsely accused of a crime, that there was much more to their Daddy than met the eye.

My Story

In the example of Atticus, I have come to see that integrity is not an abstract concept; it's a way of life. The wholeness that results when we say and do what we know is true and right requires the constant struggle to be honest about ourselves and the world. It requires overcoming the common human tendencies to view our circumstances as things that happen *to us,* rather than—far more accurately—as the sum of our own decisions, and to gloss over our personal responsibility for the pain we have caused ourselves or others.

It is my sincere hope that in the process of telling this tale—from the outside looking in on my own life—I will see clearly and be able to distinguish between the situations that I should own up to and those very few unforeseen meteors, both blessed and devastating, that crashed into my space and my time along the journey. I wish to describe candidly the things and people I have loved, as well as both the vain and the meaningful pursuits of a life of musical performance, one that has been very much in the public eye. I also wish to share a few meteor stories, which may be of value to others who are grasping for hope in the aftermath of their own tragedies, because I believe that people learn more from the struggle to overcome failings and weaknesses than from tales of glorious triumphs. Perhaps the lessons from my own failures may inspire others to live a better life.

My story is one of confession, accountability; denial; triumph; tragedy; great love and great loss; indescribable joy and heart-dissolving pain; total stubborn, vain autonomy and absolute dependence; massive self-confidence and biblical-level humility. The struggle for integrity is not a momentary event but a lifelong process, and it is a project that I am still working on "with fear and trembling" (Phil 2:12), as the Good Book says.

A Constant Hand

The image that best describes my own struggle for integrity is what I call God's "constant hand on the back of my neck". I have plainly *felt* God's constant guidance in my life from my earliest days. His guiding hand is a discernible experience of His love for me, which has manifested itself at certain distinct points in my life both for protection and for encouragement.

The experience is like that of a boy standing with his dad on the sidelines of a baseball game, itching to play. His father has his strong arm around the boy's shoulders and discerns when to keep a firm grip on the boy's neck to keep him on the sidelines and when to give him an affectionate pat on the back and send him into the game. The boy may not appreciate the full significance of his dad's embrace, but when he has a son of his own, he will understand it in a new way.

God has been that loving Father to me: tender protector, guide, and consoler. As I take the time to glance back at my life, I see even more clearly the evidence of His guiding hand on my neck, both saving me from myself and guiding me to where I would most be able to serve Him.

Faith and Family

My father, Floyd Crockett Wray, was named after the Alamo hero Davy Crockett. My exact genealogical connection to the frontier legend was never totally clear to me, but I was always told that Daddy's great-grandmother Flora Crockett was some distant cousin to him, which would make me his second cousin thrice removed—or something like that. Family trees passed down in oral tradition tend to fray at the outer limbs a little, and there is plenty of oral tradition in families from Arkansas. For bragging purposes, however, it has always been enough just to assert that I am a descendant of Davy Crockett—and I can prove it in a fight if I need to.

The story of my parents' meeting and marriage is perhaps a typical saga of the Deep South in the 1950s. Daddy was a handsome young Korean War vet who never fought in the Far East but had fixed military vehicles in Alaska during the conflict. That is certainly where he got his training as a mechanic, which was his lifelong profession. He was dashing and polite and wore his hair in the slicked-back Elvis style, as so many young men did in those days.

One day Floyd Crockett walked into the Hobnob Diner in De Queen, Arkansas, and met a pretty waitress named Lois Chandler, my Mama. Apparently, with a few more visits to the diner, he completely swept her off her feet. In the late fifties, an ex-soldier with a car, a Christian upbringing, good manners, and some interesting tales about the wilds of Alaska must have been a real attraction to a young lady looking to escape the crushing boredom of small-town life. As soon as she showed an interest in him, he wasted no time in formalizing the arrangement.

In bringing this relationship to its proper conclusion, Daddy did everything right according to Southern rules of etiquette. He made the obligatory trip to Mama's house to meet with her father, who was known affectionately by the family as Big Daddy. He was big in every way, standing an intimidating six foot four with a sometimes ornery disposition to go with his large frame. He had also been a deputy sheriff in the local law-enforcement unit, and some said he reminded them of John Wayne. Mama's mother was, of course, Big Mama, but that title wasn't considered a slight to a proper Southern woman.

During the course of his conversation with Big Daddy, my father formally asked him for the hand of his daughter. The Chandlers had nine children, four of them girls, and Lois was the youngest. Big Daddy had already practiced this routine a few times, and he didn't let just anyone into the family. If Big Daddy had a good feeling about the man, he would let him marry his daughter, but if not, there was no further discussion. A Southern family was not a democracy, and everyone respected that. In my father's case, Big Daddy liked the young man's smart looks and good manners and gave him the thumbs up.

Floyd and Lois married soon thereafter in the local Baptist church and stayed in De Queen, Arkansas, for a couple of years to be close to Mama's family. My brother, Scotty, was born the following year, 1957, and then came their little Floyd—namely, me—their second, and last, child; I sang my very first song on August 22, 1960, in the old De Queen General Hospital.

Although my immediate family would not live permanently in De Queen, it remained the place where much of the extended family lived and where the roots of the family tree were set down deeply in that Southern soil. In 1992, after I reached a certain level of popularity in the music business, the local community established the Collinfest, an annual summertime country music festival, as a tribute to me, their local boy who made it to the big time, and I am deeply flattered by this great honor from my little hometown.

My first memories of childhood are of growing up in a trailer in El Dorado, Arkansas, with my older brother, Mama and Daddy, and a German shepherd puppy named Butch. These early years were happy ones but not without their trials. I had a seizure at about the age of four, and my parents rushed me to the hospital, afraid that I might die. The only thing I remember about the episode is my mother dousing me with cold water and telling me that I would be okay, even though she wasn't so convinced of it at the time. Thank God I never had another seizure. In fact, I have never spent another day sick in the hospital—other than a few ER trips as a kid for strep throat—but in future years I would spend literally thousands of hours in hospitals with others.

My Christian faith began with my mother. She was very fervent in the practice of her religion, even though we shifted from one Baptist church to another, mostly because of our many moves. Mama was always the one who insisted on our going to church as a family, but even if Daddy didn't go, she took me and my brother with her. We didn't go to Sunday school very often, but Mama read the Bible to us and familiarized us with some of the stories and simple beliefs that come from the written Word of God. In typical evangelical fashion she emphasized that my salvation depended upon my having a personal relationship with Jesus Christ. She gave me the basis of my spirituality and my sensitivity toward the things of God. Mama had a profound understanding of her own vocation as a Christian mother, which didn't stop at the physical well-being of her kids but included their souls as well.

Fatherlessness

My father was present in my life until I was about eleven years old, and then he largely left the job of raising and nurturing me and brother to Mama. Even in the years before my parents divorced, Daddy seemed emotionally distant, although in fairness, I believe he did try his best to be a good father and did leave some positive tokens of fatherhood in my life. He was always sweet and good-hearted toward his fellow man—a trait I hope I inherited along with his looks and stature—but he was quiet. He tried to be a good father to me and my brother; he taught us to play baseball and encouraged our musical tendencies. And I recall how safe I felt when he was at home with us. But Daddy was reclusive by nature, and in time he withdrew from society and lived like a hermit. First his emotional and then his physical absence created a vacuum of self-doubt within me, but I believe that God filled that vacuum with enough confidence and drive to help me get by in life.

I do not blame my dad for being an imperfect man or father because no one has a perfect scorecard in parenting. Also, God's grace working in my heart has transformed the wound caused by Daddy's remoteness and absence into a deep desire to be lovingly present to my own kids. God's grace can bring incredible goodness out of suffering because, as we know, "with God, nothing will be impossible" (Lk 1:37).

The Marvelous Mystery of Mama

I can't think of anyone who has had a greater impact on my life than my Mama. I credit her for my parenting skills because she was the best of moms and the best of teachers in all areas of parenting. She had the innate skills for the role of motherhood, but she never took her kids or her maternal role for granted. When she married Daddy, she was not even twenty, and I remember that she always tried to be the perfect wife and the perfect mother.

Mama grew up in poverty in the cotton-growing area of Oklahoma called the Dust Bowl, but she never thought of herself as poor. From her upbringing she learned to be industrious, frugal, creative, and loving, and she put all those talents to good use in raising her own kids. Yet, as the youngest girl of a large family struggling to get by, she probably didn't get all the attention she needed. I believe some of the problems she exhibited later in life were rooted in those unmet emotional needs of her childhood: Big Daddy and Big Mama worked hard day after day just to keep food on the table, and I suspect their emotional reserves were scarce by the time my mother came along.

Little Lois discovered that Big Mama would make time for her if she was under the weather or had something wrong with her, and she developed a pattern of hypochondria that has caused a slow decline in her actual health through the years. As a child, I couldn't appreciate the significance of the number of pills she regularly took or the number of doctor's appointments she made. I just figured that was how Mama took care of herself. Later, however, I increasingly worried that some of her ailments were self-diagnosed. When I was twelve, I went with her to see a doctor in Dallas who told her frankly that she had nothing wrong with her and only wanted to believe that she did. The whole drive home she railed against the doctor's ignorance.

Now in her mid-seventies, Mama lives in a full-care facility in Texas. Although her physical needs are well taken care of, she scarcely recognizes anyone in the family but her own children. She who used to be able to talk the wheels off a wagon finds it hard to articulate her thoughts and is growing silent. I suspect that years of overmedication for real or perceived ailments have taken their toll and have either caused her dementia or accelerated its progress. It is heartbreaking to see the mother I love so much decline to the state she is in today, but I find comfort in knowing that she is in God's hands.

Singing for the Lord (and Elvis)

Mama was and still is a very beautiful woman. That is not a devoted son's pious description; everyone thought she was beautiful—even Elvis Presley. Mama would often tell the story of her "fifteen minutes of fame" singing with Elvis in the late fifties when she was seventeen. Sun Records did a concert tour through the Arklatex area—the border region between Arkansas, Oklahoma, Louisiana, and Texas—with some of the most famous artists of the day, including Elvis, who had sprung onto the pop-music scene overnight. Some other heavy hitters were on the bill too, such as Johnny Cash, Jerry Lee Lewis, and Carl Perkins; they performed five or six shows at this epic ten-day event in our humble corner of the world. It was an unbelievable billing that we would pay huge prices to see if they were performing today. The musicians in those days performed on raw talent and energy with no frills, and people loved them.

Mama and her sister Becky were booked as the opening act for every day of the series because they were local celebrities: pretty girls with pretty voices who were often asked to sing at church or town events. Big Daddy was proud to share his daughters' talents with the folks and would never let them take any money for their performances because he wanted them to "do it for the Lord". I doubt he would ever have let them attend concerts like these as spectators. When he gave his daughters permission to open the shows, he gave them a strict warning: "I'm gonna let you go," he told them, "but you stay away from that Elvis. *He's dangerous.*" Many people at the time were scared of this newcomer with the gyrating hips. He was a threat to morals. Imagine what Big Daddy would think of Marilyn Manson or Lady Gaga.

Elvis was undoubtedly the main attraction of the concerts. He drove up to the venue with his band in the back of a brand-new Cadillac convertible. All the other stars, even Cash and Lewis, were lumped together in a couple of Caddies that followed. Mama and her sister, of course, were totally enamored of Elvis, as were all young women at the time. As luck would have it, on about the third day, Elvis invited them to sing with him during his set. He personally helped Mama and Becky onto the flatbed truck— which functioned as a stage—and they sang *ooh*s and *aah*s behind him for the whole performance. It was as close to heavenly glory as a girl could get in this world.

Big Daddy experienced an Elvis conversion when he went to one of the shows. Because his daughters sang on stage, he had a chance to meet the King in person after the concert. Elvis was extremely polite, as was his custom, and shook Big Daddy's hand with a firm grip and said, "Yessir, I am so pleased to meet you, sir", "You sure do have such nice and pretty daughters, sir", et cetera. It was a total and professional schmooze job. Mama never had to prove her reputation for beauty after that—she had it from the highest authority. Big Daddy felt the glory too, and after that he began to sing a different tune: "That Elvis Presley's okay in my book."

Mama's one performance with Elvis became the stuff of an oft-repeated and ever-expanding country legend. I'm sure my brother and I heard Mama retell the story of her brief encounter with Elvis to unsuspecting listeners at least a thousand times. With each retelling, the brief encounter would expand until it ultimately became an intimate get-together with her personal friend Elvis. Mama would add gratuitous and manufactured annotations to the story, such as, "Y' know, that Priscilla never did understand Elvis." Shaking her head and looking down as she said it, she would add somberly, "So sad." She would forget that we had heard the story already and could spot the embellishments a mile away. When we would ask her how she could possibly know a certain thing, she would say it was a fact, and that was that. End of story. Scotty and I eventually gave up trying to hold her accountable for the real facts because the story *as she imagined it* seemed to make her happier. We only regret that no one ever took a picture of her fifteen minutes of fame with Elvis. If someone had, the entire state of Arkansas would have seen it.

The Rigors of Marriage

At the beginning of their marriage, Mama and Daddy were happy together, and my early childhood years were relatively free of troubles. The one complaint Mama had about Daddy, however, was that he was a "malcontent". Daddy's abilities as a mechanic made him easily employable anywhere, but the downside to this was that if he didn't like his boss or if something went wrong at the shop or if he simply grew restless, he would quit his job on the spot and go find another one in another town or even another state. Daddy changed jobs frequently, to the utter disruption of our family life.

We were like a seminomadic family, moving from De Queen to El Dorado and then to Magnolia, Arkansas; then back to De Queen for a while; then on to Texarkana, Texas, and a couple of other places before moving to Oregon for four years. Then we moved back to Arkansas. Throughout all of this moving around, Mama was the source of stability for me and my brother; she was always there, predictable and dependable, whenever we needed her. As time went on, however, the constant uprooting, resettling, and uprooting again became increasingly stressful for Mama.

After my parents divorced, Mama was forced to get a job to support us. I look back on those years with awe at what Mama was able to accomplish as a single parent raising two boys. At one point in her mid-thirties, she was working nonstop to make ends meet: she had a full-time day job driving an escort car for wide-load trucks, a second job as a trainer at a health spa, and a third job singing three to five nights a week at a local nightclub. She must have slept only an hour or two every night, but somehow she was there every morning to fix us breakfast and get us off to school. She kept up this routine for years. To this day I have no idea how one person could physically manage that kind of schedule, but she did it for her kids. Daddy gave her very little financial help in those years, and the consequences of his lack of support dawned on me the first time I saw Mama pay for groceries with food stamps. I was shocked by the realization that we were actually *poor*. The humble sacrifice that Mama was making for us with so little support made an impression I would never forget.

Little Bubba's New Uniform

My family and friends called me Bubba or Bubby, as was the custom in the South when a boy was a little brother. I never used the name Floyd for anything at all. A teacher or two may have called me by my given name on the first day of school, but I was always referred to as Bubba by everyone else. Only when I got my record contract with Sony did I change my name to Collin.

Anyone who knows me *now* would never believe that I was terribly shy as a kid and didn't like to be in the spotlight, but there was one moment of special attention that I truly enjoyed. The most wonderful story of my Mama's generosity and affection for her little Bubba had to do with my childhood love of the Dallas Cowboys. I was seven years old and in the second grade at Wake Village Elementary School in Texarkana, Texas, and I told Mama that I wanted a Dallas Cowboys uniform for Christmas. I wanted it in the worst way because Don Meredith, the Cowboys' quarterback at the time, was my hero. I just *had* to have a uniform precisely like his. Back then the only football uniforms that were available to the general public were totally white outfits—pants, jersey, and helmet—with no distinctive markings on them. My dear mother bought the white pieces and transformed them into a classic Dallas Cowboys uniform for me. She dyed the pants silver and somehow put a blue stripe down the sides; she affixed a big blue "Don Meredith" and his number, 17, on the jersey; she then spray-painted the helmet a shiny silver and emblazoned it with a big blue star on each side and a stripe down the middle.

Wearing the uniform to school—shoulder pads and all—was my first experience of celebrity; I became the instant rock star of the second grade. I remember the boys in my class coming up to me and gawking at the uniform, in a kind of reverent awe, wishing their moms had gotten them one too. They touched it all over and popped the shoulder pads affectionately, as boys do. All of a sudden I became the anointed leader of recess and the guy who made all final decisions about who was going to get into the game on the school playing field because I had the uniform.

I was never sure what happened to the jersey and the pants, but that little helmet survived beyond my childhood. When I was in my thirties, I retrieved it from Mama's storage closet and donated it to the Collin Raye Birthplace Museum in De Queen, Arkansas, where it has been on display to this day. During the height of my career, in the nineties, I got the chance to tell "Dandy Don" Meredith the funny story of the uniform through Frank Gifford, and the thought of the innocent love of boys for their sports heroes brought a big smile to his face. Meredith was the first color commentator on Monday Night Football, and in my unbiased opinion, he was the best personality they ever had. Hero worship dies hard, I know.

Music and the Northwest in My Soul

Both sides of my family had musical talent, though my mother's side had more than my father's. Daddy was a bass player, and Mama had a beautiful voice. Mama's brother John was the first member of the family to try to break into music in a more professional capacity. We called him Uncle Dub for the first syllable of the letter *W*, which is his middle initial. He was a good musician who could play several instruments very well. He cut a few independent records that sold modestly well and was always looking to get a major record contract, but he never got his big break. Nevertheless, he was a trendsetter in the family, and his ambitions and example left me with the impression that music could actually become a career.

Uncle Dub was also the direct reason we moved to Portland, Oregon, in 1968, the year I entered third grade. He moved there to pursue a musical career and eventually invited Mama to come and work with him. Knowing Daddy as I do, I'm still amazed that he was open to moving so far away from Arkansas. He must have been itching to make another change at that same time, because he agreed to move the family out to Oregon, where he immediately found a job as a mechanic. Mama began to sing with Uncle Dub in nightclubs on the weekends, and occasionally my dad would join in as the bass player. I enrolled in Joseph Meek Elementary School in Portland, where I completed the third through fifth grades.

Without a doubt, those years in Portland hold the happiest memories of my childhood, not only because our family was still intact at that time, but also because the Northwest is one of the most beautiful areas of our great country. I loved the cooler air, the gorgeous scenery, Mount Hood towering over Portland, the Columbia River Gorge, and the many sports activities that were newly available to me. Probably my best memories of Daddy are of going to Portland Trailblazers basketball games with him and my brother. We got to see some of the pioneers and greats of the game, such as "Pistol" Pete Maravich, Jerry West, Oscar Robertson, and Lew Alcindor before he became Kareem Abdul-Jabbar of the Los Angeles Lakers. Daddy also introduced us to professional wrestling, and the three of us became frequent patrons of Portland Championship Wrestling.

Music was our reason for moving out to Oregon, but as positive as music was for our family, I believe it was also the straw that broke the camel's back in my parents' marriage. Mama had good looks, a lovely smile, and a great singing voice; she was sweet, personable, and friendly. As a result, she received a great deal of attention in the Portland clubs every time she sang. Daddy became a bit paranoid and jealous of Mama, and conflicts between them became more frequent and intense. One night when they were arguing, I heard a bottle of perfume smash against their bedroom wall. For the first time in my life, I distinctly felt tension in our home, and it scared me. The conflicts continued, and when Daddy decided to move out, I was relieved. The fighting stopped, and there was peace again.

During the breakdown of my parents' marriage, I developed, by temperament or necessity, an emotional defense mechanism of detaching myself from the conflict around me. I began viewing my family members as if I were an outside observer taking notes rather than a participant who was directly affected by them. There may have been a better coping mechanism, but it was how I dealt with the situation in my childhood. All that mattered for me was that Mama was there.

My parents formally separated and then made efforts to reconcile. In 1972 they got back together one last time, and when they did, Daddy's first decision was to move the family back to Arkansas. Returning to the South was a massive culture shock for me. I loved my school, my team, and many other things about Oregon, but all that enthusiasm was short-circuited by Daddy's decision. Sadly, I never got involved in an organized sport again. Sadder still, the move failed to fix my parents' marriage. A few months later, they separated permanently and then divorced.

Watching and Playing Sports

During those years in Portland, I had discovered my own sports talents. Daddy taught us how to play baseball, and as it turned out, I was pretty good at it. The only year I ever played Little League was the 1971–1972 season in Portland, and I absolutely loved it. I was not much of a runner, but I hit extremely well and played a mean first base.

Batting was my real strong point. I could hit the ball so well that I was considered a threat to our opponents. Teams would often try to walk me so that I couldn't get hits against them. I had a .500 batting average, which was remarkable for Little League. When our team went to the finals, the opposing pitcher kept pitching the ball away from the plate to walk me. Old Coach Anderson took me aside and said, "Now, Bubba, they're gonna throw 'em high and outside, so you just step over the plate and hit it. They won't be expecting it."

"Really? I can do that?" I asked. That was a new concept to me as a ten-year-old, but it was fun and exciting to think that I could outsmart the opposition and have the coach back me up. His call was perfectly on target. On the next pitch, I stepped over the plate and knocked the ball into the outfield for a double that cleared the bases. My hit won the game and made us Little League champs.

I rarely saw Dad laugh with joy, but on that play he was beaming brighter than a lighthouse. I will never forget how good it felt to have done something that made my dad proud of me and made people happy! Perhaps that victory was also a sign of things to come, because my coach, all my teammates, and all their families were overjoyed that I had won the game for us.

In time, I would learn one very important parenting skill from the decision to leave Oregon. I learned to respect the delicate nature of a child's development process, especially as he discovers his own talents. When a child finds joy in doing something, he begins to understand his own self-worth, but he requires a parent to give him time and attention during that process. It was a lesson learned at great cost to me.

Although I missed baseball terribly in Arkansas, there was a silver lining in the loss: without sports as a consuming activity, I was able to engage my interests and talents in another direction—in music—the path that God had chosen for me. It took me a while to appreciate this. Not until later in life, when I read the words of the prophet Isaiah, who said that God's ways are not our ways, nor His thoughts our thoughts (cf. 55:8), did I understand more clearly that God can take a painful disappointment and turn it into a blessing. Often, when we are in the midst of a difficult situation, we don't see its full significance.

Needing a Male Role Model

During one of the periods in Oregon when my parents were separated, my mother dated a man named Ron Newton. To two preadolescent boys, Ron was the definition of cool. He worked at a health spa and was fit, tough, and muscular. He wore those tight turtleneck shirts that were common back in the early seventies and was the picture of a man's man, someone a boy could get excited about. An added benefit was that he was from Texas, near where we grew up. We were glad that Mama liked him, because he fit the need for a male role model in our lives at a time when Daddy was absent. I even remember the three of us taking a vacation with him back to Texas one summer. We spent three or four days driving from Oregon to Texas in his big Cadillac Coupe deVille, and it was on that trip that I saw my first real "man fight".

On some lonely highway in the middle of New Mexico, we began to be harassed by three young men in another car who were pulling up parallel to us and giving us the finger and doing other threatening things. At first Ron stayed cool about it, but eventually he got fed up with them, rolled down his window, and told them to pull their car over. Scotty and I immediately sensed the tension and knew we were going to see some action. Ron drove onto the shoulder, calmly reached into his glove box, and pulled out a .38 snub-nosed revolver. He gave it to my mom and said, "If they get by me, shoot 'em." She was nervous—to say the least—but she had her orders and tried to stay calm. My brother and I ducked behind and then peeked over the front seat to watch what was going to happen. What we saw was better than a movie.

Before the other guys could get fully out of their car, Ron began pounding on them with his fists. He pulled one guy completely out of a window and stomped on him. I was worried because one of the guys was bigger than Ron, but apparently those guys—combined—were never the slightest challenge to Ron's power and skill. He looked like a professional boxer taking on three little kids. I don't think they even landed a punch on him, because in the end the only things bleeding on Ron were his fists. The other guys, in contrast, were bloody messes. The whole incident was frightening, but Ron was so cool about it that he inspired confidence in us.

Ron brought two of the men over to our car and told them to apologize to my mother for their behavior; the third guy couldn't even get off the ground. "Ma'am, we're very sorry for giving you the finger and for our behavior" was all they could say as they pathetically wiped blood off their faces.

Then Ron left them with the lesson of the day: "You boys remember this the next time you try to bother a man and his family who are just minding their own business."

That fight had a huge impact on me. For those young men, the beating was a hard lesson in respect, but for me and Scotty, it was such sweet justice. As a kid, I felt pretty scared when a real live danger presented itself; I was glad that Ron was there acting as a surrogate father when we needed it most. The incident showed me that *real men* defend innocent women and children—even if it means going toe-to-toe with scoundrels.

Scotty: the Prodigy and the Rebel

My brother is two years older than I am and one of the most talented guys I know. We were raised in the same environments and did everything together when we were kids, especially in sports and music, but we couldn't be more different in every way. If music brought us together, worldviews and personalities separated us, sometimes radically. In looks, I favor Daddy and Scotty favors Mama. In temperament, I'm happy-go-lucky and he's intense and brooding. As time went on, I became more conservative politically, while he continued to espouse just about every liberal cause and doctrine. He is nostalgic for the peace and free love, Neil Young and John Lennon culture of the sixties, and I'm only too glad that the sixties are over.

Scotty always wore the problems of Mama and Daddy on his sleeve. I tended to shrug things off and do my own thing, but Scotty used their problems as an excuse to rebel, especially against Daddy, with whom he didn't get along very well. Scotty has the same personality now as he had at age seventeen in Texarkana. His basic temperament hasn't changed much, and he doesn't want to change. I am glad, however, that his destructive anger at the world has abated as he has grown older and that now he is a very funny, big-hearted guy and a lot of fun to be around. I accept him as he is. I didn't always like him, but I've always loved him. I think the nicest thing he has ever said to me was at the time I was successful and was helping him and his family; he looked at me and said, "I'm so proud of you. I'm so proud to be your brother."

Scotty was undoubtedly a music prodigy. I have vivid memories of him picking a guitar, playing Buck Owens/Don Rich solos, at the age of six or seven. He was responsible for my very first musical performance when I was about four years old. I still have a picture of the two of us at the Lions Club in De Queen with our flattop haircuts and button-down shirts. Scotty is standing up front, managing a guitar so big he can hardly hold it. I'm banging on a snare drum behind him. He played and sang the song perfectly, which won him high praise from the locals.

Along with his musical gifts, Scotty had a defiant and self-destructive streak, which nearly got him killed the summer before I entered seventh grade. While Dad and I were watching *The Getaway* at the old De Queen Drive-In, we got a surprise visit from Uncle Ken, my Aunt Becky's husband, who told us that Scotty had been in a terrible car accident. Uncle Franklin, a deputy sheriff in De Queen, drove in front of us the fifty miles to Wadley Hospital in Texarkana at what seemed like a hundred miles an hour. It was a brutal ride and an even more brutal experience.

When we arrived at the emergency room, I had what was to be my first experience of utter tragedy: my brother was lying on a table in the emergency room wearing an oxygen mask and covered with blood. It was a shocking, horrific image that has remained with me all these years. Mama was hysterical, Daddy was distraught, and everyone else was speechless.

After being out all day with friends, Scotty had come home to change clothes before going out again. He and his friends might have been smoking pot, and they were driving a huge old Buick Electra 225, which was as dangerous as a cruise missile in the hands of irresponsible kids. Mama told Scotty that he had to eat dinner before he went out again, but he ignored her and walked outside with a flippant attitude as if to put on a show for his friends. When Mama ran out the door after him, he jumped on the hood of the car, and the girl at the wheel drove off. Mama had a premonition that something bad was going to happen and screamed, "Stop! Stop! Stop!", but my brother was in no state of mind to listen.

Scotty "surfed" on the hood until the driver hit the brakes as a joke and he flew headlong onto the asphalt in front of the car. The girl then panicked, took her foot off the brake, and the car rolled forward on top of him. Making matters worse, the long-bodied Electra was lower to the ground than most cars of its day. Its low floor crushed and mangled Scotty horribly. The girl panicked again and *backed up*, pinning Scotty to the ground with the hot tailpipe touching his flesh, causing third-degree burns in several places. Mama tried in vain to lift the heavy car off him, but there was nothing she could do to help her son. Scotty had to wait almost half an hour in excruciating pain for the rescue squad to arrive. It was a complete nightmare.

When the total damage was assessed, Scotty had a crushed pelvis, several broken ribs, a broken shoulder and elbow, a cracked skull, and a great deal of internal damage. He had several massive third-degree burns on his back, legs, and elbow from the car's exhaust pipe. The fact that he survived the accident was a miracle, as was his almost total recovery. Mama's premonition couldn't have been more accurate; if only he would have listened to her that night.

The accident occurred the summer before I entered the seventh grade. I was only twelve years old, but my "job" for the rest of that summer was to stay with Scotty in the hospital while he recuperated. That proved to be the first of my many vigils at the bedsides of loved ones in hospitals. I responded to my brother's agony by going deep inside myself and detaching myself from the pain and pressures he was experiencing. It was the same instinctive, self-protective reaction I was having toward my parents' marital problems.

Scotty eventually healed well enough to live a normal life, which to us was a life of music. After many years of personal difficulties, he became Miranda Lambert's first band member when she was getting started. In fact, I credit Miranda with saving my brother's life. Her loyalty and strong principles made the difference for him. Scotty's addictions had built up over decades, and at one point, Rick, Miranda's father and manager, wanted to fire him, but Miranda simply refused. She knew there was another way to handle my brother; instead of firing him, she got in his face and straightened him right out. She insisted that he beat his addictions, and he listened to her. May God bless her for giving me back my brother.

The Time I "Got Saved"

Even though my family had not been going to church as regularly as when I was a small boy, after Scotty's accident I "got saved" in a ceremony at a local Baptist church. In typical evangelical fashion, I "accepted Jesus Christ as my Lord and Savior" and was baptized by full immersion. The pastor, whom I don't remember very well, said a few words and then pushed me down into the water, which was warm enough to keep me from being shocked into the Kingdom. Although people were really happy for me, the ceremony was a rather unemotional experience. I did it mostly because Mama wanted me to do it. In God's perfect timing, however, my baptism was probably the exact grace-filled experience I needed to get through the difficulties that had come upon me and my family.

Life is a mix of good and bad, and my twelfth year had a big dose of both. My family moved back to Arkansas, my brother had his accident, and my parents divorced. Yet many good things were in my life too: I had an extended family that loved me, a decent education, the gift of faith, and a lot of music in my life. Music would be the gateway into my future.

2

Music Was My Future

Thank You for the Gift

(1973–1979)

Teach me your way, O LORD, that I may walk in your truth;
unite my heart to fear your name.

—Ps 86:11

If someone would have asked me at age twelve what I wanted to be when I grew up, my first answer would have been Carl Yastrzemski. The Yaz, as he was called, was the Boston Red Sox left fielder and first baseman for twenty-three years and one of the greatest baseball players of all time. When I was going through my baseball phase, my ambition was to be like him. I sometimes wonder what my future would have been like if I had stayed with baseball, but I will never know. I can only say that God's ways are always a whole lot better than ours. Baseball was not the path that God wanted me to take through adolescence and into adulthood; the path He chose for me was music. Each day I thank God for the precious gift of music. Second only to my family and my faith, music has brought such joy and meaning into my life.

Rock 'n' Roll Memories

Even though country music would eventually be my career, rock 'n' roll had a profound impact on my sense of self as I was growing up. I started listening to rock 'n' roll and mainstream pop music on the radio when I was a preteen in Portland in the mid- to late sixties, which means I'm old

19

enough to remember some of the early days and bands of rock music. Rock was so good back then, and I was captivated by this new genre of music.

There were so many great bands. Among my favorites was, of course, the Beatles. I don't honestly remember many specifics about the Beatles in their heyday, but I listened to "Let It Be", "Get Back", and "Hey Jude" on the radio. In the nineties, I recorded a version of "Let It Be" for a *Country Beatles* album with other country artists, and doing so brought back such great memories. In the sixties, the Beatles appeared to be a fixed part of the universe, and I distinctly remember when that universe started to fall apart. The breakup in 1970 of what I thought was the greatest rock band of all time was an epic event that shook my world. Even at that age I found it strange that John Lennon separated from the band under the influence of Eastern religions and his second wife, Yoko Ono. All Beatles fans, it seemed, were confused and grieving over the breakup, but no one could do anything about it except rush out and buy more of their albums in the fear that they would soon be gone. It was my first glimpse of the instability that often haunts the lives and relationships of the very talented people who achieve stardom. I was to see a great deal more of that in the years to come.

Believe it or not, the Partridge Family was a favorite of mine too. (Of course, I was only eleven or twelve then!) I snatched up singles of "I Think I Love You", "Point Me in the Direction of Albuquerque", and "I'll Meet You Halfway" as if they were going to sell out before I could get one. I had the same passion for the smooth voices and style of Crosby, Stills, Nash, and Young. I just loved "Teach Your Children", "Our House", and many of their other classics. The beauty and genius of the Beach Boys I would discover later in my life, but in this period I didn't grasp how cool they were.

In my early to mid-teens, I began to listen to "power" rock 'n' roll and was enthralled by the legendary bands that produced it: the Who, Led Zeppelin, the Rolling Stones, Jethro Tull, Queen, and others. In an era when access to music was becoming more and more immediate, kids were highly, often unduly, influenced by the music of their generation, and I was no different. Since my parents were musicians, my mom tended to be somewhat permissive in letting me and Scotty explore different musical styles, even if my folks didn't always appreciate our distinctive tastes. By that time I had already memorized close to a thousand songs by other artists, many of which I used later in my own concerts.

My absolute favorite band at the time was the Eagles, who were either legendary or notorious, depending upon one's perspective. To me, they were supermen. I loved their harmonies, their intelligent lyrics, and their style. There was an aura of mystery surrounding them that appealed to my teenage soul. I could listen to their albums for hours at a time and never tire of them. Their drummer, chief lead vocalist, and primary lyricist, Don Henley, was well known for his dark and divisive personality, but I judged him only by his musical talent and either ignored or forgave the rest. I couldn't get enough of the Eagles in those years. Their originality and creativity in music influenced me greatly as an artist, so much so that I would consciously attempt to imitate their style when I began to write songs myself. At various points in my musical career, I had the chance to meet three of the original Eagles and to perform on stage with one of them, Randy Meisner. These moments I count as some of the most sublime experiences of my career.

Foghat and Finding My Vocation

The seminal influence on my desire to be a performer, however, did not come from music on the radio or from listening to albums; it came from a direct experience of the very cool blues-rock band Foghat. The band was playing at the Hirsch Memorial Coliseum in Shreveport, Louisiana, about seventy miles from where I lived, and Scotty allowed his pesky little brother to go with him and a few of his friends to this exciting event. We had to travel that far because no bands or star performers bothered coming to our hometown of Texarkana, Texas—an uneventful place with a population too small to make a visit worth their while.

In those days concert venues were less organized and controlled than they are today, and the Hirsch Coliseum had no special reserved seating sections. Their arrangement was called "festival seating"—a euphemism for *standing*—which meant that anyone could get up front if he elbowed and pushed his way through the crowd. Our efforts to squeeze and wend our way through hundreds of admiring fans to get to the front, where we could see the performance in the blazing lights of the stage, symbolize for me what it took to make it to the top in the music business: the passive resistance of people in the crowd, our persistent desire and concerted effort to get to the front, a few creative detours around obstacles, et cetera were all elements of the journey Scotty and I made to fulfill our dreams of performing on the glorious stage.

At the Foghat concert, Scotty and I got our first taste of performance magic, and it truly had a magical effect on us. I was fourteen going on fifteen, he was sixteen, and we were exhilarated at the very idea of seeing a real rock band in person. The concert was literally an all-around electrifying experience of intense volume, overwhelming beat, blazing lights, and the awesome thrill of being somehow connected to those long-haired, bawdy British guys jumping around the stage like madmen. I've forgotten what band opened for Foghat that night, but I will never forget the moment those lights went down and my emotions shot sky-high with the euphoria of being in rock paradise. I was in awe of those men on stage and spent the whole night thinking how cool that whole experience was. I remember saying to myself, "Oh, I want to do this *so bad*!" I was hooked on the idea of being a performer like the Foghat guys. I wanted to be on stage and play like that.

The concert was sort of a vocational experience for me because it defined my understanding of what I would dedicate my life to and profoundly inspired me to pursue it. For the first time in my young life, I felt excited about something to the depths of my being with an emotion that was so positive and so new to me. The Foghat concert had lit a fire of joy, passion, and enthusiasm in my heart and imprinted it with a single desire that I could neither resist nor ignore: to be a performer in a band. I believe it was God's guiding hand that, surprisingly, used a rock band like Foghat to put me on the pathway that could lead me to fulfill my dreams and hopefully do His will.

From that point on, my brother and I were united in a single-minded goal to perform for others, to be creative, to gain a following, and to live in that fascinating world of professional musicians. Nothing else mattered to us. Some dynamic force had penetrated deeply into our souls, discovered a door hidden under layers of rubble, and opened up a passage to a secret treasure chamber below. Very few events in my life have ever led to such complete clarity of purpose as that.

How I Became a Singer

Soon after that concert, I played my very first band gig. I had sung on stage with my mom when I was six or seven, but this experience of playing in a band was an almost spontaneous event that took place in a friend's garage. I had had Daddy's old bass guitar for only three weeks when I got together with my friends Mark Harper and Robin McMillan to play some songs. After one rehearsal we discovered that we had a band. Our impressive repertoire consisted of a total of three songs: the Chuck Berry rock classic "Johnny B. Goode", Brownsville Station's infamous "Smokin' in the Boy's Room", and the Rolling Stones' "Jumpin' Jack Flash". As I said: impressive. Robin was a year older than I, and he was a cool, handsome, popular kid whose family had a little more money than the rest of us. Mark's parents were pretty cool too, because they were okay with our playing a gig in their garage and inviting all our friends. That gig became the innocent beginning of my singing career when one of the boys asked, "Who's gonna sing?", and I said, "I guess I will." It was all history from there. It's amazing what God can do with a person's yes even when he is not sure about what he is agreeing to do.

That night about forty kids turned out for the concert, including a lot of girls, and we delighted them for three solid hours with the same three songs that we played over and over again. We lacked a sound system, but my mom lent us a microphone, which I plugged into my bass amplifier, and it made my voice sound a little like the squawky adult voices in the Charlie Brown specials. I am sure the music was perfectly hideous, but the audience of adolescents was undemanding, and the whole experience turned out to be a watershed moment for me. It was my first actual rock 'n' roll band and my first chance to experience audience reaction to musical performance.

A Bit Too Much Self-Confidence

The reaction of the girls was what most surprised me. In particular, I was taken aback by Robin's stepsister, Jerita, who was absolutely beautiful. I had always liked Jerita, but she never seemed to notice me—until, of course, I was in a band. At the end of our gig, Jerita bounded up to me enthusiastically and said in her irresistible voice, "Oh, I really like the band! You're so good!" I was smart enough to know that the band was no good at all, but *she* didn't seem to care. Clearly Jerita was paying attention to me precisely because she had seen me rockin'. That night I had my first kiss ever—from Jerita—and among the many things racing through my mind at that time was the thought, "Oh, I'm a rocker! I have found myself! This is good!"

Eighth and ninth grades, the dawn of my teen years, were great years for me. Being in a band, I had to look the part. I grew my hair down to my elbow and became one of the most popular guys at Westlawn Junior High in Texarkana. I guess my peers thought I was cool. What more could a guy ask for? The previous year I was still that shy kid who had moved in from another state, but during these two years I grew in self-awareness and self-confidence. I developed a strong sense that I was my own person.

Frankly, some of my self-confidence was due to my popularity with the girls. I freely dated many girls, including a few of the more popular cheerleaders, and my conduct was not what it should have been. I was a kid without a dad living at home and with too much freedom at a time when morals in general were taking a nosedive all around. The challenges of keeping the Sixth Commandment at a time when promiscuity was rampant among my peers were too much for me, and my morals declined accordingly and predictably. Few people my age had much guidance in the area of sexuality during the so-called sexual revolution. Behavior that was permitted, or even encouraged, for young teens in the seventies would have been taboo for them just a decade earlier and utterly unthinkable in the fifties. I am not evading responsibility for my actions, but only describing the era in which I came of age.

As I entered my ninth-grade year, I met Cathy Huddleston, whom I dated for the whole year—a record for me at that time. My relationship with her was different from those I had had with other girls; this was the first time I felt a real kinship and close friendship with a girl. She was my first love because with her I learned the difference between liking girls and really loving someone.

The Closest I Ever Came to Being a Statistic

At that time race issues in the South were thicker than molasses, and my junior high school was not immune to them. Alex Haley's television series about slavery, *Roots*, ignited race tensions beyond what I had ever experienced before and caused me to reflect a lot on the reality of racism. I cannot remember in my family any negative attitudes toward blacks, but at this time in my school, which was a fifty-fifty mix of black and white, violence was being directed against white kids just because they were white. One incident in particular made that clear to me.

Down the street from where our school bus picked us up, there was an abandoned gas station where we used to hang out and smoke cigarettes et cetera while we waited for the bus. The coolest thing of all was the regular presence of an older kid named Danny Womack, who played running back for the Texas Senior High varsity football team; he was a monster of a guy who ran all over other teams and put Texas High on the map. To my eyes, he was superbig and superfast and became like the dashing older brother of our little group. We basked in the glow of this star. Everybody knew that if Danny Womack hung out with you, then you must be cool too.

One day we heard some commotion down the street near Sears, where some of our girlfriends had gone to shop. On their way back, a group of black kids of different ages were yelling racial slurs and throwing *bricks* at them, and the girls were, not surprisingly, scared. Everyone froze, uncertain as to what to do about this situation, except Danny, who immediately jumped up and started yelling obscenities at the group and taunting them to "come here and try that." Even with no experience of street fighting, I knew that challenging a group of thirty to thirty-five armed and angry kids to "come here and try that" was a bad strategy. I had a sick feeling about the turn of events and quickly asked my friend Randy Newsome to run back to the bus stop and get more guys to come and join us, but as he ran off, *all the other kids* in our group ran off too. That left just me and Danny to face this group of hostile kids, who were forming a circle around us and bending down to pick up pipes, rocks, and other debris that were plentifully scattered about. I was truly afraid that I was going to be killed, but I was not going to abandon Danny. I was going to be a man of my word: I was there at the beginning, and I would be there to the end. My mind's eye flashed back to Ron Newton defending my mom and me and Scotty against those three punks in New Mexico, and it seemed as if defending those girls was the chivalrous thing to do, even though the odds were totally against us.

As soon as we were surrounded, Danny went to work, and was he impressive! He picked out the one really big guy who looked like the leader of the group (the guy seemed to be about thirty years old), went directly up to him, got in his face, poked his finger into the guy's chest, and screamed a string of choice words and phrases to convince him that the best course of action was to take his friends and go home. By this time the group was circling like a pack of hyenas waiting to pounce. Remembering the gang scene in *West Side Story*, I thought, "Oh boy, we're gonna die." For a brief second, I imagined my weeping mother making my funeral arrangements.

Incredibly, Danny's strategy worked. The big man—who was considerably larger than Danny—froze as Danny got in his face and read him the riot act. General Patton once said, "When I want 'em to remember something, I give it to 'em loud and dirty", and Danny sure did that.

The group of kids was still circling around, batting their palms with their weapons and saying, "Hey, man, do something", but their burly leader hesitated just a bit too long, and Danny's dirty language and physical intimidation wore him down. After a few minutes, the tension broke and the group leader began shaking his head and saying, "Man, it's cool, it's all right." He actually shook Danny's hand and hugged him. He obviously wanted no part of young Danny Womack. A minute later, the two guys were sharing cigarettes. I couldn't believe what I was seeing. It was a miracle. All the other guys who were itching for a fight just laid down their weapons and walked away confused. And I breathed a sigh of relief.

I learned two valuable lessons that day—one about myself and the other about life. I learned how much I valued loyalty: I would not abandon a friend in need. That incident was the closest I ever came to being a statistic, but I am glad that I stuck with Danny because it was the right thing to do. And as a result, I learned something about handling conflict: Danny was just a country boy, but his gift was the ability to go right to the center of the opposition and use *intimidation* to protect those who needed it. If he had any fear at all, no one knew it. Thanks to his quick thinking and nerves of steel, the crisis was averted, and I'm still alive to tell about it. Once again, I witnessed a real man who went toe-to-toe with scoundrels to protect the weak and innocent.

A Surrogate Father at a Good Time

When I look back at my adolescent years, I can see why the Ron Newtons and Danny Womacks of that time impressed me so much. I was suffering from the lack of a strong fatherly figure and was awed by their examples of male strength. It doesn't take a genius to see that a father makes a huge difference in a boy's life because a father is a *male* authority that boys can't ignore. In addition to modeling masculine virtue for his son, a father can apply punishment in a way that a mother can't, and boys know it.

During my ninth-grade year, Mom started dating another Ron—Ron Etheridge—whom I liked a lot. He was dashing and tall with dark hair and a dark complexion and was a real Southern gentleman, not a hillbilly type. He had a positive personality and could joke around to a certain degree, although we knew better than to cross him, because he was a manly man who wouldn't put up with any nonsense, especially toward Mama.

Ron entered my life at a critical time, because Mama was losing control of her two boys. She had bonded more closely with Scotty after his terrible accident; nearly losing him had flipped some kind of maternal switch inside her, which was not a bad thing in the short run. In the long run, however, her mothering spoiled him; she let him do pretty much whatever he wanted. He became disorderly and quit high school. By the time Scotty was seventeen, he was on a dangerous and self-destructive path. I was fifteen and could have followed my big brother, save for the countervailing force of a good man who acted like a surrogate father to me, at least for a time.

I distinctly remember the day I mouthed off to my mom in Ron's presence. He witnessed the incident in silence, but when Mama left the room, Ron took me out into the front yard and said to me in no uncertain terms, "If I ever hear you talk to your mother that way again, I will whoop your &#@$! all over this yard. I love you, but you are not going to talk to your mother like that again. You hear me?" My stunned and wide-eyed response was simply, "Yessir."

I was very self-confident with my friends, but it was a lot harder for me to be cocky when confronted by a strong male authority figure who could—and would—*hurt me* if I got out of line. I soon learned to make decisions based upon the likely consequences of my behavior with Ron. Looking back, I am so grateful for Ron's presence in my life; his influence kept me on a better path than I would have walked without him. When I saw Ron some years later at a concert in Shreveport, Louisiana, I thanked him for being there for me at a very vulnerable time in my life.

Ron also taught me something critical about being a man, though it would take me some years to understand it fully; he showed me how a man takes responsibility for those entrusted to him, even if it means tough love.

The Frenzy Band

Ron was very supportive of Scotty's and my musical ambitions and for a time acted as our quasi-manager. He helped our newly formed band, Frenzy, put on three concerts in our town. These three heavy-metal concerts were memorable for their brilliant audacity and total absence of professionalism. Smart enough to know that the events needed good promotion, we took out an ad in the *Texarkana Gazette*, bought some radio time, and printed posters announcing that Frenzy was appearing at the Texarkana College Auditorium. Our intent was to create the impression that we were a big-time band from somewhere else because people wouldn't come if they knew we were locals. That's also why we wore masks! We charged only three dollars for a ticket and almost filled the auditorium the first time around.

On the technical side, we proved ourselves to be total neophytes. Experienced performers would have rented a concert-grade sound system for the heavy-metal music we played, but we had only the auditorium's sound system, which was totally inadequate. Our friend Terry Bridger, who wanted to be a light man, improvised a few light trees with tin cans to create a kind of makeshift light show for us, while another friend climbed up on the catwalk with bags of confetti to dump on the fans when the time was right. Basically, the choreography was good but the music stank. The audience received the performance moderately well, but the after-show reviews were pretty brutal—all well deserved, of course.

The coup de grâce of the show was to be the guitar smash during the drum solo. If Pete Townsend of the Who could do it, we could too. Scotty and I only had one good guitar each. Not wanting to destroy those, we went to Sears and bought a couple of cheap guitars to bring out on stage at the right moment and smash together in midair. We did not realize that the bands that did this stunt used hollow-body guitars, which would shatter dramatically when they hit, and bought instead *solid-body* guitars. When they collided, we felt as if we were slamming bricks together. They didn't break! They only sent shock waves through our arms and into our bodies, and I can't describe the rude feeling of pain and embarrassment that ran through every fiber of my being. Both Scotty and I stood there in a panic at the failure of our trick, and of course we tried it again—smack! Still the guitars didn't shatter; the second crash only jolted the pain further into our limbs and increased our sense of horror.

Scotty and I looked at each other and asked with our eyes, "What are we going to do?" Then we saw the orchestra pit at the front of the stage and had the *exact* same thought: "Let's dump the guitars down in the pit and see what happens." We ran to the front of the stage, raised the guitars over our heads, and simultaneously chucked the instruments down ten feet into the pit. They burst into kaleidoscope pieces right before our very eyes, but unfortunately no one but us saw the spectacle As we stood there in awe of the beautiful display of smoking guitar shards below us, three or four concertgoers in the front row jumped to the edge of the pit to see what had happened, but our brilliant demonstration had already fizzled out.

Although we got better at performing our antics on stage, fewer and fewer people came to the next two shows—which signaled both the beginning and the end of our power rock days.

What a Difference a Good Teacher Makes

Despite a shaky start, our commitment to a future in music was solid, and for me, still in high school, that meant that I didn't put a whole lot of effort into classes that didn't interest me. College wasn't in my plans. I did, however, excel in subjects that I liked, which were those that didn't have to do with numbers. I absolutely loved literature and history and got straight As in both. My high school English teachers exposed me to some of the best literature of all time, and, even more importantly for my future career, I developed a deep appreciation for the talents of great writers. F. Scott Fitzgerald, Edgar Allen Poe, Charles Dickens—these and other gifted authors have become my permanent intellectual companions on life's journey and have provided inspiration for me as an artist.

I took an elective course on Shakespeare in my senior year because someone said it was an "easy A", but much to my surprise, the course absolutely fascinated me. Naturally, the *teacher* made all the difference. Nancy Ferriger was noticeably in love with Shakespeare and had a way of communicating that to a generation of Texas teens who probably couldn't have spelled the Bard's name if they had tried. She would put on records of his plays and stand in rapt admiration of the inspired words. Although she had probably heard or read the lines countless times before, her innocent awe gave the impression that she was hearing them for the first time. She must have been a pure soul, because tears would well up in her eyes at the artistry displayed before us. Every student who took her class ended up loving Shakespeare in the same way, and her appreciation for timeless beauty appealed to the lyricist in me. My favorite songwriters over the years—Hugh Prestwood and Karen Taylor-Good, to name two—have been the ones who could combine great poetry with great music.

Ms. Ferriger's course was also very timely, as the beauty of Shakespeare provided a counterbalance to the degradation of the seedy bars I was playing in during that same period.

Forty Bucks a Night and All the Pride You Can Swallow

Even as a teenager, I knew that the road to success would be a challenge. Scotty and I would need a lot of grassroots experience to make a name for ourselves—and that meant playing in a lot of bars. We didn't mind, though; we were dying to play anywhere we could, which translated into gigs that paid forty bucks a night and all the pride we could swallow.

During my teens, I had tried my hand at a couple of temporary jobs, but nothing appealed to me, or held the same potential for income, as music did. By age fifteen, I was playing music in some establishment every weekend, and the band was the single focus of my life. During my sophomore through senior years of high school (1975–1978), I kept a schedule that few kids could imagine, probably spurred on by my mother's work ethic and unusual sleep habits. I went to school during the day and played in bars five or six nights a week from 9 P.M. to 2 A.M. When I played on weeknights, I got to sleep at 3:30 A.M. and was up again to go to school by 7. As a result, I spent more time with my brother and his friends than with my peers, and I soon felt as though I had outgrown my own age group in my desire for the one thing that was important to me: musical success.

The Cedar Shake and Other Classy Establishments

Texarkana and its environs was the location of numerous low-class drinking establishments that needed a musical backdrop to all the fighting and other disorderly conduct they encouraged. Texarkana's premier seedy bar was the Cedar Shake, the default place for all the people who didn't fit into the better drinking hole down the road, the Pines Club. The Cedar Shake had absolutely no redeeming value. It would be an understatement to say that its appearance and clientele were shabby, but the only thing that made it worth our while was that we could make two hundred dollars a week playing there from Tuesday through Sunday rather than just playing on weekends.

All musicians were required to play from 9 P.M. until closing time, which was always between 2 and 3 A.M., but since hardly anyone even got to the bar *until* 2 A.M., most of our playing time every night was an exercise in utter, life-sapping drudgery. The few drunks and prostitutes who populated the place before 2 A.M. seemed totally uninterested in the music; with such an indifferent audience, we were bored stiff playing our six sets every night. It was such a soul-killing gig that many times I stood on stage in a stupor and had a recurring conversation with myself: "Now *why* am I doing this? Gosh, I hate my life. I am going nowhere fast. Man, I should go to college." The Cedar Shake was awful. There was no way to develop a following at that place—it had no respect, no dignity, and no future—so we learned to diversify.

During those years, Scotty and I and some friends would drive about seventy miles to play music in the little city of Idabel in McCurtain County, Oklahoma, which at one point was considered the most corrupt county in the country. Everyone knew that all the local cops and sheriffs were on the take, due in large part to the county's reputation as a marijuana-growing region. Law enforcement made it a point to look the other way when drugs and other shady dealings went down in and around the three infamous bars that were the main attraction and source of revenue for the area. Apparently the local bar owners had cut a deal with the authorities not to come into the bars unless something took place that the bouncers couldn't handle, and I witnessed uniformed cops standing guard over areas where illegal things were going on. The bars were thus a safe zone for all kinds of unruly and dangerous behaviors.

Of the three establishments, the Black Hat was the "classiest" and a true window into the lower depths of humanity. The huge place could hold as many as 1,200 people and always had at least three very diverse and often conflicting constituencies: the Bikers, the Hippies, and the Cowboys. Thankfully, the guys in the biker gang, the Road Barons, liked us for some reason and protected us from the fights that would break out three or four times a night on a regular weekend. The owner was a bowlegged older man with white hair. Always wearing a coverall/jumpsuit as a uniform, Ed Frazier set down the rule that when a fight broke out—not *if* but *when*—we were to launch into an animated rendition of "Under the Double Eagle" and play it as fast as we could until the fight ended. Apparently Frazier liked music with his destruction. Thus, whenever we would hear something break or a bottle crack over someone's head, one of us in the band would yell, "Okay, boys, one, two, three", and we would light into "Under the Double Eagle" until things calmed down or until Frazier drew his finger across his throat, which signaled for us to stop. Then it was back to playing "Hello, Darlin'" and our calmer repertoire again. There were times when the place looked like a scene from *Gunsmoke*, with up to ten people brawling at once. If you saw that kind of thing in a movie, you would think it was pure fiction. Needless to say, the Black Hat was a rough joint.

A further step *down* from the Black Hat, on the other side of town, was the Far East, where we played the following year. That was the venue where I witnessed the most vicious, blood-curdling fight I have ever seen— and it was between two women. At first glance, we wondered why even the bouncers and cops stood aside and let it go on, but we soon figured it out: the girls were fighting over some dimwitted cowboy and were so sadistic that no one dared get in the middle of it. The stronger one was on top of the other, cussing up a storm, ripping at her clothes, and pulling out chunks of hair just to humiliate her. It was a terrifying spectacle. Apparently, the winner got to go home with Slim.

Playing in seedy bars was an interesting lesson in human nature for a sixteen-year-old kid, but it was also a necessary step to realizing my dream.

The Many Faces and Lessons of Integrity

Periodically I think about the men and women I encountered in the bars as a teen. Ironically they taught me something about integrity. These characters could be outrageously funny, seriously messed up, or just plain tragic—and sometimes all of the above—but even as a kid I realized that they were just people, with lives to live and souls to save. As I now view them from some distance, I am grateful for their presence on my life's journey. I learned something from them that can be learned only by personal contact with fallen human nature: everyone carries some secret burden of pain, abuse, deprivation, injustice, or just plain sorrow that no one else can comprehend. Every person's pain is unique and often deeply hidden, and what God requires of us all is a heart of compassion for our fellow man as we make our way together through the sufferings of life.

I am also grateful for those real-life Atticus Finches that God put along my path to adulthood, who gave me the precious gift of themselves. They taught me to strive for integrity and lit the pathway into my future. What kind of person would I be without my mom and dad, Coach Anderson, Danny Womack, Nancy Ferriger, Ron Etheridge, or the preacher who immersed me in the waters of baptism? It is said that our lives are built on the sacrifices of others, on their many acts of generosity, which give us a foundation and reflect the sacrifice of God Himself for our salvation. I look back with immense gratitude at the people who unselfishly shared their talents, resources, and wisdom with me at a vulnerable time in my life. It is my hope that I can give to others as many blessings as I have been given and offer the rest of my life to God for whatever purpose He deems fit. I know His strong, constant hand will guide me and protect me—as it always has from the very beginning.

3

Two Defining Moments

Faith and Fatherhood

(1980–1984)

*So shun youthful passions and aim at righteousness, faith, love,
and peace, along with those who call upon the Lord from a pure heart.*

—2 Tim 2:22

I was born in 1960, baptized in 1972, and literally born again in 1983. That was the most important year of my life and my initiation into the adult world. In 1983 God blessed me with the two greatest gifts I have ever received from His loving hand: faith and fatherhood.

I spent many years learning my craft, establishing my reputation, trying to fit into the world, and trying to become a man. These activities were important, but they were not enough to form the basis of my *identity*. I truly learned who I was only when I made an interior commitment to live for others. That happened when I became a Catholic and a father at virtually the same time. Everything that preceded my entrance into faith and fatherhood was a dress rehearsal for a life invested in the things that really matter, and I am certain that these two events were the wellspring of the only force that helped me survive the ups and downs of my twenties.

Don't Tell Me I Can't

After I graduated from high school, Scotty and I were playing music most nights of the week—and going nowhere. Texarkana was still a stifling little town, and we encountered a spirit of discouragement there like none I would meet again. There was a steady stream of people who would give us the "Ain't nobody from here ever made it big" speech whenever they heard that we wanted to be successful musicians. I would always tell them that plenty of folks from small towns actually made it big in music—Elvis himself was from Tupelo, Mississippi, for crying out loud! But that didn't matter: the cloud of failure over that place was simply overwhelming. We had become musicians, and they didn't mind having us in their band, but they gave us no credit for being good, and no one supported us or urged us on to accomplish great things.

Whenever they hit us with their negativity, I felt a kind of inner revolt well up in me: "Well, I'm just gonna prove you wrong!" It was my way of being rebellious, I guess. Their disbelief had the opposite effect of what they intended. It fired us up. Our determination to fight the naysayers grew in direct proportion to their skepticism. We were going to make it big, no matter what it took, but we also knew that we would never make it big by staying in Texarkana.

It's funny how life sometimes goes in circles. When we complained to Mama that we had to get out of Texarkana to a place where people would actually like us, she called her booking-agent friend in Oregon, Billy Ray Guerin, to see if he could help us, and he promised to find us some work there. The only gig Guerin could find for us was playing in a bar in Bend, Oregon, for a *month*, but we were so desperate to get out of town that we jumped at the chance. We loaded a van with all our earthly belongings and drove the 2,100 miles back to the great Northwest just to play for a month with hopes of something better. Piano player Randy Altenbaumer and drummer Jim Covert joined us, and we started a new life as the Wray Brothers Band. We were filled with the somewhat rash and unbounded optimism of youth: "Nobody's gonna tell us we can't." I, for one, was elated to be going back to a place that had very dear childhood memories for me.

A New Chapter Begins

A year or so before we moved to Oregon, I met a very pretty and well-put-together young lady named Connie Parker when we were playing at the Master Host Inn, which was just down the street from the dreaded Cedar Shake in Texarkana. A friend of hers was dating a musician friend of ours, which was the reason she and Connie made the two hours' drive from Greenville, Texas, every weekend. Connie and I hit it off right away. She had been married before, but at the time I didn't see that as an obstacle. She was a few years older than I, which seemed cool, and she had a nice car and a good job at a title company. She appreciated my plans to advance in music and wanted to help me reach my goals. Connie was aggressive in her pursuit of me, but I kind of liked that because at that age I was still pliable—maybe I was looking for someone to guide me. Pretty soon we were dating, and soon after that we were living together.

Part of Connie's appeal to me at that time was her huge personality. Before my performing days, my core temperament was essentially shy and laid-back, and—as often happens in relationships—I was attracted to people whose traits complemented my own. Connie's somewhat brash take-no-prisoners style attracted me at the beginning. She didn't mind telling people what was on her mind, and I found her assertiveness engaging.

Connie was raised essentially the same way as I was, with a strong, believing Christian mom and a religiously disengaged dad. She went with me to Oregon, and soon after that she told me she was getting pressure from her parents, who wanted us to tie the knot. She asked me if we should get married, and as an indication of just how serious I was about marriage, I replied, "Sure. Why not?"

There was no possibility of a big wedding because our families were back in Texas. With Scotty as my best man and his future wife, Cathy, as the maid of honor, we trotted down to the Benton County Courthouse in Corvallis, Oregon, and were married before a justice of the peace on June 2, 1980. Neither of us was seriously practicing the Christian faith at the time, and as a result, our decision to marry was a pragmatic one with almost no religious significance for us. Our wedding was not the celebration of faith and family that God intends this occasion to be. In fact, if we had courted properly, I doubt we would have gotten married at all.

Heaven Is for Real and So Are Babies

At the beginning of a marriage, young people are forward-looking and optimistic and don't generally consider that suffering will ever enter their lives, and Connie and I certainly fit that mold. In 1982 we greeted the news of her first pregnancy with great joy. We really wanted a baby and were totally unprepared for one of the harsher realities of married life that many couples have to face: miscarriage. Our band was playing in the Stuart Anderson Steakhouse in Portland when Connie suddenly ran to the ladies room; soon after I learned that she had lost the baby. I was saddened by our loss, and Connie was really broken up by it. We were deprived of the joy of welcoming our first child into the world.

After recently reading the wonderful little book *Heaven Is for Real: A Little Boy's Astounding Story of His Trip to Heaven and Back* (Thomas Nelson, 2010), I saw the miscarriage from a new perspective. Todd Burpo's book recounts the near-death experiences of his three-year-old son, Colton, who almost died from a burst appendix. After Colton recovered, he described with great precision the things he saw while on his own personalized tour of heaven, and his story is amazing. He told his parents in some detail about his operation and his family's reactions to his crisis as if he had been looking down on them from above. He also described sitting in Jesus' lap and looking at the "markings" on His hands and feet and meeting John the Baptist along with a man who fit the description of a great-grandfather he had never known.

His most compelling testimony, however, was about meeting a *sister* of his whose existence was unknown to anyone but his parents. The sister had been lost in miscarriage before Colton was born, and the parents didn't even know that the child was a girl. In heaven, this child ran up to Colton and hugged him and told him that she was his sister who "died in [her mother's] tummy". When his mother asked what her name was, Colton simply replied, "She doesn't have a name. You guys didn't name her." He then added, "Yeah, she said she just can't wait for you and Daddy to get to heaven." He went on to explain with childlike directness what she looked like, that she was okay, and furthermore, that "God adopted her". After that, Colton kept on repeating that "Jesus *really* loves the children"—all children.

My heart was so touched by reading this book that I had a discussion with Connie about the baby we had lost through miscarriage. Our baby all of a sudden became *real* to me, to us, but like Colton's parents we didn't know the sex of the baby since it was impossible to tell that so early in the pregnancy. We decided to name the baby, and it was our daughter Britanny who came up with a name that could fit either a boy or a girl: Jamie. Such a perfect name! More than anything, the very parental act of endowing the miscarried child with a name helped me to restore the bond with the lost child and to recognize his humanity and value. I am the father of *three* children, one of whom is in heaven and, as Colton said, "can't wait for me to get there".

The book gave our own miscarriage experience a new interpretation. If every child is infinitely precious to God, no matter how small the child may be, then our society's practice of abortion is truly abhorrent. I always knew that abortion is wrong—no one had to teach me that—but as a young man I never paid attention to the issue, which I always thought was just a political thing. Little Colton's reflections helped me to understand the truth about the humanity of every unborn child. Each one is totally and fully human from the moment of conception. We have to recognize the value of unborn children and put our efforts behind every attempt to save them from abortion. I trust that God adopts all the innocent victims of abortion, but after reading that book, I can never again be silent in the face of such a great evil. God indeed reveals truth "out of the mouths of babies and infants" (Mt 21:16).

Too Much Mountain for Me

Among the reasons I relished going back to the great Northwest was the chance to climb Mount Rainier in Washington, the second highest mountain in the lower forty-eight states. Mount Rainier is where American expeditions train to climb Mount Everest because it is similar in terrain to the famous peak in Nepal. Its towering presence over the city of Seattle challenges adventurous types like me to scale it, and when I was twenty-two years old, I wanted to conquer that magnificent wonder of nature. It turned out that the natural wonder conquered me.

My trainer for this expedition was Pete Whittaker, the son of Lou Whittaker, the first American to scale Mount Everest. Pete and his brothers were literally mountain-climbing royalty and led expeditions up Mount Rainier; they were in immaculate shape with huge lung capacity because they climbed the mountain two or three times a week. As my climb date approached, I went to a training session with a group of about fifteen eager climbers; we practiced using an ice axe, crampons, and ropes. As we had to be in excellent physical shape to make a climb like that, I worked out

intensely and ran up and down bleachers to get my lungs in shape. I even
loaded fifty to sixty pounds of dumbbells into my backpack, put on my
hiking boots, and went jogging to imitate the kind of rigorous conditions I
would find when I got to the mountain. I was doing too much.

One day when jogging, my bootlace came undone, and instead of taking
the load off my back and propping my leg up to retie my boot, I squatted
down and felt something come apart inside my knee. The injury immediately alarmed me but didn't cause me any pain—at that moment. I resumed
my jog, and about two hours later, I felt as if a little man with a pick axe
was scraping away the back of my knee cap. I was in serious pain. The
climb was about two weeks away, and I had paid my money and was determined to do it. Anyone with sense would have cancelled, but I nursed the
knee as well as I could and hoped for the best.

The two-day excursion started with a hike to windy, frigid Camp Muir
at about ten thousand feet, where we stayed in a rustic shack until the wee
hours of the morning. Up to that point, my knee held out well. A few hours
into the next day's climb, we arrived at the appropriately named Disappointment Cleaver, a sheer cliff face rising fifteen hundred feet in front of us at
a very stiff incline—only a few degrees off vertical. Scaling it required the
climbers to be roped together, four to a rope, and *now* my knee was killing
me. During the climb, I could feel the rope tugging on me, which meant
the other climbers were pulling me and compensating for me; to be holding
them back was terribly humiliating. Still, I didn't want to admit defeat, and
when the guide told me that I should get off the rope, I just responded, "No,
I'm fine." I wasn't fine. My knee was hurting very badly, and I should have
gotten off. I experienced some consolation when I made it to the summit
and saw the immense beauty that can be experienced only at that height. I
took my pictures with the team and then went back down in extreme pain.

I'm sure the combination of the barbell jogging and climbing with an
injury—as well as a good dose of stubbornness—damaged my knee forever. To this day I can't jog. Rainier had been too much mountain for me.

"I'm Going to Be That Guy"

The bar in Bend, where Billy Ray got us a gig, was the China Ranch. It was
a second-rate place, but it was a job; and we felt good being out of Texas

and on our own. We played five sets every night, and Billy Ray came to our performances to see if we had some potential. After a month he offered us another opportunity to play at a better place about two hours away in Corvallis, the home of Oregon State University. The new gig was at the Lamplighter, a barely respectable bar on the ground floor of the Benton Hotel, which was a pretty dumpy old place. Within four months, the Wray Brothers Band brought the bar a fame it had never known, and lines of people were stretching down the street and around the corner for several blocks just to hear us play. It was our first exhilarating experience of having real live *fans*!

The local people liked us mostly because we were from Texas and acted the part well. An outlaw country band— with cowboy hats and drawls— was no news in Texas, but these were the days of the *Urban Cowboy* craze. Oregonians, especially the college kids, just ate it up. We rehearsed a great deal and worked very hard to stay professional because, now that we had some popularity, we didn't want to lose it or blow the opportunity for more.

It didn't take me long to figure out that there is a big difference between getting an audience and *keeping* an audience. The former is sometimes the result of dumb luck, but the latter never happens without a lot of hard work. Previously my goal had been to be a singing bass player in a good band, not a front man, but I realized that to keep our audience and to expand it I needed to make some changes. I took my cues from a musician in Oklahoma named Troy Ruffin, who taught me that there is no show at all unless someone makes the audience feel a connection to the band. Ruffin had no musical talent to speak of, but he got jobs because he worked his audience table by table and knew everyone in the bar. He was the performer the customers wanted, less for his talent than for his ability to connect with them. Seeing him in action, I thought, "So that's how it's done! I'm gonna be that guy!"

From that point on, I began to force myself to get better at public relations: stepping up to the mic and talking more, greeting people before and after the shows, developing friendships, making the rounds of the tables during breaks, et cetera.

I also learned to be more aggressive at promotion. We were way beyond putting up Frenzy posters for our show at Texarkana College. Our stated goal was to make it to the big time, and it couldn't be accomplished without some serious promotional effort on our part. Because I was the lead singer, I became, by default, the public face and front man for the band; and in order to find new ways to move us forward, I took on the jobs that would promote us—the interviews, the meetings with people, the bookings—and it was tremendously hard work.

The extra effort paid off as we began playing at public events, such as county fairs and local Fourth of July celebrations, and packing in crowds everywhere we went. Eventually we started performing in casinos. I saw these gigs as opportunities to increase our exposure, to go beyond the bar scene. But they meant the band members had to do more work, which wasn't always welcome. Good intentions sometimes have bad consequences, and the inevitable popularity that came from my promotional role led to tension within the band. I found out from Connie, who was always talking to the wives of the band members, that a couple of the guys in the group were growing resentful of me. Honestly, I wasn't trying to get all the attention; I was just trying to keep us working.

First Recordings

Our first real recording opportunity came in 1980. Although this wasn't a record deal, it was a possible gateway to greater opportunity. I had written the song "Everybody Wants to Be a Cowboy", and to my great surprise, it became a hit in the local area. I wrote it as a kind of spoof of the *Urban Cowboy* phenomenon, but the folks didn't get the sarcasm in it—thankfully. The song was so popular that we decided to record it and sell it as a single.

I contacted the Kaye-Smith Studio in Seattle and booked a date, and when we got there, we were assigned to Studio B. Amazingly, the rock group Heart—Ann and Nancy Wilson—were recording in Studio A across the hall from us, and to be honest, I was thunderstruck to be in the same building with a couple of real live rock stars. The sense of disproportion I felt in their presence was overwhelming: they were already megahit stars with three Top Ten albums, and we were there recording a single about cowboys. A little humility is good for all of us. We cut our single that day in the studio and went back to Corvallis, hoping that we had made something people would like—and buy.

Nashville freelance promoter Bill Wence offered to promote our single for a contingency fee. He pitched it to radio in an attempt to get it charted nationally, and although it didn't set the world on fire, "Everybody Wants to Be a Cowboy" became a regional phenomenon. I learned a valuable lesson from Bill Wence: people don't know you exist unless you put yourself in front of them. Self-promotion is the cardinal rule of generating and keeping an audience—but it's never cheap.

In 1982 we were approached by another promotional outfit, CIS Northwest, which was looking to do a series of albums in different genres: country, Southern rock, and jazz. They picked us to be their country act and offered us our first actual record deal! CIS offered to pay all the recording and promotional costs, which was good for penniless musicians, so we signed a contract and went to work. Scotty and I were in our early twenties at the time and probably had more enthusiasm than brains, but we pooled our talents and came up with a list of pretty good songs that became our first real album. We called it—tongue in cheek—*Cowboy Sangers*. It was a phonograph album, one of those old vinyl LPs prior to the advent of CDs that would make the snap-crackle-and-pop noises between the grooves. Every now and then, I meet a person who asks me to autograph an original album cover of *Cowboy Sangers*, and I marvel that there are still some copies floating around. They're probably collector's items now.

The back cover of the album had a picture of the Wray Brothers Band members squatting by a hay bale, playing poker in cowboy hats. I'm certain I was holding back a smile as we all tried to look rugged and country tough for the picture. I was 160 pounds at the time, but I looked as if I weighed about a hundred pounds soaking wet. CIS got behind the album and promoted it the best they knew how, and even though it was a mediocre performer, it had the effect of solidifying our regional reputation, which made us feel we were at least moving toward the big time.

First Defining Moment—Faith

By the time I was in my early twenties, I knew a few things about myself: I loved music, I was determined to make it big, and I was married. Yet, beyond these concrete realities, I discerned an inner longing for something deeper than the party environments I had been immersed in since high school. The seedy bars were growing old, the fairs were fun but superficial, and the casinos, though initially exciting, were spiritually draining. My mom had done her best to make me a true Christian man, but now that I was on my own, I felt a distinct separation from God. I always prayed—there was never any question about that—but I had very little desire to go to the evangelical churches I had attended with my mother. Although I loved the Bible, I didn't feel attracted to the evangelical style of worship. Yet I felt empty. My heart told me there was something missing in my life and more to be discovered about faith.

We were packing in crowds all around Portland in 1982, but one night at the Fireside in Beaverton, Oregon, I happened to meet Lil and Dick Ellingson, a sweet couple who were so kind and gentle that I felt attracted to them like a moth to the light of a flame. They had followed the band for some time, but I never really spoke to them until that night at the Fireside, when I decided to sit down and talk to them about religion. Little did I know then what a role they would play in my faith from that point onward. Dick was a pure gentleman, and Lil seemed to exude holiness. I noticed that Lil wore a chain with a crucifix around her neck, and since I had seen priests use crucifixes in Bing Crosby and Dracula movies, I decided it was a good bet that they were Catholics. I've noticed that God has a way of putting people in our paths who will help us along the road to heaven. Lil and Dick were His instruments for me.

Growing up in the Bible Belt, I had heard my share of negative comments about the Catholic Church, but my only exposure to Catholics was through movies such as *Going My Way* and *The Bells of St. Mary's*. In those films, Catholics looked to me as if they were pretty Christian, despite what some people I knew might say, but the only way I could uproot those seeds of doubt was to check out the Catholic Church for myself.

I have to admit that Catholicism looked attractive to me at that point primarily because of Lil and Dick. They were witnesses of such a wholesome goodness that I wanted to see if their religion was the reason for it. One evening, after finishing a set, I sat down with them and outright asked if I could go to church with them the next Sunday. They were a bit surprised at the request but also delighted, and they immediately said, "Well, sure!" They told me where the church was, and the next Sunday I met them for Mass at Our Lady of Sorrows Catholic Church in Portland. I had my Bible in hand, of course, because that was how I had always gone to church.

The quaint little parish church was a box-like structure covered completely with off-white wooden siding, and from the outside it looked like any one of a thousand little Protestant churches I had seen growing up. I knew Catholics were devoted to Mary, but it struck me as strange that they would put the word "sorrows" in the name of a church; nevertheless, I didn't give it much thought because I truly wanted to experience what a Catholic service was like without prejudging anything.

The church was hardly large enough to hold a congregation of a hundred people, and my first impression from the outside was that everything was very neat and orderly. As I walked up the steps of the little rustic church on that Sunday morning, I was unprepared for the sensation that immediately came over me when we opened the door and walked through the small entranceway. I was half expecting to be greeted by some smiling person telling me how welcome I was there, but no one greeted me, and no one handed me a bulletin or a song sheet. Instead, as I walked over the threshold, my senses were invaded with the most profound sense of peace and comfort I had ever experienced in my life.

I hadn't grown up with the sacraments as a normal part of worship, so I believe my senses were more attuned to the sacramental action of the Church than they might have been if I were a cradle Catholic. I was like an empty vessel into which God could pour His grace. What I felt can be described as a gentle but deep sense of awe and reverence that washed *through me and over me and in me* all at once. I will never forget it.

The interior of the church was simple: wood-paneled walls with a slanted white ceiling and no decorations. There were two statues flanking the back wall, one of the Sacred Heart and one of Mother Mary. Inserted in the wall between them was an ornate golden box. At that time I didn't know that the box was a tabernacle, or what its purpose was, but I would find out soon enough. At the head of the main aisle, in the center, was an altar, and it looked as though anyone could just walk up to it and touch it. A pulpit was to the side of the altar. The arrangement was unusual for me. I was accustomed to churches with a raised platform mounted by a preacher's pulpit, front and center.

From an aesthetic point of view, Our Lady of Sorrows was somewhat ordinary but lovely; the people, however, were impressive without trying to be so. Distinct from the congregations at the many non-Catholic services

I had attended, the people weren't looking around or talking before Mass—they were *praying*. I said to myself, "Wow, no one knows I'm here", and that was an immensely refreshing thought. The solitude in the presence of the Lord was both totally new and comforting to me. I felt I could be myself in that church, with no one to distract me, no one to ask me questions, and nothing between me and God. It occurred to me that something awe-inspiring and beautiful brought those people to church, not just a feel-good experience of community. I was later to learn that the Real Presence of Jesus in the sacrament of the Eucharist was what drew them there; it was the same Presence that filled me with such peace when I walked into the church that morning. In an instant, and without anyone saying a word to me, I understood why people are Catholic.

Lil used the missalette to walk me through the Mass. Just as I had hoped, there was nothing weird about the service at all. Any vague anti-Catholic prejudices I might have had from my upbringing were dispelled—I saw no one worshipping statues or trying to deify Mary during the whole liturgy. In fact, the Mass was all about Jesus Christ. I was surprised to hear readings from the Old Testament, the Psalms, the New Testament, and the Gospels, which was probably more Scripture than the typical Protestant service includes on any given Sunday. Above all, there was *silence* at certain points of the Mass. This was totally new to me. Even though the music wasn't much to write home about, it was, nevertheless, humble and reverent and didn't overwhelm the silence that allowed people to pray to God on their own, especially after Communion. I believe it was also the first time in my life that I ever kneeled to pray. In this church, praying on my knees felt so natural, and everyone did it, so I didn't feel awkward.

From beginning to end, the Mass in that little church gave me a totally new sense of worship and of God. I didn't expect a Catholic church to *feel* that way; in fact, I didn't expect any particular feeling at all. Even though I was churchless at that time, I had expected that I would intellectually examine Catholicism to find out if it met my exacting standards of what a church should be; I would refuse to settle for anything that didn't make sense to me or didn't measure up to everything I knew about the Bible. Thus, I was rather pleasantly surprised to find that *I* was the one who had to measure up to a higher standard of faith altogether. I had visited a church whose roots were deep, whose worship was pure, and whose heart was with Christ in a way that I had never expected to encounter. The experience of just one holy Mass seemed to fill the void that I had felt for so long. Christ Himself was truly present in the Catholic Church, and I had happily found Him. I was finally home.

I left Mass with a voracious appetite for everything Catholic and wanted a systematic approach to learn as much as I could in the shortest length of time. Within a few days of that Mass, I entered the parish's RCIA (Rite of Christian Initiation of Adults), which is the standard program for adults who wish to convert to the Catholic Church. It usually consists of several months of classes until Easter, when people are formally accepted into the Church. It's hard to overstate my joy in being on this new path to faith. It had everything I needed: intellectual study, prayer and piety, and companionship for the journey.

Thankfully, a delightful and well-prepared nun, Sister Sheila Marie, was in charge of the program, and she did a marvelous job of answering all my questions. Given my upbringing, I needed to understand things in a biblical context. Even though I had a wonderful first experience of Mass with Lil and Dick, I was a little bit afraid that if some doctrine couldn't be squared with Scripture, I would have difficulty believing it. Luckily, Sister Sheila Marie knew her Bible well. She met my biblical challenges and showed me how everything added up. In fact, much to my surprise, it all added up perfectly.

Protestant churches are weak at teaching the history of the Church and the history of the Bible. Knowing this, Sister didn't get defensive when I said, "I won't believe it unless I find it in the Bible"—the old *sola Scriptura* line. Rather, she recognized this objection as a kind of Protestant blind spot and asked me where the Bible came from. It suddenly occurred to me that I had been reading the Bible for twenty-three years but had no idea where it came from. Then she told me that the New Testament was actually produced *by the Church* under the inspiration of the Holy Spirit, and I began to understand that Church authority has a role in interpreting Scripture, as opposed to the Protestant idea that every man is his own authority. Likewise, since the Catholic Church could trace her origins back to Jesus as no other church could, I recognized it as the *original* Christian Church: the one, holy, catholic, and apostolic Church, as we call it in the Nicene Creed. That insight burst all the antipope and anticlerical arguments about Catholicism I had ever heard.

When we discussed the Eucharist, she directed us to read chapter 6 of John's Gospel, where I was finally exposed to a passage that for some reason had always been glossed over in the Bible churches. They always emphasized the more famous John 3:16, the "born again" passage, but never seemed to read three chapters later in the same Gospel. Reading Christ's words about the Eucharist as if for the first time was truly astonishing for me:

> I am the bread of life; he who comes to me shall not hunger, and he who believes in me shall never thirst (v. 35).... I am the living bread which came down from heaven; if any one eats of this bread, he will live for ever (v. 51).... Truly, truly, I say to you, unless you eat the flesh of the Son of man and drink his blood, you have no life in you; he who eats my flesh and drinks my blood has eternal life, and I will raise him up at the last day (vv. 53–54).

Oh my! What sublime beauty resonates from those passages! Here the whole treasure of heaven, the Body and Blood, Soul and Divinity of Christ, was in the Catholic Church—and no one had told me about it.

When it came to the touchy subject of confession, my Protestant ears were ringing with the many disparagements I had often heard in the South, such as, "Man doesn't have the right to forgive sins; only God can do that." Sister Sheila Marie had a biblical answer for that too, of course. Both Jesus' commission to the disciples in Matthew's Gospel (cf. 16:18–19) and His words after the Resurrection in John's Gospel set me straight on this one: "And when he had said this, he breathed on them and said to them, 'Receive the Holy Spirit. If you forgive the sins of any, they are forgiven; if you retain the sins of any, they are retained'" (Jn 20:22–23). Jesus Himself gave His Church the power to forgive sins—what a revelation that was to me.

The place of Mary in the Catholic faith was also a constant subject of derision in the Bible churches I had attended. Even though Mary figures prominently in the Bible, many non-Catholic Christians look selectively at the scriptural evidence for her role in the history of salvation. Sister Sheila Marie taught us that the Hail Mary is a biblical prayer (consisting of passages from Luke's Gospel, chapter 2) and that the Wedding at Cana in John's Gospel, chapter 2, shows very clearly Mary's intercessory role with Jesus, which is something Catholics take seriously. If Jesus Himself performed His first miracle at the request of His Mother, then there is no reason why Mary cannot be an intercessor for our needs too. Mel Gibson's 2004 movie, *The Passion of the Christ*, showed the unique rapport between Mother and Son very well, and no one seemed to think that his portrayal was too Catholic. Jesus loves His Mother so much, and I began to wonder why most of the non-Catholic Christian churches didn't.

I am ever so grateful to God for answering when I knocked on the door of the Church and for giving me the fullness of the Christian faith in Catholicism. I became a Catholic at a critical time. In my early twenties, immersed in the secular, often pagan, environments in which I performed my music, I was vulnerable to going down the road of addictions and dysfunctions, which leads to a crash-and-burn ending. I'm convinced that Jesus saved me from disaster and gave me a new reason to live—the fullness of His Truth.

Second Defining Moment—Fatherhood

Connie generally supported my conversion to the Catholic Church, although she carefully reserved judgment about my newfound zeal for the faith at that time. I think she wanted to see if I would stick with it, and she might have even thought I was overdoing the religion thing a bit. During those several months of RCIA, I was spending a lot of time with Lil and Dick. I was reading something about the Catholic faith every chance I could get, and I was praying and going to the sacraments regularly, all of which was a change from the lifestyle that I had lived at the beginning of our marriage. Connie flexed with me and asked a few questions here and there about what I was going through, but she had some other things on her mind.

The same year I was in the RCIA program, Connie became pregnant for the second time, and we were afraid of another miscarriage when she started having early contractions. She also had sharp abdominal pains, and her doctors admitted her to the hospital and gave her a drug to stop the labor. The abdominal pains were a forewarning of the problems that would come upon her in a later pregnancy, but we didn't know it at the time. We spent Christmas of 1982 in the hospital to make sure Connie would carry the pregnancy to term. It was all worth it because she held on to the pregnancy, and on February 10, 1983, our little Britanny, the love of my life, was born—the second defining moment of my existence.

The results of the ultrasound had indicated that the baby was going to be a boy, but when the baby arrived, the nurse's surprised reaction was, "Oh, it's a little girl!" We were finally parents!

When I saw my baby girl being born, I understood for the first time in my life what unconditional love is. As if peering through a tiny window into heaven, I glimpsed the love God pours out when He creates a new human being for His Kingdom. He has revealed Himself as Father for a reason. We all love many people in our lives, but there is no love that compares to a parent's love for his child.

What a radically new existence began for me at that moment! Without this child knowing me or being able to communicate with me, I began to speak in the most courageous and categorical terms about her: "I will do *anything*, anything at all for this child. I will lay down my life *right now* for this child if need be"—and I meant it. What is it about defenseless little babies that can turn men into blathering fools and mighty heroes? It must be divine grace, because up to that point, I had never uttered that phrase for any other human being, including my mother, father, brother, or wife. Those bold sentiments were the purest indicator of the change that was beginning inside of me. In fact, I hardly remember the man I was before that, because Britanny's birth became the new reference point for my life; all my decisions, all my thoughts, and all my actions related to her well-being. I would never be the same man.

With my personality and upbringing, I was cut out to be a dad. I already had by nature a passionate love for kids, and I was equipped with good parenting skills, thanks to my mom's excellent example and the positive images of fatherhood that my dad had given me. Britanny's birth was the real beginning of my adult life because I finally had someone to whom I could dedicate my best years, my best efforts. If up to that point, I had lived pretty much for myself, I could no longer justify such an existence. Without even trying, that little darling brought me into the fullness of my manhood by making me a father. I am grateful to God and Connie for bringing me into this new phase of my life.

Although Connie was not Catholic at the time, she came to the Easter morning Mass two months later—April 3, 1983—to see Britanny and me both received into the Catholic Church. Britanny was baptized, and so was I. Even though I had been baptized before, I asked to be baptized at that ceremony so that I could experience baptism as a sacrament rather than as an obligation to make my mom happy. The parish priest agreed to my request and baptized me conditionally—that is, in the event that my first baptism had not been valid. It was a beautiful privilege that Britanny and I were baptized together; it was a symbol of our father-daughter bond of unconditional love. I also received confirmation and first Holy Communion and was so happy to be one with Christ and His Church, with my little baby in my arms.

At the time I entered the Church, the situation of my marriage was not brought up by those who taught me the Catholic faith. I now understand that a civil marriage between Christians is incomplete in the eyes of the Church and that my wife's previous marriage made ours even more problematic. Not knowing anything about annulments or marriage tribunals— and I suppose such ignorance was and still is pretty common—we did not seek to have our marriage blessed by the Church.

Glass-Half-Full Kinda Guy

By the time Britanny was born, we had moved to Portland. I knew that if the band were to have any chance at success, we had to go where the better opportunities were. Before leaving Corvallis, we hired Lin Phillips, who was a jazz/country guitar player, a wonderful soloist who could make his instrument sound like a steel guitar and other things; having him was like having two or three instruments in one. In Portland we played at a real chic place called Jodie's, and within a year or so, we were top dogs in that city. We found ourselves in competition with Buckboard, which was the established group in town. The band was led by guitarist and songwriter Kraig Hutchens, who seemed to be a bit jealous of us because we were stealing his thunder and a good portion of his audience. Ironically, Kraig became my first band leader when years later I got the big CBS/Sony contract, and he accompanied me on the journey to stardom.

As already mentioned, I was trying to branch us out beyond bars to keep our talent fresh and to reach larger audiences. It was promoter Ed Dougherty who had suggested we play at county and state fairs in the summer. He had said that the money would be better in the fair circuit than in the bars, which turned out to be true.

The fair circuit, however, was a mixed blessing. On the plus side, it taught me more about the visual aspects of show business, and I developed a few bits of showmanship that eventually became trademarks. For example, when I realized that the fair crowds reacted well to a medley of Beach Boys songs we had put together, I donned a Hawaiian shirt and ran around the stage like Mike Love to ramp up the crowd. It worked. On the downside, my brother thought my antics and the music were dumb and a sellout of our outlaw brand. He had a point, but being a glass-half-full kinda guy, I saw that the showmanship was making us money. We could not see eye to eye on this, and eventually Scotty left the band, which was a relief for me. We always seemed to get along much better when we weren't playing in the same band.

Ed Dougherty also suggested that we could find work in Reno, where we could make even better money playing in casinos, and it seemed like a good idea. If we played Reno in the winters and the fair circuit in the summers, we could have the best of both worlds. He introduced us to two booking agents, Steve Cox and Ted Files from the Scott Dean Agency, who had a lot of booking strength in Reno. They were both slick, nice guys, and I was immediately drawn to Steve, who seemed manly and decent, with a good sense of humor. Steve would eventually become my sole manager for a dozen years or so and have an immense impact on my life. Steve and Ted were able to get us a lot of dates that year playing at the Peppermill and Western Village casinos; best of all, we would be able to do them without leaving Oregon. In 1984, with a new baby, neither Connie nor I wanted to move, so the arrangement seemed like a perfect scenario.

The Tough Stuff Ahead

The period after my entrance into the Catholic Church was one of great peace and productivity. Several converging forces had a positive impact on me for a while: marriage, a stable job with opportunities for advancement, a precious new baby, and a newfound faith. During that time, I struck a balance of spiritual and physical discipline that I have rarely known in my life. I was working out a lot, reading voraciously, and staying focused spiritually and mentally on the right things. Yet this period of peace was the calm before the storm because, as I would find out, there were serious trials around the next bend in the road.

If the eternal things give a person his identity, it's the tough stuff that molds his character and helps him realize that God is always faithful to him. By this point in my life, I was developing an ability to take a punch, but I hadn't felt the hardest punches that life had to give me yet. God knew that I would need faith—and kids—for the next leg of the journey.

4

Meteors

Impact and Aftermath of the Reno Years

(1985–1989)

I will all the more gladly boast of my weaknesses,
that the power of Christ may rest upon me.

—2 Cor 12:9

More than that, we rejoice in our sufferings, knowing that
suffering produces endurance, and endurance produces character,
and character produces hope, and hope does not disappoint
us, because God's love has been poured into our hearts
through the Holy Spirit who has been given to us.

—Rom 5:3–5

The best year of my life, 1983, was very shortly followed by what was, up to that point, the worst year of my life, 1985. A meteor came crashing into my world that year, and both its immediate impact and aftermath were devastating. When my brother, Scotty, was run over by a car in 1972, I was just a kid and was able to detach myself to some extent from his trauma by escaping into the things that interested me, such as music and movies. In 1985 I experienced a tragedy from which I could not escape. Nothing could hide me from the brutal reality that my wife and newborn son were on the brink of death. At the ripe age of twenty-five, I was not expecting a trial of such proportions.

Palm Sunday Code Blue

At the end of 1984, Connie became pregnant again, and we were surprised but happy that another child was on the way. Needless to say, this time we were even more cautious about prenatal care because of the previous premature labor issues. The pregnancy went well enough during the first six months that in mid-March Connie's doctor let her go with me to Reno, where I was booked to play for a month at Western Village. He connected her with a Reno obstetrician to give her a safety net if she needed it, and little did we know how much she would need it.

Prior to leaving Portland, Connie was complaining a lot about stomach pain, which was unusual because she never whined. She was tough. Connie was still in pain when we joined the rest of the band and their families in Reno. Then on the afternoon of Saturday, March 30, after we finished playing at a lavish wedding party, Lin came running up to me with a worried look on his face. He said that his wife, Cathy, had taken Connie to Saint Mary's Hospital and that we should go there quickly. When I arrived at the hospital, I found Connie sitting on a chair, doubled over and hardly able to talk. A nurse informed me that the emergency staff had already looked at her and released her.

I insisted on talking to the ER doctor and told him how sick my wife was, but he explained somewhat dismissively that Connie had nothing more than gastritis. They had checked the baby, he said, and everything was normal. He had prescribed some medicine for Connie and discharged her. I was so shocked at his callousness toward my wife's suffering that I was speechless. Connie was so clearly in severe pain; I couldn't believe he expected her to tough it out. But he was the doctor, and I grudgingly took his word for it and ignored the evidence of my own eyes. At age twenty-five I didn't confront this outrageous situation as I would today. Instead, I *carried* Connie out of the emergency room, brought her back to our hotel, and put her to bed.

Scotty and his wife, Cathy Jo, looked after Britanny while I reluctantly went to work that night, hoping Connie would improve while I was away. It was wishful thinking, because when I got back at about 3:30 A.M. her condition had not changed. In fact, she woke me at about 5 A.M. and moaned, "Bubba, I'm dying. Take me to the hospital." There was clearly something worse than gastritis happening, and I rushed her back to Saint Mary's. When I explained to the emergency admissions nurse that my wife was still experiencing severe pain, she sighed one of those big, obnoxious sighs and made us wait a full twenty-three minutes for a doctor. I asked numerous times for immediate help, but the emergency staff ignored me. Those twenty-three minutes were devastating; by the time the doctor came Connie was barely conscious.

When the doctor asked Connie questions and she couldn't answer, he sent her right to Labor and Delivery (L and D), the first sensible decision the ER people made. The L and D doctor recognized at once that *the baby* was in major distress and needed to be delivered by an immediate C-section to save his life. They asked my permission to do the surgery, and of course I told them to do whatever they needed to do. They wheeled Connie away, and I sat down and prayed that everything would be all right. Suddenly I realized it was Palm Sunday, the beginning of Holy Week.

A short time later, a code blue, the alarm for a life-and-death emergency, sounded on the floor, and I saw all kinds of people in green scrubs running around. It never occurred to me that the code blue was for Connie, but it was. A nurse came out to the waiting room, looking shaken. Connie's heart had stopped when they opened her up for the C-section, she said, and they were trying to resuscitate her. I looked into the surgery room and saw the anesthesiologist on the table, straddled over my wife's body, pumping her chest to get her heart going. My own heart must have skipped about ten beats as I looked at that scene and thought, "Oh my God, she's dead." To make matters worse, our newborn baby boy was blue, with barely a heartbeat, and on a ventilator. It dawned on me that my family was in the midst of a total catastrophe.

About twenty-five minutes later, the doctor came out and gave me an update. They had restored Connie's heartbeat but had to put her on a respirator. They also had discovered the reason for the whole incident: an ulcer the size of a golf ball had perforated her stomach lining (probably the day before) and caused her stomach literally to explode when the knife went in for the C-section, spilling its toxic contents into her body. She suffered cardiac arrest and a stroke at the same time; it couldn't have been worse.

I was paralyzed by the news. I flashed back to my brother's car accident when I was twelve, but this was so much worse than that or anything else

I had ever experienced. The helplessness I had felt at seeing my brother in the emergency room was magnified a hundred times at seeing my wife in far worse condition. The only consolation in the doctor's information was that now I knew what the problem was.

The doctor explained further that Connie had lapsed into a coma after the surgery and that he did not know whether she would come out of it. She should have had the C-section *the night before*, he added. No kidding! What had started as an emergency had turned into a calamity, and it had all been preventable.

As soon as I was able, I called Connie's parents. Naturally, they were shaken by the news of their daughter; yet at the same time, they exhibited a certain calm that comes from maturity. They had been through a few crises of their own and knew that being present with their loved ones during times of trial was the best way to handle them. They flew in from Texas on the next available flight and stayed with us for the duration of the crisis, which was a great support. We didn't know at the time that Connie would spend over a year in the hospital, and I am so grateful for Connie's mom, Doris, who spent the majority of those long months at Connie's bedside. The wives of my band members also helped us during what proved to be one of the most trying years of our lives. I will be forever grateful for Cathy Phillips, wife of our guitarist Lin; Cathy Jo Wray, Scotty's wife; and Bonita Covert, wife of our drummer Jim.

After Connie was stabilized, she was taken to the ICU, and when I went to see her there, a nurse directed me to a curtained-off room. Lying in the bed was a large body attached to multiple machines, but it wasn't my Connie. Thinking I was in the wrong place, I went back to the nurse's station, but the nurse assured me that I had looked into the right room. When I returned, a new reality slowly came into focus, and I was horrified. Connie's head had swollen to the size of a basketball, and her entire body was bloated. She had tubes and wires coming out everywhere, and she was twitching like someone getting electric shock treatments in a horror movie. My heart just broke for her. Connie didn't respond to anything I said or did, but I told her everything would be okay, hoping that maybe she could hear me in her unconscious state.

After a little while, I went to check on our Jacob. This beautiful baby had it rough from the beginning. When they took him out of the womb, he was purple. They immediately put him on a ventilator and rushed him to the neonatal intensive care unit (NICU). When I got there, I told the nurses that I was his dad, and they allowed me to put on some rubber gloves and hold him. Both the tininess and the suffering of that innocent child made me love him even more than a father normally would, if that were possible. When I picked him up, he was totally unresponsive. His limp little body barely stretched the length of my hand. His legs were skinnier than my pinky finger. The ventilator mask was much bigger than his face, and just like his mom, he had tubes and wires coming out everywhere. Oh, I felt so sorry for the poor little boy.

"How very fragile life is", I thought. Literally *half* my family was in intensive care, struggling for dear life, and all I could do at that moment was to be there with them and pray. I can't say that I even knew what to pray, because I was totally out of my league with this crisis. I needed God more than I had ever needed Him before.

Jacob was stable at the moment, but the doctors couldn't say whether he would make it through the night. I asked for Father Anthony, the hospital chaplain, who baptized him and made him a child of God. Poor Jake was so sick, and his Daddy could do nothing to help him. I needed His Father in heaven to heal him.

Short-Term Care

With one major exception, the Saint Mary ICU nurses, doctors, and specialists were marvelous, dedicated individuals, who impressed me deeply by their professionalism. I can't say enough good about them. The champion of the entire year that Connie spent in the hospital was undoubtedly Dr. Susan Buchwald, the seasoned physician and surgeon who was in charge of Connie's overall care. She kept track of an infinite number of details, specialists, treatments, and protocols that needed careful management on a daily basis. She was amazing. What I liked most about her was that, despite being a consummate professional, she was blunt and brash and could swear like a sailor when she needed to!

Connie was in a coma for nine weeks. During that time she had eleven thoracic surgeries; afterward she didn't remember a single one. Because of the amount of bile and poison that had entered her system, it seemed as if she had every possible illness ending in -*itis* along with other Greek-sounding conditions—pancreatitis, peritonitis, sepsis, anemia, toxemia, et cetera. At one point the monitors registered her body temperature at 108 degrees, which I didn't think was even possible to survive, but the nurses assured me that they had it under control. I think they were being nice and trying to keep me hopeful when there seemed to be very little hope for Connie's survival.

The New Normal

During that year (1985–1986) all of us in the family and in the band had to accustom ourselves to a new normal as Connie and Jake lay in hospital beds trying to recover. It would be impossible to condense all the ups and down of that period into a few pages, but it was undoubtedly the greatest test of faith and courage I had ever been through. Despite some upheavals we experienced in April, we were blessed with a certain amount of stability during the rest of the year and eventually saw the recovery of *both* Connie and Jake. We just had to be patient and prayerful and allow God to do His work.

My daily routine remained the same for about a year. While Cathy Jo took care of Britanny, I would visit the hospital in the late morning, accomplishing nothing more than getting updates on the constantly developing situations of Connie and Jake. In the afternoon I would spend time with Britanny. Then in the evening I went to work at the casino, where I tried to be entertaining and fun for the audience. It was a brutal schedule, but at least it was stable and predictable, which brought us a sense of normalcy.

Our two-year-old Britanny was such a trooper during this time. She seemed to handle the traumatic situation with a positive spirit, which is indicative of the sweet character she has had all her life. Soon after Connie and Jake went to the hospital, I had some father-daughter time with her, which gave me the chance to explain to her in kid language what had happened: "Baby girl, Mommy is real sick right now, but she loves you and misses you very much. Don't you worry at all; everything's going to be okay. Just be patient while Mommy gets better, and we'll all be together again." I explained in the same way about her new little brother, and she handled it all with a maturity beyond her age. In fact, I think she took it a lot better than I did!

It was many months before I let Britanny see her mom. Connie was hooked up to so many machines and looked so bad, and I just didn't think it would be good for Britanny to see her in that condition. She did see her little brother in the NICU, however, and she acted like the perfect big sister, holding him so tenderly, whispering words of encouragement to him, and kissing him. She knew that Jake was struggling to survive, and it was touching to see her treat him with so much love and sisterly affection.

Day in and day out, we followed the same routine, hoping and praying for a miracle. Then one day God came through for us. Out of the blue, after nine long weeks, Connie woke up!

A Sad but Touching Reunion

I was at home when I got the call that Connie had miraculously awakened from her coma. As I rushed to the hospital to see her, I could only marvel to myself, "Wow, wow." I had never experienced anything that was such a direct answer to prayers.

I found Connie awake but incoherent: she wasn't recognizing anybody or anything around her. She just looked afraid, and I felt very bad for her. Her mental confusion persisted for four or five days until I could finally break through her fog and get some measure of recognition from her. She could only communicate through yes and no blinks of her eyes because a trachea tube impaired her vocal chords. I looked her in the eyes and said, "Hey, Connie, you know who I am, right? I'm Bubba. Can you blink your eyes if you recognize me?" She blinked. What a relief that was! As with all married couples, I had been used to a daily back-and-forth with her on all matters for several years. After nine long weeks of silence, it was an amazing experience to be reconnected with her.

I told her that Britanny was fine and that Jacob was too, but at the mention of Jake she gave no response. Consistently over the period of about a week she made no reaction at all to his name. When I asked her if she wanted me to bring him into her room so that she could see he was alive, she grimaced. Finally the nurses brought her the baby, but she looked away and refused to touch him. I couldn't understand what was going on inside of her.

It occurred to me that maybe she needed someone to tell her what had happened; after all, she had been unconscious for nine weeks. I asked her if she remembered certain things about the Palm Sunday morning we returned to the hospital and got no response. I explained the whole course of events to her, and when I got to the part about Jacob being taken by C-section and kept alive all this time, she mouthed the words, "Jacob's alive?" Yes, Jacob is alive! Astonishingly, Connie didn't know that. Apparently, while in the coma, she had dreamed that she saw Jacob die. She was sure that we had shown her another baby only to make her feel better. Oh my! No one could have imagined that.

When we both realized that she understood at last, the tears came down in torrents for both of us. She mouthed, "Oh God! Oh God!" She had overcome her grief-stricken nightmare. One of the more privileged moments of my life was bringing our little son from the NICU to Connie's bedside and showing her that he was alive. There was very little need for words at a time like that. Although she couldn't hold him, she turned her head toward him and looked at him with the tender eyes and smile of a mother, and we cried at the sad but touching reunion. Mama and baby were together again.

Jake spent a little more time in the hospital than his mom and developed gradually as the months rolled on. He grew a bit from when I first held his fragile little body in my hand—in two months he had grown to almost eight inches. He also added some needed weight, but he still took his nourishment through a tiny feeding tube for a long while after that. Because he was oxygen-deprived during the birth, the doctors told me that he would probably be blind and brain-damaged, and they predicted that he would have severe cerebral palsy. In fact, none of this happened. He did develop a slight touch of cerebral palsy, but it has not prevented him from functioning, either as a child or as an adult.

The doctors also gave Connie a pessimistic prognosis. They expected her to survive, but they had little hope for her quality of life. My glass-half-full attitude was an asset at this very difficult time; I didn't care what her prognosis was, or Jacob's. I was just glad to have my wife and child back and would accept them in any condition.

Angel of Death in a Lab Coat

Reflecting back on the whole catastrophic experience, a disturbing encounter with a doctor stands out in my mind. About ten days after Connie's incident, we had to deal with a neurologist who was a member of Dr. Buchwald's team. He was considered the resident expert regarding Connie's coma, and he insisted that she had no chance of recovery. I regret that I did not take down his name because he deserved to be reported to the Board of Medicine for his lack of professionalism and compassion.

Due to oxygen deprivation during the trauma, Connie could have suffered irreparable brain damage, and during her coma we did not yet know whether she would end up in a permanent so-called vegetative state. With a condescending attitude the neurologist scoffed at us for "wanting to believe" that she could fully recover. He belittled me for holding out hope when I felt Connie squeeze my finger. He put his finger in her hand, to no avail, and said, "You see? There's nothing there; you're imagining it."

Connie's parents and I were at a disadvantage because we didn't understand all the medical issues and terms, but we did understand the value of life. The critical point was when the doctor said to me, with a wink and a nod, "You know, you have the option of *putting an end to this*" (emphasis mine). He added, "She doesn't have to be kept suffering like this."

"Excuse me?" I thought. "He's telling me I can kill my wife! I don't think so."

Doris was sitting right next to me, and I was stunned at how callous the man could be to say that in front of a mother who loved her daughter and would do anything to save her. Not able to articulate my shock and animosity very well, I waved him off, saying "No, no!", and walked away.

At the time, I was unaware of the exceptionally clear Catholic teachings on end-of-life issues, but I discovered later that my basic intuition had been correct. The Church teaches that although we are not morally obligated to continue extraordinary medical treatments if the patient is beyond any hope of benefitting from them, deliberately and directly killing an innocent person is never a moral option. In Connie's case it was too early to declare her a terminal patient or her treatment futile. We still clung to hope for her recovery *because there still was hope.*

God was not done with Connie yet, and somehow I knew it. When Connie woke up after the many weeks we had kept vigil at her bedside, we felt vindicated. The hope we had placed in the God of life was not disappointed. The neurologist, however, had been dead wrong. Physicians are supposed to be angels of mercy, but he was a minster of death. I find it hard to distinguish him from the Nazi executioners who eliminated sick and disabled people because their quality of life was deemed inferior to theirs.

Even though there are some truly menacing individuals who come into our lives from time to time, the pathway through life also has angels of mercy posted at every juncture. A real angel in my life at that time was Lou Martinez, the entertainment buyer for Peppermill Casinos. Since we could not leave Reno because of Connie and Jake, he booked the band for a year as a favor to us. Up to that time, we had been playing gigs that lasted three weeks to a month, so Lou's offer was extraordinarily generous, and at a time when we needed it most. I will be forever grateful to Lou, because the new arrangement allowed us to live in Reno, and to all the band members, who were okay with moving there. My brother and friends in the band, and especially their wives, were my daily, ongoing, angelic support. They were such a huge help that I will never be able to repay them.

Out of the Frying Pan and into the Fire

Connie got stronger as time went on. When Dr. Buchwald decided to remove the tube from the trachea device and let Connie talk again, I got a call to come over to the hospital. As I got out of the elevator, I could hear Connie's old, familiar foghorn voice echoing down the hallway. She was chewing out everyone in sight with several months' worth of pent-up emotions. She apparently had been saving up all her gripes for just that moment, and she came out firing at the doctors, nurses, and me. It was ugly.

Dr. Buchwald stood there in a shocked state, saying slowly, "What have we done?" She even asked me if I would like her to put the tube back in! Seriously, Dr. Buchwald was probably the best and most competent person to deal with Connie because she was as strong-willed as my wife and refused to put up with any of her nonsense. In fact, she sometimes gave it back to Connie in this tone: "Listen to me, you little &#@$! You're not going to talk to me like that. I saved your life, and you're going to cooperate with me." Indeed, she had saved Connie's life numerous times during the nine weeks of her coma, but that didn't stop Connie from fighting her once she was able. It was clear, though, that the doctor really cared about Connie, and that made all the difference. I am so grateful God put her in our path.

Before Connie's discharge, the nurses gave me a crash course on how to manage all the medical devices that would home with her: feeding tube, colostomy bag, oxygen machine, et cetera. I really couldn't learn it all in a day, but I was a typical twenty-five-year-old male and assured them, "I can do this." I guess I hadn't learned my lesson after presuming to climb Mount Rainier with a seriously injured knee. I still had my stubborn pride that would shortly bring me to the point of another disaster. I believed that I could handle this new situation *myself* simply by taking more responsibility and working harder. In fact, we were going from the frying pan into the fire, and I didn't realize it. I seriously overrated my ability to handle everything.

During her hospitalization, Connie had been through what seemed like endless therapy sessions and was considered well enough to live at home with some assistance. The prognosis was that she would gradually regain most of her motor functioning and health if she kept going to therapy and working to get better. A struggling artist playing all night in casinos, I couldn't afford the type of home nursing care that would have been best for her at that time, and I believed that I could provide for all her needs. But in a few more weeks Jake would come home, and he too would have special needs. I *hoped* everything would work out, but my optimism—this time—didn't take into account the magnitude of the problems facing us.

A Man Must Know His Limitations

Our new routine was a delicate balancing act. The wonderful women who helped us on a daily basis took turns caring for Connie and Britanny when I was working and sleeping. When I was home and awake, I did my share of taking care of my wounded family. With a mentality that didn't admit failure, I was bound and determined to make it all work.

One of the biggest challenges to caring for Connie at home was the complete change in her attitude. In the hospital, Connie was actually proud of the way I had handled the crisis and expressed it in her own strange way, in comments such as, "I didn't think you could do it." But almost as she crossed the threshold of our home, she sank into a terrible and almost aggressive negativity, which was understandable given the helpless condition she and her baby were in. The woman I married, who had always been so vivacious, had become an emotional black hole—she hated God, she hated life, and she hated me. Of the three, I was the easiest target of her bitterness, and I took her criticisms personally. Whenever she found fault with me, I defensively replied, "Thanks a lot." I sometimes added, "This was not my idea either, and I'm sorry that it happened to you, but we can't change it, and we're doing the best we can." I became resentful of her resentment, which, needless to say, did nothing to pierce her cloud of desolation.

I was dealing with my own increased stresses too. The very thought of Jake coming home scared me to death, because he would be another dependent being with more problems to manage. My joy at his arrival didn't last long, because I took upon myself the whole responsibility for the devices that kept him alive. Many nights I raced back home on my half-hour break at the casino to rethread Jake's feeding tube or to calibrate a machine, and then rushed back to play the rest of the night. It was this mad daily dash to do it all that paved the way for another catastrophe. I should have trained our friends to manage Jake's care when I was working, but I guess I had a hard time admitting that I needed more help.

The redeeming grace in all this was my relationship with Britanny, who was the one constant in my life at that time and remains so to this day. I had afternoons and evenings with her, and she coped well with the stress at home simply by playing games with her dad and watching the little kid movies she liked. Because she was so young at the time, she hardly remembers anything from that episode except many of the fun things we did together, such as going out for milkshakes, delicacies she termed "shaky milks". To this day, "shaky milks" are our favorite drinks. The Gospel says that we cannot enter the Kingdom of God unless we become like little children, and Britanny was a living example of how children teach us the most important lessons in life and love.

The event that haunts me to this day involved a life-threatening incident with little Jake soon after he came home. Connie called me at Western Village early one morning to tell me that Jake was very pale and that she was very concerned for him. After finishing my last set I was utterly exhausted. I raced home to see what the issue was, and when I got there, Jake was very pale indeed. His skin was almost see-through, and it struck me immediately that something was very wrong. I quickly ran through the list of the things

I was supposed to check on every day, and there was nothing out of place. All his vital signs were good at that moment, and all the machines seemed to be working. He looked his normal, content little self; he was even smiling. I presumed that if there was no blood or apparent trauma, everything would be fine. Out of sheer exhaustion, mixed with some apathy, I went to bed while Connie chewed me out for ignoring the problem.

Chalk it up to mother's intuition—Connie and my mom, who had come from Texas to help us for a while, didn't wait for me to take action. They rushed the baby to the hospital and met Dr. Buchwald in the emergency room. There was a good reason why Jake looked so pale: something had caused his internal feeding tube to dislodge, and he wasn't getting any nourishment. Dr. Buchwald told them that if they had waited another hour or so, little Jacob would have died. It's hard to say which was more jarring: the phone ringing at 7 A.M., waking me out of a sound sleep, or Connie's angry voice on the other end, calling me every name in the book for *what I almost let happen*. In all fairness to her, she was upset, understandably so, because Dr. Buchwald had read her the riot act for both of us being so negligent on this important matter. Nobody barks an "I told you so" like Connie, but this time she didn't need to say a word; I was utterly crushed by my own negligence that almost cost my precious little son his life.

In one of his Dirty Harry movies, Clint Eastwood said, "A man must know his limitations", and this situation with Jake taught me one severe limitation of mine: a bad habit of overestimating my own abilities. I was totally out of my league in trying to be primary caregiver, provider, husband, and dad at the same time. That morning I called Connie's parents in Texas and related to them the whole sorrowful incident. I confessed to them that I needed their help. Truth be told, they had offered to help earlier, but in my pride I had refused their gracious offer. This time I was willing to admit that I could not do it all on my own. Life had brought me to my knees. I had experienced my own crash-and-burn failure—something that I never thought would happen to me.

Soon thereafter, Connie and I agreed to move her and the kids to Greenville, Texas, where her parents would look after her and Jacob's needs better than I could. It was clear to me that Gary and Doris would be the perfect caretakers for Connie during her ongoing recovery, which was predicted to be total if she had the right environment and help. The Parkers provided both of these, and I was so grateful. They also took great care of Jake, who needed constant attention during that early period of his life. Jake too made a full recovery in time, thanks in large part to his grandparents' love and care.

I moved into a free housing unit provided by Peppermill and stayed in Reno to work. I fulfilled the role of provider to the best of my ability by sending Connie every dollar I could from my wages. I lived very simply in Reno so that I could give my family all they needed, but I also lived with a lot of guilt, not only about my failure to do everything that I had promised to do as a husband and a dad, but more importantly, about not being present to my family. For the next several years I would never be able to spend as much time at home as my heart desired, and I was haunted by the specter of the fatherly absence I had experienced in my family, a pattern I did not want to repeat. I believe that my guilt about being absent for that period led to a later tendency to overcompensate for that.

My big reservation about the arrangement was that Britanny would have to go with Connie to Texas, and I would be separated from her for an indeterminate amount of time. I knew that would be hard for both of us. Dads are supposed to do what is best for their kids, and I felt that this move was best for her—a decision I would greatly regret—but I missed her like crazy. Every spare moment I could afford to take off from work, I flew down to Greenville to be with my family and to do my best to make up for my absences.

A Momentous Decision

During this period, when I was traveling back and forth between Reno and Greenville, a separation that had been growing between Connie and me for several years grew wider, and our relationship deteriorated further. Connie's negativity seemed to have become a fixed part of her personality. We were fighting often now, about everything. Our physical distance had been great for some time, but our emotional distance was even greater.

One evening in Greenville, Connie cussed me out right in front of the kids for folding a bathroom towel in two instead of in the trifold way that she preferred. It was one of our worst fights and was symbolic of how badly damaged our marriage was. I knew deep down that the real issue was not the towel; it was the animosity that we had allowed to grow between us.

After that fight, I knew that I didn't want to be married to Connie any longer. We could not stand to be around each other. We had reached the point of no return in our relationship

Similar to the way my parents dealt with my brother's accident, Connie and I let our own family tragedy drive us apart. The decision to divorce after eight years of marriage was one of the hardest decisions of my life. Nothing short of the death of a loved one is as painful as divorce. I knew that I should honor my commitments, and I felt guilty about breaking my promises to Connie. I initiated the divorce and prayed that God, who sees all, would understand.

With hindsight, I can see that our marriage had not been built on a strong foundation. Couples who live together before marriage often form selfish habits that remain essentially the same the day after the wedding as the day before. When questioned about marriage, Jesus quoted the book of Genesis, "For this reason a man shall leave his father and mother and be joined to his wife, and the two shall become one flesh" (Mk 10:8, cf. Gen 2:24), in order to point out that marriage entails a total, lifelong commitment and an actual change of life for both spouses.

Had Connie and I not lived together, we probably would never have gotten married or our marriage would have had a more secure foundation. The birth of our daughter made Connie and me very happy and united us for a while, but we were too different in temperament and values and too lacking in resolve to stick together no matter what. Looking back, I see that one of the reasons we didn't stay together is that our marriage was not a sacramental union, that is, an unbreakable covenant relationship endowed with God's full blessing. Yet the fruits of our marriage are a daughter and a son who are the most precious blessings we have ever received. My faith has grown in the intervening years, and I certainly have come to a greater appreciation of the Church's teaching about marriage.

Although divorced from Connie, I continued to provide for her and our children. After I signed my record deal with Sony, we lived very close to one another and did many things together that revolved around the kids. The one accomplishment of mine that makes me most proud is that I have honored my commitment to provide for Connie, Britanny, and Jacob. I rest secure in my conscience that I have fulfilled my sweet, blessed obligation to my family as a father and a provider—and have loved every minute of it.

First National Record Deal

The year Connie and Jake were both in the hospital was also, ironically, the year the Wray Brothers Band got its first national record deal. I was like a thirsty man traveling through a vast desert who had suddenly come upon an oasis.

The band was playing for Peppermill Casinos in Reno with some degree of success, and I was wondering whether we had any future in the record business. Thankfully, my manager Steve Cox was able to secure us a record deal, which made us feel that at least there was some movement forward toward the ultimate goal of hitting it big in Nashville. Steve had connected us with Nashville producer Stan Cornelius, who signed us with the major record label Mercury/Polygram, an outfit that already had several big names such as the Statler Brothers and Kathy Mattea. Every producer and label in Nashville was looking for the next Alabama, and Mercury/Polygram was willing to take a look at us. They were giving us a shot at a *national* record deal.

Our first trip to Nashville was a long and tedious one filled with many disappointments. It was our first exposure to the business aspect of Nashville, which was a rather rude awakening for us. For example, all the members of the band went to the studio, but they were prohibited from playing or singing on our own album. We had to use studio musicians and cut only the songs that Stan chose for us. Some of them were pretty cheesy too, such as the highly amusing "You Lay a Lot of Love on Me". It had inspiring lyrics such as, "Hey, little lady, you lay a lotta love on me. You got a little bitty body with a heart big as I've ever seen." It may have reached Number Forty on the charts—maybe—and my voice was the only element of the Wray Brothers Band to be heard on the album. It was very disappointing for everyone.

We were even more disheartened when we found out that Mercury/Polygram would never release the album. We shouldn't have been—admittedly, it wasn't a very good album. The executives at Mercury thought only two singles from the album were actually good enough to release to radio; of these, only "You Lay a Lot of Love on Me" had any success at all—and that was marginal at best. The whole album was back-shelved, and that was our short-lived national record deal. We had better success with *Cowboy Sangers*.

I admit with some regret that I didn't put a great deal of effort into this first chance at hitting the big time. I was preoccupied with the health of Connie and Jake and with taking care of Britanny; I basically went through the motions when we were in Nashville. Perhaps the rough year I had just been through left me too exhausted and distracted to do a good job. I was feeling the accumulated stress of trying to be the perfect father to my kids while trying to advance my career, and I'm sure that was taking its toll on me. I only know that we were better than our lackluster performance on that trip to Nashville, and I still held out hope that we would get another shot at it. When the record failed, I wondered whether we had really blown our one and only chance at national exposure. I had many doubts: maybe we as a group weren't good enough; maybe I wasn't a good enough singer; maybe we just weren't cut out for the big time. At the end of it all, I felt kind of lost, professionally.

My Purgatory on Earth

The next four years were the darkest years of my life because I was in the proverbial no-win scenario and saw no clear exit. I was locked in a job that paid well but that was an absolute soul-buster. Playing in Reno was very good for my career and provided great support for my family, but, personally, it was very devastating to be apart from the ones I loved and wanted to be with all the time. It was a classic catch-22 situation that I dealt with in the way that many divorced dads do: I compensated like mad to be with my kids as much as possible and make sure that they didn't suffer on my account.

My schedule for that whole period was appallingly rigorous. I performed in Reno six or seven nights a week for six weeks straight, and then I took a week to ten days off to play Superdad in Texas. I talked to the kids every day on the phone, multiple times, and prided myself on being at most of the major events in their lives during that time. Nonetheless, my coming and going was pretty hard on them, more so on Britanny than on Jake. Whenever I would have to leave the kids to go back to Reno, Connie and her parents would bring them with us to the airport to see me off. In those days, families could go with their loved ones to the gates in the terminal, and Britanny always cried, sometimes powerfully, as I walked down the ramp to get on the airplane. Her tears ripped my heart out every single time. Jake was still very small then and thought I was just going into another house when he saw me walking through that door to get onto the plane. He used to tell people, "My Daddy lives at the airport!"

After the emotional upheaval of leaving the kids in Texas, I was back on stage in Reno four hours later, pretending to be happy, doing my job, and pleasing audiences. It was an absolutely brutal experience each time. It had the effect, however, of toughening me up for things to come.

Sparring with the Pros

To keep my sanity during this period, I lifted weights and learned to box. Most of my band members were well on their way to addiction and/or self-destruction, and I definitely did not want to walk down the same path. Playing in casinos was lucrative but was also potentially soul-killing: we faced audiences that, night after night, didn't care that we were there. The routine left us absolutely numb. Being away from my kids, I needed to be focused on something that was healthful. I could have filled the emotional vacuum with the plethora of addictive substances or bad relationships that are readily at hand in casinos, but I chose to get out my anger, frustration, and aggression in a positive way, and am glad I did!

As a routine, I got up about midday and went to the Hans Gym in Reno to work out. In a few short months, I went from 175 pounds to 215 pounds, but it was all muscle weight. I also began to train with a crusty old boxing coach named Moe Smith, who looked and sounded uncannily like Burgess Meredith, the seasoned Philadelphia boxing trainer in the *Rocky* movies. Moe trained professional boxers for a living, and after a session one day he asked, "Why don't you come in here and start sparring with the pros?" I wasn't sure about that because I thought sparring partners needed to be licensed, but he said it would be okay as long as I didn't tell anyone! Moe wanted me to spar because he was looking for someone who didn't mind getting hit but could stay up with the pros.

The boxer I most remember sparring with was the heavyweight Phil Brown, who at that time was ranked in the top twenty in the world. Phil weighed 220 pounds, while I was 207 pounds at that moment but very fit. Moe wanted me to get low, the way Mike Tyson did, and put pressure on

Phil by hitting him as much as I could. He was trying to teach Phil how to fight guys who were smaller than he, who were the majority of boxers. I did this with several of Moe's other boxers and apparently performed a valuable service for their careers—without too much damage to my face or ego. When I would go to work after an afternoon of sparring with the big boys, I would often find that my band members had spent the whole night drinking and drugging and were still in their clothes from the day before. I would make a point to greet them cheerily, "Guess what I did today?", and tell them about the cool guys I had sparred with at the gym. None of them was impressed, but I was doing it to make a point. I knew that God was protecting me from the most dangerous aspects of the entertainment lifestyle, and I was grateful.

I Almost Quit Music

Between the failure of the Mercury/Polygram deal in 1986 and the time I would sign with CBS in 1990, I was reevaluating my singing career. On the plus side, I was having some great quality time with the kids, especially during the summers. Britanny was five years old in 1988, and Jake was three. Little Jake didn't spend as much time with me as I would have wanted because he liked to stay with his grandparents. He was developing well, thanks primarily to Doris, who spent endless hours training him to walk during that period. He may not have learned to walk at all, had it not been for her infinite patience in helping him to develop the proper coordination of his little limbs. I will be forever grateful to her for that.

Britanny and I had some of the best times of our lives during those summers, and she remembers it all very well. Reno was close enough to San Francisco for us to go there on a regular basis. We saw Fisherman's Wharf and Pier 39, the Golden Gate Bridge, Alcatraz, the Great America amusement park, and many other attractions. We also took that special ride *down* the notorious Lombard Street, which prides itself on being the most crooked street in the world. We have so many fun, precious memories of those days, and Britanny was always nonstop joy, the light of my whole life. Those were magical summers with my little girl.

Professionally, I was both gratified at my progress as a musician and frustrated at the same time. I had gotten noticeably better at singing since

I had been in Reno. My voice was getting more pronounced, and I was hitting higher notes with greater ease. Usually a man's voice gets lower as he ages, but mine got higher. My voice seemed to have opened up, and as a result, I was doing things that I could never do before, such as singing classic rock tunes that had a very high range. I was singing in the range of Zeppelin's lead singer, Robert Plant, who was known for his intense, high-pitched vocal prowess, and it felt great to be able to do what few guys could do. The payoff for years of constant applied effort in my profession was a greater level of confidence in my abilities as a singer.

At the same time, my band was in a shambles. I had to change a few band members over the course of our time in Reno, and the band members who were left—with the exception of Lin Phillips—all seemed a bit dysfunctional or addicted to something. Clearly their years of partying had taken their toll on them. My frustration level was extreme. It reached the boiling point in the late summer of 1989 in Laughlin, Nevada, when we had a gig playing at the Ramada Express for a whole month in what must have been 120-degree heat. We had no following at all there and no enthusiasm for our task; the boys didn't want to be there any more than I did. Britanny had just gone back to school, and I was missing the kids and missing home. I was just miserable.

My manager, Steve, came down to see me there, and we had a heart-to-heart talk about my emotional state and my career. I started our conversation bluntly, "Steve, I'm quitting. This is ridiculous; I'm done with this. I'm gonna go back and be with the kids. I've hit bottom." I unloaded all my frustrations on him, and I know that he was keenly aware that I was suffering from being away from my kids. Fun vacations and phone calls home, even on a daily basis, were no substitute for a fatherly presence in their little lives, or their presence in mine. I had even made some inquiries with my brother-in-law back in Texas about getting a *janitor's* job at the Raytheon plant in Greenville. I was actually considering working for the government! Lord, what was I thinking?

Steve read the situation perfectly and took matters into his own hands. I remember him taking the cigar out of his mouth, putting his left hand around the back of my neck, looking me straight in the eye, and telling me to hang on for a little while longer, just a few months more, while he worked some more angles for me. "Bud, you were *meant* to do this", he said. "Just give us a little time." In his noble way, he assured me that he believed in me and my talents. More importantly, he sized up the overall situation accurately and gave me some good advice. Knowing that the band was falling apart and that I was floundering, he said something that changed my life: "Maybe it's time to forget the band. We'll get a deal for you alone."

A solo career—it was not exactly a new idea, but it was as if I were hearing it for the first time. In fact, going solo was an option I had discounted in my mind many times before, but it suddenly became the one that God wanted me to choose. Steve saw me standing as if paralyzed in front of a door, one too massive for me to open on my own, and insisted that I walk through it. He pressed the issue. He knew that there was nothing left for me in being part of a band, and he believed that I *needed* to go solo. Sometimes a devoted friend can be more objective about your situation than you yourself can be, and in this case, Steve had the sight and the maturity to point out the way.

Steve's guidance turned out to be critical for my whole career. His strong grip on the back of my neck at that moment was a *literal* experience of God's hand leading me where He wanted me to go. God used this wonderful, fatherly man to put me on the right track to my future. I sat with the "going solo" idea for a while, and it grew on me. The more I reflected on it, the more it made sense, and I soon recognized it as God's will for my life. I decided, finally, that I would take his challenge to be a solo artist, and it was the beginning of a new life for me. I'll never be able to thank Steve enough for that heart-to-heart talk or for his keen insight into my deepest self. He was the cool head in the 120-degree Nevada heat.

A dear friend in Reno, Bob Dee, put Steve and me in touch with Jerry Fuller, who was a pop-record producer from Los Angeles looking to break a country act. Jerry looked and sounded like a Texan right out of a John Wayne movie, but earlier in his career, he had been a top executive at Columbia Records in New York and was a well-known pop-music writer. He wrote Ricky Nelson's famous "Travellin' Man" and some big hits for Gary Puckett and the Union Gap, such as "Young Girl" and "Woman, Woman". He was an awesome songwriter and producer. His production partner was John Hobbs, who was a pianist and without a doubt the best musician I had ever met. Hobbs would end up producing at least six of my albums and was to have an unparalleled impact on my career.

Jerry came to see me at Bob Dee's Western Village and immediately liked my voice. He told me that I sounded great and promised to bring me down to his studio in LA. We would cut a demo, he said, that we would pitch to the major labels and hopefully land a record deal. I appreciated Jerry's offer, but I had heard that line many times before; I didn't hold out much hope that anything would come of it. Yet, about eight months later, Jerry came through. I flew down to LA to cut the demo in his own studio in 1990, and my life was never the same.

Jerry got top-drawer musicians to help me make this demo. I brought my guitarist Kraig Hutchens with me, and John Hobbs arranged the music and played piano. We also had on steel guitar J. D. Manus, who had worked with Buck Owens and the Desert Rose Band. To top it off, bluegrass legend Herb Peterson, who had played with John Denver, sang harmony with me. These guys were real pros. It was a dream come true.

We cut six or seven songs for the demo, none of which ended up on any album, but we knew at the time that we weren't producing an album. We were producing a demo, and it needed to impress only a few key people in Nashville to get me in the door. After shopping the demo, Jerry connected with his good friend Bob Montgomery, the head of A and R (Artists and Repertoire Division) at CBS, who wanted to come to Reno to see me live. He came with his radio promotion man, Jack Lameier, and after they saw me on stage at the Carson Station Casino, they offered me a record deal with CBS Records right on the spot. "Yeah, you're great", said Bob after he saw me perform. "We love your demo. You got a deal."

I said to myself, "You mean it was as simple as that?" After all the years clawing my way through the business, after catastrophes in my personal and family life, a couple of near misses with recordings, doubts about everything I was doing, a disintegrating band, and thousands of hours playing in squalid bars, I was finally a solo artist wielding an eight-album record deal with one of the biggest record companies on the planet. Then another thought hit me like a ton of bricks: eight albums is a whole career's worth of albums. Thank You, Lord!

A Name Change   .

I now had a record contract with CBS (soon to be Sony) and was eager to start recording, but my initial excitement was dampened when Steve called me and said that Sony was insisting on a name change for me.

"A name change? Really?" I asked.

"That's what they want", he replied as diplomatically as he could.

I had been called Bubba for thirty years and, as any other person would be, I was fairly attached to my own name. In my mind, Bubba was a good country music name, but to the leadership at Sony, it wasn't a *marketable* name in radio. The Sony people said that there were some radio stations on the East Coast that would not even touch a song by a guy named Bubba, and I had to bend to that reality. In today's country music environment, the more hick-sounding a name is the better it works, but in 1990, Bubba had to go.

My last name, Wray, had to go too. I knew my dad wasn't going to like the change of surname—and he didn't—but Sony didn't leave him or me with much of a choice. Again, Sony's logic was all about marketing and sales: most people trying to find a Bubba Wray album in the record store would naturally look in the *R* bin rather than search for it under *W*; thus, my last name needed to be spelled "Raye". I understood the concept and was happy that at least my new last name would *sound* the same. I look back on my name change as symbolic of the radical transformation of my life from small-time performer to big-name performer, and the name was a critical element of that.

I was nominally included in the name-change process, but I don't think my input was ever taken seriously. Steve asked me to make a list of twenty possible names to submit to Sony for consideration. The only name I remember from my list of cool names was Tom Bowie. I liked that name. I grew up in Bowie County, Texas, and loved the famous Jim Bowie, one of the heroes of the Alamo, but I knew they wouldn't let me use his name. I also always liked the name Tom or Thomas for some reason, although I would have settled for James or John, if it came down to it. But they ignored every single name I submitted, including Tom Bowie, and four days later announced the new name that would identify me until the day I die: Collin Raye.

I remember the night I got the call from Steve announcing my new identity. I was playing one of my last shows at Stockman's Casino in Elko, Nevada, and when I picked up the phone, I could tell he wasn't totally comfortable on the other end, which was out of character for a guy who was normally very laid-back. I didn't know at that moment that he had an unusual piece of news to give me. Then, with no lead-in, he cleared his throat and announced abruptly, "Well, bud, your new name's Collin Raye."

"Collin?" I asked.

"Yep, Collin."

"Hmmm. Collin … Collin … hmmm. Well, I don't know, Steve."

In fact, the name had never even crossed my mind as an option. The only mental connection I made at the moment was to General Colin Powell, and I wasn't thrilled with the idea of having a name that sounded too similar to the famous army general. I also remembered that in the movie *The Great Escape* there was a half-blind character named Collin, who was played by Donald Pleasence. The character was a bit odd, though, and didn't give me a good impression of what a Collin should be like. I remained concerned.

"Sounds kinda English to me", I said. "Does it sound *tough* enough, Steve? Does it sound *rugged*?"

"Well, that's what they picked", he replied matter-of-factly, ending his formal process of discernment on the matter.

The real reason they chose Collin was less than encouraging. One of the executives at Sony had just welcomed a newborn grandson who was given a name the exec really liked—Collin. This was a reason to change *my* name? I think Steve tried to soften the blow by telling me that he remembered a pretty decent rodeo cowboy with the name Collin somewhere in the vast annals of Western lore. He meant well.

At that point, my mind was attempting to force together the discordant images of an odd British actor, a rodeo cowboy, a newborn baby, and a four-star general—all named Colin or Collin—and it just wasn't working.

"Well, I guess I'll have to get used to it", I said somberly.

I accepted the need for a new name but wasn't entirely sold on the one they chose. After all, what was wrong with Tom Bowie? I levied just one condition on the name before I adopted it; namely, that it be spelled with two *L*'s instead of one. There were two very practical reasons for wanting the double *L* in *Collin*. First, I didn't want people confusing it with Colin Powell, and second, I didn't want them pronouncing it with the long *o*, making it sound like *colon*! Call me picky, but, I refused to go through life being called by a name that sounded like that of a digestive or excremental organ. Essentially, I was making a statement that I was going to be my own man with my own unique stage name, or not at all. Sony acquiesced to my one condition, and the process of creating a new country-music personality was thus complete: *Collin Raye* was born.

Even I was surprised at how quickly I got used to the new name. Within a week, I was comfortable with people calling me Collin, and an interesting transition took place inside me. The name soon "felt" better to me and began to fit like an old shoe as time went on. The transformation eventually became so total that when people would call me Bubba or refer to me by my legal name, Floyd, I would feel uncomfortable with *those* names. Anyway, Collin wasn't so bad after all. I am fully comfortable with it, and making it my own was easier than I thought it would be.

Of course, the only names that really matter to me are the ones I hear from my kids and grandkids: Daddy and Poppy.

Second Chances

From a distance of more than twenty years, I am still assessing the damage from the meteors that crashed into my life during the eighties. The meteors left their trails of destruction, and, to this day, I look back with amazement at how my family survived all that upheaval: moves to three states, medical and personal catastrophes, agonizing disruptions of our lives, divorce, and years of separation from the kids. This was by far the darkest period of my life; the pain of it was to be equaled only by the passing of my grandchild years later, but I was glad to emerge from it with my identity, my personality, and, thankfully, my relationship with my kids intact and thriving.

Most of the eighties were brutal years in every way, but by 1990 I had a new name and a new status, and the sun was dawning on a new day.

5

Real Life, Real Love, Real Loss

The Agony and the Ecstasy of Country Music

*But we have this treasure in earthen vessels, to show that the
transcendent power belongs to God and not to us.*

—2 Cor 4:7

The story of my albums and songs cannot be told unless I first recount the
tale of my passion for music from my earliest days. Irving Stone entitled
his 1961 biography of Michelangelo *The Agony and the Ecstasy*, which is
an iconic title that captures both the passion an artist has for his work and
the rigors he endures to create it. The title is certainly a fitting description
of my own experiences as a professional musician. The many moments
of agonizing losses, immense sacrifices in following my dream, and sufferings resulting from my own faults and those of others always seem to
have been balanced by the ecstasy of sublime musical experiences and
fascinating encounters with some of the most incredible and gifted human
beings on the planet.

There is no denying that music has had a mystical effect on my soul and
has helped to form me into the person I am today. From a very early age,
I was able to absorb effortlessly every kind of music, memorizing easily
both the lyrics and the tunes of songs, which, in hindsight, was an early
sign of my growing talents. My musical appetite was insatiable, not only
because I came from a musical family, but especially because music was
my calling. God had given me the innate capacities to be a musician and
the deep love of music that I needed to be a performer, and I have no doubt
that the musical gifts I have are not mine; I am aware that I must use those

gifts for the benefit of my fellow men and always try to leave the world a better place than I found it, through music.

My First Musical Love: Country

Even though my desire to be a *performer* was crystallized by the insanely cool and seductive personalities of rock 'n' roll, my first musical love was country and my childhood heroes were the icons of the trade: Waylon Jennings, Merle Haggard, George Jones, Hank Williams, Willie Nelson, Buck Owens, Johnny Cash, and Glen Campbell—the real poetic men of country music. There were many more.

In contrast with today's music—both pop and country—which is saturated with promiscuity, the sixties were luminous years of musical purity, when country music experienced a kind of heyday or golden age; it was the predominant music of my family and social environment during the period of my childhood and adolescence in Arkansas and Texas. In the South, country music is in every nook and cranny of culture and society: being broadcast from most radio stations, playing on the jukeboxes in every diner, and pumping through the loudspeakers in many stores and malls. Even my mom's foray into singing with Elvis in the late fifties was a *quasi*-country music experience, because in those days the line between gospel, country, and rhythm and blues was still a bit blurry. The legend from Memphis was actually born in Tupelo, Mississippi, and got his musical start singing gospel songs in an Assembly of God church long before he ever became the King of Rock 'n' Roll. His music was technically called "rockabilly", essentially a new fusion of country and rhythm and ("hillbilly") blues.

Oh yes. Elvis was country too—and if he wasn't, please, no one tell my Mama.

The Genius of Country Music

The true genius of country music is Merle Haggard. I remember him when he was just getting his start. I first heard him when my dad brought home his single "(My Friends Are Gonna Be) Strangers", and he sounded *so good* to me! He was clearly different from most of the other country stars at the time, mainly because he was a singer/songwriter. While there were others who wrote their own songs, no one did it quite like "the Hag", as he was called. His songs had so much character and beautiful poetry: "Mama Tried", "Branded Man", "The Fugitive", "Mama's Hungry Eyes", "Sing Me Back Home", and countless others are among the classics of country music. I rank Merle as the greatest singer/songwriter in country music history. Hank Williams is perhaps the only one who rivaled Merle and might have even surpassed his life's work had Hank not died at the young age of twenty-nine. We'll never know.

In any case, the country stars of my childhood years imbued my whole being with a respect and love for country music that has never left me. The country greats were artists, first and foremost, but they were also representatives of the culture that formed them. I listened to their songs and absorbed their unique perspective on life the way thirsty ground drinks in the rain. They all sang about real life, real love, and real loss. That has always been my rather idealistic view of country music's contribution to culture, and the purity of my ideal was never diminished by the reality of the performers' lives. These men and women made a career of entertaining, consoling, and even healing people through their music; I am certain that their music healed me in many ways by its beauty and power to inspire. Their lyrics memorialized the ups and downs of the human drama that normal people live on a daily basis: abandonment, lovesickness, loyalty, family, God, simple joy, sorrow, suffering, and pain were the concerns of country songs. I grew up wanting to sing about those things before I ever imagined I could be a solo artist.

There is no doubt that the old-time country music had a penchant for dwelling on the negative, and for that reason there emerged a later tendency of country radio stations to want songs that were "positive, positive, positive", but those always seemed false to me. Merle and Hank and company had taught me that country music, by definition, was almost always sad because it dealt with the real sorrows of ordinary people. Many things in life are sad. Of the dozens of songs in Hank Williams' repertoire, not one was "positive", except perhaps "I Saw the Light" and "Jambalaya". Virtually all of my top-ten favorite country songs are sad and deal with the problems caused by our weak and fragile nature.

Not everything about that generation of music was wholesome, however, nor was it always very sophisticated. It was just *real*. It had its own salacious element. When Travis Tritt did a remake of that early Elvis song, "T-R-O-U-B-L-E", I wondered why I had ever liked it. The silly piece is about a guy lusting for a woman who walks into a bar. Songs about marital infidelity and drunkenness were also quite common, but the difference between songs of that era and songs of today is that these phenomena were never celebrated; they were parodied and displayed as some of life's many problems that needed remedy, comfort, and perhaps even compassion.

Yet, for all the earthiness of the genre, the bygone country music culture was rooted in something called respect: respect for God, religion, tradition, timeless values, and the institutions of marriage and family. The olds songs might have related in tongue-and-cheek fashion the many foibles of the human condition, but they didn't justify or glorify them—they sought to raise fallen man from them. Rousing tributes to faith and references to God were an essential element of the music of that era precisely for that reason. The time-honored tradition of ninety-year-old Little Jimmy Dickens ending shows at the Grand Ole Opry by singing his classic songs such as "Life Turned Her That Way" or "The Bird of Paradise", followed by a gospel song, is an expression of the classic country values that used to reign throughout the industry as a whole. In other words, after the fun and entertainment, real country music roots its listeners in the ideals that we all hold dearest in our hearts.

Many readers will remember the country humor and variety television show *Hee Haw* (1969–1992), featuring Buck Owens, Roy Clark, Grandpa Jones, Junior Samples, "Stringbean" Akeman, and Minnie Pearl, among others. My favorite part of the show was undoubtedly the hilarious "Gloom, Despair, and Agony on Me", a skit that would mercilessly parody country music's tendency to dwell on the tragedies of life. It ended with one of the most memorable refrains of the golden era of television: "If it weren't for bad luck, I'd have no luck at all / Gloom, despair, and agony on me!" *Hee Haw*'s humor was clever, fun, and earthy. Its music was always top-notch and usually included a segment of gospel as a natural part of the programming.

The old-time country music also had phenomenal artistry and color that is hard to reproduce today. In the era of my heroes, Glen Campbell was as different from Buck Owens as Johnny Cash was from Charlie Pride. Each was uniquely his own man with his own artistic style and flair because he was not trying to conform to industry expectations about record sales. In fact, I would go so far as to say that these musicians were not trying to be stars at all; they were essentially artists, and stardom caught up to them because they were *good*. Like oil, real talent has a way of rising to the top. The greats were simply the best of the best in their field, and they achieved stardom the old-fashioned way: they earned it.

Artistic, well-written songs that address human suffering tend to touch people's lives. That was the genius of country music. Music is consoling for people when they feel sad or defeated, and even as a kid I wanted to sing in the authentic country music tradition of the greats with songs that heal broken and hurting hearts whether or not a fiddle or a steel guitar was featured.

The Incomparable Waylon Jennings

I recorded Waylon Jennings' song "Dreamin' My Dreams with You" for my 1994 album, *Extremes*, and because of that song I had the opportunity to meet Waylon in person and to get to know him and his wife Jessie fairly well. It meant so much to me that he liked me and my version of his song; he even said that he admired my talent, which I think may be the greatest compliment I have ever received. I will never forget the day, a few years later, that Waylon himself came with his publicist to the studio where I was working and pitched me a song that he wanted me to do. It was a truly surreal moment; I wondered how it could be that my childhood hero was pitching *me* a song.

Waylon's place in my heart can never belong to anyone else. He was the one who taught me to love country music all over again when I was fifteen or sixteen years old and getting drawn into rock 'n' roll. He was a brilliant artist and a great writer whose songs reminded me of the true beauty and common-man wisdom of the genre. They were pure and raw and aimed at touching the very souls of people. Waylon sang with deep emotion and never oversang his songs or overproduced his records with too many vocals or instruments. His low, gravelly voice and rugged style were inimitable. Because my voice and style are so different from Waylon's, many people are surprised to learn that Waylon is my favorite country singer of all time. He isn't my hero because I want to imitate him; I admire him because no one could ever do what he did; he was unique and deeply inspired me.

Country music has never been as good as when Waylon was the biggest thing there was.The last time I saw him before he died was in 2001 at the Ryman Auditorium in Nashville, and I have to say that I miss him greatly.

Nashville's Modern Sellout

The "real life" country that nurtured me and fed me in my youth is not the country music of today. The movers and shakers of Nashville have largely abandoned the reality-based, moral message for the common man that made country music a strong cultural force for good. There are still many great singers and songwriters in Nashville who can write a touchingly deep and meaningful song, but in my opinion, some of the most gifted country songwriters water down their talents on shallow, trashy music designed to sell records by appealing to the lowest common denominator. They've settled on an ethic of "give 'em what they want" in the pursuit of the almighty dollar, and that is a violation of the artist's unwritten oath to raise men's hearts to a higher place. I doubt that the public really wants that kind of shallow music. They may *consume* it—as they consume fast food—but it leaves them destitute of nourishment. One cannot listen to Top Forty "hot" new country stations and hear even three songs in a row *without* a vulgar celebration of drinking, partying, or girls going wild. Songs about superficial love, pickup trucks, and happy-go-lucky rednecks are not authentic country.

My judgment is less about the artists who are hungry to break through, perform, and prosper in Nashville and on the world stage than it is about what record labels push as the "hot new country". The industry has gone from "Something in Red" to "Somethin' 'bout a Truck" with the following profound lyrics:

> Somethin' 'bout a truck in a field
> And a girl in a red sundress with an ice cold beer to her lips
>   begging for another kiss.
> Somethin' 'bout you and me and the birds and the bees
> And Lord have mercy, it's a beautiful thing
> Ain't nothin' 'bout it luck, somethin' 'bout a truck.[1]

Quality songs are too few and far between nowadays.

My granddaughter Mattie and her generation are on the verge of growing up thinking country music is about buzzkill, tattoos on a girl's back playing peek-a-boo, and the art of being redneck crazy. The following lyrics are indicative of the sad state of the genre today:

"Crank up a little Hank, sit on the hood and drink. / I'm about to get my [expletive] on."[2]

"You're a buzzkill every time you come around. / Those beers might as well have been poured out.... Baby, you're a buzzkill."[3]

"It's hard to drive with her hand over here on my knee. / When she's all over me, I'm all outta control / All over the road."[4]

"Pour a little Crown in a Dixie cup. / Girl, you make my speakers go boom boom.... That kind of thing makes a man go mmm hmmm.... Hey, I'm a little drunk on you / And high on summertime."[5]

"I got a dress that'll show a little uh uh / But you ain't getting uh uh if you don't come pick me up [expletive]!"[6]

"Make me want to go ouuh ouhh when you dance like that. / You got that little tattoo playing peeky boo on your back.... All you got to do is put a drink in my hand."[7]

These songs are not isolated excerpts from the dregs of country music. Songs of this stripe are legion today—and extremely popular. I highlight them simply to point out the current trends. Lowbrow behavior is the common theme of most of country music today. Instead of lifting people up by giving meaning to their suffering, this kind of music demeans the dignity of people by emphasizing, even glorifying, base and immoral pursuits. It used to be that rock 'n' roll was the reservoir of promiscuity, intoxication, and vulgarity, and its influence on country music is beyond evident. Why are country music artists now eagerly imitating the worst aspects of hip-hop and rock 'n' roll?

Bottom-line business criteria have always played a role in deciding which songs get played on the radio, which singers get the big label push, and which acts will be the winners of the coveted country music awards. I regret to say that these decisions are not made on the basis of sheer artistry or talent. They are made on the basis of what does the most business and who can sell the most beer, and they generally favor yuppie boys in cowboy hats trying desperately to sound as if they have a chew of tobacco in the lip, singing about the sentimental value of getting drunk a lot. The breweries and distilleries that rule the day in Nashville may soon ruin the country music genre. It's time for Nashville to come home to its roots planted deeply by Hank and Haggard, Patsy and Dolly, George and Waylon.

Country Music Should Be Different

One could argue that the trends of superficiality, vulgarity, and commercialism are endemic to every aspect of our society, especially entertainment, but I would argue back that country music should go beyond that. Country music has always been about reality—*real* life—which means it has to be based on themes that touch on the noble struggles of man to overcome the problems of life. The term "pop music" has always meant trendy, flash-in-the-pan, here-today-gone-tomorrow superficiality, and the themes of pop music reflect that capricious spirit. I would challenge today's young artists and tomorrow's superstars to believe that country music has much more to offer than a superficial view of life and that it should dig deeper, reach farther, and try harder to be true to its founding legacy. Country music should be a "secluded" genre, that is, one that bucks passing trends and maintains its essential identity, even if that becomes a stumbling block for the politically correct. Country music can be trendy and current without selling its soul.

Jazz music is a good example of a genre that is secluded and deliberately so. Those who play jazz and those who listen to it are not interested in how popular it is or in how much money or glory they can make from it. Jazz is not "popular" in a strict sense; its appeal is limited to a certain audience that has an appreciation for the particulars that make the music great. Folk music fits the same mold. Generally speaking, there are no trends in jazz music, nor are there any folk acts on *American Idol*. They are exclusive clubs, and they like it that way. Country music is not as exclusive—by definition, it's bigger and has wider appeal—but it can and should remain true to its heritage of greatness and should not try to imitate pop. It should hold its ground and not change with the times. The risk of straying from its heritage is that the industry may never discover the next big voice like a

Trisha Yearwood, a Pam Tillis, or a Travis Tritt, artists who will not lower their moral standards in order to sell records. That would be a great loss both to country music and to the world.

Cookie-Cutter Stardom

The other awful trend of modern Nashville is its nagging penchant for instant stardom. Instead of being a *culture* able to produce talented artists like Merle, Johnny, Waylon, Willie, and George, Nashville today is an *industry* that produces celebrities and their records. The two realities are diametrically opposed. Country music is unfortunately going down the overnight pop-star path of *American Idol*, which leads to solo vocalists who have a bit of flash and good looks but no maturity as artists. And while a few have done well in the business, such as Carrie Underwood and Kellie Pickler, most of these young people are not prepared for stardom because they haven't had the years of experience needed to hone their craft or to mature their voices and styles. Most of them are pop entertainers, not real artists, and their desire for fifteen minutes of fame meshes perfectly with the music industry's desire for fast dollars.

Nashville songs are now written to match the celebrities created to sing them. Dumbing down lyrics, not getting too wordy, removing any challenging vocabulary, making each line and image so blatantly obvious that a chimpanzee could understand it, zealously purging songs of any metaphors or symbolism that could possibly inspire someone—this is how so much of Nashville writes its songs today. Poetry, apparently, doesn't sell. Or perhaps because good poetry takes more time and effort to produce, it does not result in the same profit margin.

Nashville stardom in recent years has become a one-size-fits-all mold, which contradicts the rugged individualism that was characteristic of the early country legends. The standard image of the country bumpkin stud muffin singing about girls, trucks, and whiskey gets rather boring after a while. Often those who are intent on being "unique" end up looking the same as all the others who are looking for an artificial persona.

The world of sports offers the best contrast to Nashville's instant stardom machine. I believe the reason men like sports so much is that its method of evaluating talent is fair. The competitive dimension of sport has a single standard: the best team or player wins. No matter how unpopular an individual player may be, he is judged by his performance, not by his personality or his image. The sports media hated Barry Bonds during the course of his career—his personality was caustic, and he was arrogant to one and all—but he put the ball over the fence a lot; thus the media put up with him, the fans adored him, and he won all those MVPs (five—Mickey Mantle won only three). In sports, success is that simple. Winning is the standard in the sports world, and sheer competitive performance—a combination of talent, hard work, discipline, and aggressive output—is the measure of success. The rewards of the sports industry, money and fame, go to the best performers, period. This is not always the case in "political" Nashville.

Politics That Kill

Every industry has its political dimension, and Nashville is no exception. Someone has to call the shots, and others have to tow the line. The rest quibble about the details. I get that. Even the Lord said, "Where two or three are gathered in my name, there will be politics." (Just kidding.) The difficulty is when the politics of an industry end up strangling the culture that made it what it is. I do recognize that political correctness is a national problem that is destroying our country, and I believe the Nashville culture is just the country music version of it, a microcosm, if you will, of the larger cultural problem: selling out moral values in favor of profits; coveting success, awards, and prestige; and valuing power over artistry. If Nashville can overcome the politically correct seduction of the general culture it can get back on track. I won't hold my breath, but I can hope.

When I went to Nashville, I wanted to be a worker and an artist, not a politician. Because of that, I got to the top of the charts, but I never got *ahead.* I did not adopt the feel-good, party-happy, money-focused mentality that was already taking over the country music business in those years and eventually changed it to what it is today, and that kept me an outsider. The other thing that made me an outsider was simple geography: I was one of the few major artists, other than Lee Greenwood, who didn't have roots in Nashville. Greenwood came from Vegas, and I was discovered in Reno. I also did not wear a cowboy hat or sing about being a redneck. On top of this, my voice was a little bit pop sounding. I wasn't one of the "good ol' boys" of the Nashville circuit, and there were many times when I was made to feel it. I accepted it as a fact of life, but it did bother me at times.

Fatherhood was also a determining factor in my relationship with Nashville. I had growing kids to care for at home and chose not to exchange my kids' well-being for the sake of personal success. Every man has to make trade-offs if he wishes to be faithful to his priorities, and for me, giving up being a Nashville insider for the sake of my kids was overwhelmingly worth the sacrifice. But it was not easy. For many years, I lived a sort of divided existence of getting along in an uncomfortable environment with harsh rules in order to advance my career while striving to tend to the needs of my kids. My twofold goal was to be successful and respected in Nashville and to make my children my number-one priority.

I respectfully acknowledge that there were a number of artists who successfully managed both career and family during their years in Nashville, and I admire their achievements. Yet, for every artist who successfully negotiates Nashville politics, there are dozens who lose their individuality, or their humanity, in the fight to make it to the top of the pile. The pressure to be "one of us" is a powerful motivator, and those who don't conform don't reap the rewards. Conformity to the expectations of the movers and shakers in Nashville also has a deadening effect on artistic quality, which shows in today's superficial and commercialized country music culture.

The Legacy

A song from my 1994 *Extremes* album, "A Bible and a Bus Ticket Home", tells the story of a son who launched out into the big wide world to fulfill his dreams only to discover that leaving home also left something missing in his life. When his parents pass away and he returns to pay his respects, he reminisces about a simpler time in his life when he was rooted in faith and love. As he lays flowers on his parents' graves, he feels the pull of his own family legacy; he says, "I can almost hear my Mama calling, saying, 'Son, come back where you belong. You've got all you need to get here; a Bible and a bus ticket home.'"

The world of country music has changed significantly since the nineties, and in my opinion, the change hasn't been for the better. Nashville's tradition of excellence in writers, artists, and producers of great music is unparalleled in the modern entertainment industry; as one who has had a small part in building that legacy, I hope for nothing more than Nashville's return to its roots. Those of us who have had the honor to be involved in the country music industry know that we have a tradition of excellence to fall back on. That legacy is our true home. I hope and pray that, in time, Nashville can get back to being a crucible for the development of real talent, rather than a self-absorbed community dominated by glitter and money, which may lead to the death of the genre. Only time will tell if Nashville can find its way "back where you belong".

6

All My Dreams Came True in Music

The Albums and Songs of Collin Raye

(early 1990s)

Do not be deceived; God is not mocked, for whatever a man sows, that he will also reap.... And let us not grow weary in well-doing, for in due season we shall reap, if we do not lose heart. So then, as we have opportunity, let us do good to all men, and especially to those who are of the household of faith.

—Gal 6:7, 9–10

I believe that the universe is an immense work of art for those who have eyes to see and a beautiful symphony of joyous music for those who have ears to hear. Who could look at the Rocky Mountains or the Grand Canyon without seeing the brush of an eternal Artist painting beauty everywhere or hear the sounds of nature without being in awe of their harmonies? The beauty of the world is anything but skin-deep: it is transcendent. It enters creation from a source beyond the material world and lifts the spirit of man so that we can become more like the angels than the animals. The vocation of an artist should imitate the project of the divine Artist by raising people up: healing hearts that are broken, strengthening limbs that are weak, and touching souls that need relief from the burdens of life.

When I first entered the world of entertainment, I can't say that I fully understood that truth. The desire was in me, but it was like the mustard seed that had to grow in my heart as my career progressed. I went to Nashville telling God that I wanted to do His will, but in reality, my true desire was to make hit records. Over time, seeing music's impact on the world

93

matured me and nurtured that mustard seed so that it grew into a coherent philosophy of life. I have continually witnessed the power of music on other people's souls and have come to the conviction that it is an intimate and blessed sharing in the work of the divine Artist.

I believe that an artist's real success is in the quality and artistry of his work, not in ticket sales or his bank account. Money can be a strong motivating factor but should always be seen as a by-product of the artist's true commitment to inspiring others with his music. This principle doesn't exclude simple and sometimes secular enjoyment in performing. I have sung quite a few ditties and two-steppers in my life to know that these too can be part of the work of creating a better life for others, bringing joy into the world, and helping people get out of the drudgery of everyday existence. Yet my belief that music is for the betterment of people is essential to how I have lived my life and pursued my career. For this reason, I have tried to give many of my songs a double or triple layer of meaning to help listeners experience the transcendent dimension of music. Many of my love songs, in particular, can be messages about the love of a man for a woman, or the love of a parent for a child, or especially, the love of God for a soul.

The tale of this artist's life would be less than complete if I omitted the stories of my albums and songs and what went into their creation. In a sense, it is the story of my heyday and the commemoration of some of my fondest moments. I think that all my dreams *have been* fulfilled in the wonderful gift of music.

All I Can Be *and "Love Me", 1990–1991*

Even though the illustrious *Cowboy Sangers* was the first album I made, *All I Can Be* was the first album of my CBS contract and the one that would immediately push me onto a national stage. I wanted it to be perfect. During that transition out of Reno, I made a few trips to Nashville with Jerry Fuller to "hunt" for songs at the big publishing houses. While many artists write their own songs, the vast majority of country artists sing songs written by a talented group of Nashville songwriters who work at various establishments in one area of the city known as Music Row. I think some of the best songwriters on the planet inhabit that small square of interlocking streets near downtown Nashville, and every year they produce a load of songs that keeps the country music business hopping. I don't always like their songs, but I admire their talent.

On one of my trips to Nashville, Jerry and I were pitched a song that was to become the signature song of my career, "Love, Me". When I first heard it, I was actually confused by the lyrics. Skip Ewing's folksy style on the demo seemed to rush the refrain, making it hard to understand the meaning of "love, me". Initially, I thought the words meant "I love you, and I want you to *love me*", or something along those lines. Then Jerry said, "No, Bubba. It's like he signed a letter." Bingo! A light went on. "Love, me" was the closing line of a letter. "Oh! Now I get it!" I said. "This is great! Can we have it?"

To this day I am amazed and humbled that Opryland Music Group, the owners of the song, gave it to an unknown singer like me, but I will be forever grateful. Charlie Monk and Troy Tomlinson, the publishers, believed in me and told me that they thought I was going to be a star. I didn't share their confidence at the time, but I did feel as though "Love, Me" could be a big hit. It turned out to be more successful than anyone would have imagined.

When I decided to do the song, I knew that the last part of the chorus had to be emphasized artistically so that the listener didn't think the phrase "love, me" was the man's demand that the woman love him! To do that, I inserted a dramatic pause between "I'll be loving you" and the sign-off, "Love, me". I also paused ever so slightly between "love" and "me". I've often wondered if the pauses were what made the difference in driving home the point of the song and giving it the impact it still has today. In twenty-one years of singing this song—at approximately one hundred shows a year, plus television appearances and other events—I'm sure I have sung it more than five thousand times. (Even that number seems low!)

The song took the airwaves by storm. In the space of about three months, it flew up the charts—twelve to fifteen spots a week—and eventually became the Number One song by Christmas of 1991, a position it occupied for three full weeks into the new year.

People loved the song, I believe, because it touched their hearts and made them think of the value of romantic love, spousal love, family love, and eternal love all at once. That combination of values is the best of country music songwriting—of any songwriting for that matter. On top of that, the song is immeasurably beautiful and lyrical. It was perfectly suited to my high-tenor voice, and I sang my heart out when performing it; I still do to this day. In the ensuing years, literally more than a thousand people have told me that they played the song at the funeral of a loved one or even engraved the words of the refrain on the tombstone as a reminder that they would one day be reunited with their loved one in heaven. "Love, Me" is sometimes mistakenly called "If You Get There Before I Do" because of the first line of the chorus; some fans even ask me if I can "do that grandpa song, you know, the one with the letter on the tree." Of course, I always know what they mean!

I might add that we made a music video for "Love, Me" in which my own children appeared when they were little kids. I still can't watch that video without being filled with such love and nostalgia for a simpler time in our family's life. It was the first of several instances when my kids (or grandkids) appeared in my videos or onstage with me. If I may say so, they were adorable in this one. In one of the scenes of the video, I'm the grandson who is looking through some boxes of his grandmother's belongings. When I open one box, I pluck out my little Jacob and pick him up for the camera just as if he were a human teddy bear! Dressed in precious little overalls, he looks cuter than any other little boy I've seen. I'm being totally objective about my own kids, of course.

Here, at the beginning of my solo career, indeed, with my very first hit song, God was revealing to me my higher calling in music, which was developing in me as an artist and helping me to grow as a person. When I saw that "Love, Me" touched so many people's lives as powerfully as it did, I began to realize that I had a mission and a platform from which to pursue that mission: quality music was my way to touch people's hearts. I would have that lesson reaffirmed many times after that first hit, right up to this very day.

The album name, *All I Can Be*, was the shortened name of the title song, "All I Can Be (Is a Sweet Memory)", which was the first single released prior to "Love, Me". It is a cool, haunting song with a rolling rhythm that Bob Montgomery thought would be a great single. It was written by the late Harlan Howard—arguably one of the greatest country music writers of all time—who was in a league with Hank Williams and Merle Haggard. Harlan wrote mountains of hit songs over a six-decade career and had a huge impact on country music. He kicked off Pam Tillis' career with her Number One hit, "Don't Tell Me What to Do", and wrote such other favorites as "I Fall to Pieces" by Patsy Cline, "Busted" by Ray Charles, and Ray Price's "Heartaches by the Number". Harlan was a consummate songwriter and one of the all-time greats of Nashville. As friend, mentor, and skilled professional, he also had a huge impact on me, and I will always appreciate how he helped to make me a better artist in the early days of my career.

The famed Vince Gill, whose silky-smooth tenor voice is as high as mine, did me the honor of singing harmony with me on this song; I remember how well our voices blended. My pianist and producer, John Hobbs, knew Vince well and suggested that Vince might sing with us on the album.

"Do you really think he would?" I asked.

"Well, let's find out", said John, and, after a simple phone call, Vince was in the studio an hour later singing with me as a favor to John. It was my first chance to meet him, and I will never forget Vince's kindness in doing that for me when I was still a nobody.

"All I Can Be (Is a Sweet Memory)" was my very first music video, and for the first time in my career I felt the excitement of putting my music into a visual format. It was a new experience for me. We filmed it in a dilapidated barn in West Memphis, about ten miles outside of the city, and I recall that it was raining the whole night. Honestly, it was the most arduous day's work I had ever done. It was physically and emotionally exhausting. I had watched music videos for as long as I could remember and always presumed that filming a video would be a fun and easy task. How wrong I was! Since I was the only one who appeared in the video, I did all the heavy lifting and was on my feet for the entire sixteen or seventeen hours of filming. When we finally wrapped up the filming, it was eight o'clock in the morning; we had worked all day—and all night. I got to the hotel that morning and don't remember my head hitting the pillow.

A final note about *All I Can Be.* Another song from that album that performed very well and hit Number Two on the charts was "Every Second", written by Gerald Smith and Wayne Perry. It was a clever, two-stepping tune that helped me to establish a reputation as a versatile artist. Billy Ray Cyrus' "Achy Breaky Heart" flew at supersonic speed to the Number One spot that year and prevented "Every Second" from making it to the top of the charts, but I can't say I begrudged him that. "Every Second" stayed at

Number Two for three solid weeks, and that was another major success for me.

Thankfully, my first album with Sony, *All I Can Be*, performed extremely well, reaching platinum status (that is, a million records sold); it had two Top Two singles and two Number One videos. My career was off and running, and I was grateful for a strong beginning.

Interim: Buses, Bands, and Kids

Backtracking slightly, my CBS record deal came in 1990, but working full time in my solo career didn't come immediately. I was in transition. Nothing good comes easily or quickly. A musician who enters the limelight without having been slow-cooked for years in the lowlight of sleazy bars and foul-smelling honky-tonks is a musician who is being set up for failure, burnout, personal disaster, or all of the above. A life in the public eye, under constant and intense scrutiny, is very difficult. The inside of a star's world looks very different from the outside. I knew that an artist has to be tested and weatherworn, as it were, in order to manage the rough sledding in Nashville, and I was glad for having paid my dues during long years of hard work to get to where I was now, even if that way of doing things took a little longer.

That same year, as soon as possible, I moved to Greenville, Texas, where Connie and the kids lived near her parents. I was looking forward to being with my kids again. It took me a few months of traveling between Reno, Greenville, Nashville, and even Los Angeles to get through this transitional period. I thought I was a musician, but I felt like a juggler and a high-wire acrobat. I was doing a delicate balancing act of holding up multiple responsibilities at once: I had to satisfy all my obligations in Reno and start recording *All I Can Be* in addition to bouncing back and forth between Nashville and LA. If that wasn't enough, I also began to branch out into my new touring schedule as Collin Raye.

Steve Cox was now the manager of a man who had a major-label record contract, and he wanted me to get on the road immediately and to travel as much as I could. He knew it was good for my career and record sales. Having worked with me for several years by now, he knew that I excelled at live performance and wanted me to be on the road performing constantly.

Steve, who was a former booking agent, never fully lost his natural instinct for that aspect of the business: he kept the act working and making money.

The immediate reality I had to face was a diminishing money supply. The simple fact of having a record contract didn't mean that I had money, and that surprised me initially. In fact, as I made the transition from playing casinos in Reno, where I could make as much as $1,500 a week, I took a pay cut to go touring. I didn't launch into full-time touring right away because I couldn't *afford* it. The full benefits of being a music star would come slowly, and so would the money.

By far the greatest benefit of this new period was the chance to be with the kids again. As excited as I was to have a record deal with a major label, to have songs playing on the radio and a chance at breaking into a higher level of musical performance, nothing was more satisfying to me than being able to be with the kids. I could now be on their home turf. This was one of the most joyful times in my life, because Britanny and Jake were still young enough to have that wonderful innocence of childhood (Britanny was seven and Jake was five at the time), and I got to share their childhood with them. The desolation of being physically separated from them during most of my four and a half years of playing casinos in Reno was coming to an end. Even the prospect of continuous touring didn't worry me because the ability to be my own boss meant I would be coming *home* to the kids like a father should, rather than just *visiting* them from exile in another city. Psychologically, it made a huge difference in my relationship with my growing kids and in my comfort level with the new touring schedule, which would keep me on the road about 260 days that first year.

I even had the opportunity to bring the kids with me on selected trips, especially in the summertime, which was an immense joy. I must admit that I even got them out of school a few extra days during the year just to be with me for a tour or a special event. Far from being an impediment to my career, my kids were the saving grace of this whole new period of my life. I felt like a true father again rather than just an artist who visited his kids once in a while. That sense of wholeness was extremely positive for me after so much desolation. I was deeply grateful to God to be with them.

Jake was still quite attached to his grandma Doris, so he stayed home more often than his older sister, but he toured with me from time to time. Thankfully, I had an excellent road manager, Randy Cudd, who took care of the kids when I was occupied with the business of performing. I knew they were always safe and taken care of whenever they were on tour with us. Britanny especially loved touring with Daddy and accompanied me everywhere I went, except on stage. When she got older, she would sing with me on stage a few times, but during these early touring days she sat in her own special VIP seat, which was a little stool by the monitor desk right next to the stage. She thus had a bird's-eye view of every performance, and Randy watched her until the show was over. Then she would sit at the table with me when I was signing autographs; needless to say, the fans just loved to see their star with his little daughter next to him! It made the whole star experience more human and down-to-earth. I can't recall any major problems having the kids with me on tour. It was utterly delightful.

A single traumatic incident occurred on tour when Britanny was about ten years old, which caused even her dear old dad to marvel about the character and sweetness of that child. It was one of those moments in a parent's life when he realizes that his child's innate personality and spirit gifts from God. On this occasion, I was standing outside the door of the bus while Britanny was getting off. My bass player, a wonderful man named Joe Alford, was getting on the bus and didn't see that Britanny's hand was on the doorjamb. He unintentionally closed the heavy metal bus door on it. In fact, he slammed it pretty tightly on her little fingers. Naturally, she screamed in terrible pain, and I rushed to get the door open. I had seen the door slam on her fingers—I was sure that each one was broken—but her hand was somehow miraculously spared any real damage. Joe's head dropped because he felt so bad for what he had done; and as soon as Britanny looked up and saw his head bowed, even though she was in severe pain, she began to console *him*. "It's okay, Joe. It's okay", she said. "I'm gonna be fine; don't worry." Then she started hugging him! What an awesome girl! That sensitive and caring girl turned into an even more remarkable woman.

Touring brought two major problems with it: I needed a road band, and I needed voluminous amounts of cash to make it all possible. Only my guitarist, Kraig Hutchens, stayed with me from the dissolved Wray Brothers Band, and I tasked him with the job of pulling together a band to play with me on the road. This wasn't an easy assignment, due to the demands of the job. A touring band has to be road-ready, which means being able on short notice to travel across the country to play in nightclubs and festivals for weeks on end. More importantly, they had to be good musicians. Kraig tapped a local band, Silver State, which was quite good. Geno LeSage, a friend of ours and a dynamite pianist and vocalist, joined us and later was my musical director for a number of years. Kraig had worked with one of the other members of the group in a Portland-based band called Buckboard some years before. My new band consisted of Kraig, Geno, and the Coffee Brothers, Van and Tony. We then added a sixth member, who would be my drummer for the next dozen years, Sammy Wray (no relation), one of the best people I have ever had the honor of working with.

Family Vacations

Despite being so busy touring, my focus was always on the kids. I orchestrated many family vacations—at least twice a year—so that I could have significant quality time with Britanny and Jake and give them a chance to do some extraspecial things that kids love. I wanted them to have the childhood I didn't have. Every year I took them to Disney World, so that they would have their fill of Mickey Mouse and the Magic Kingdom. The alternative vacations were usually to Europe or Hawaii. My kids got to enjoy the beauty and serenity of the Hawaiian island three times during their childhood, and they experienced many famous European sights, such as the Tower of London, the Matterhorn in Switzerland, the Marienplatz in Munich, and the Eiffel Tower and the Arc de Triomphe in Paris. What blessed times those were for all of us!

As a little kid, Jake would say the funniest things. On one of our trips to England, when he was about eleven years old, we were standing outside the gates of Buckingham Palace and noticed six little economy cars for various palace staff parked inside the courtyard. Britanny said, "I wonder whose cars those are?" Then Jake added, "Yeah, I wonder which one's the queen's car?" He thought the queen of England drove herself to work in a cheap little car every day! Jake was full of that kind of innocent humor.

He was also a reflective child who—in his unique way—learned a great deal from our historical visits. On a tour of Leeds Castle outside London, he wanted to know about Henry VIII. Jake had a cute way of pronouncing *-ing* words by adding a *k* to the ending which made the word *king* sound a little like "kingk". I told him that old Henry was not such a good guy: I recounted a little about his break with the Church of Rome and his affectionate treatment of his seven wives, et cetera.

Then, after a little reflection, Jake asked, "Dad, was Henry VIII the worst kingk England ever had?"

I said, "No, that was probably Richard III, the guy whose life was the basis of Disney's *Lion King* story." (I was using an analogy an eleven-year-old would understand!) I told him how nasty Richard had been and how he had killed his father, his son, his nephew, and quite a few others.

The tour concluded with a nice repast of scones and tea, and we got on the bus and headed back to London. About halfway into the return trip, as most of us were dozing off from midafternoon fatigue, I felt a tap on my shoulder from Jake, who was sitting behind me. As I turned, I noticed that he had a very pensive look on his face. He must have been mulling over what he had learned that day.

"Dad?" he asked with a serious tone "Do you think that Richard III was happy when he was kingk?"

I couldn't help but laugh, almost to tears, at such a profound question from a reflective little kid with such a delightful way of speaking.

Fame but No Fortune Yet

Although I tried to keep the reality of new-found stardom in perspective, the adrenaline rush of fame was powerfully addictive. In the dog days of playing honky-tonks and sweaty bars, I had everything I could do just to get a couple of people to clap! People usually go to bars for reasons other than music, and they pay as much attention to the people on stage as they do to the beer signs on the wall. If the band didn't show up, they might notice it and complain, but when the band was there, bar crowds took the music for granted. Touring, however, was an altogether different reality.

Even during the days when we started to experience real fan enthusiasm in Oregon, it was different from the electric pulse of crowds that were now packing an arena or theater just to see me. I had been performing for over half my life by this time, and I was accustomed to being in front of people, but now I was giving concert performances, not playing dance sets, and the dynamics were totally different. It was adulation, fan attention to the tenth power. The feeling of adrenaline rush is the only way I can adequately describe it.

The other force that had a huge impact on singers' popularity in those days was the new influence of music videos on television. TNN was the main music video channel at that time, before CMT got big. CBS had done a good job of getting my first video, "All I Can Be (Is a Sweet Memory)", onto TNN. In fact, it garnered the Number One spot, and as a result, I was a known quantity, even in physical appearance, before I even walked out on stage. No more was I just a phantom voice singing to them on the radio. The genius of the music industry was its ability to marry the visual and audio media for a double sensory impact and then deliver that impact directly into people's living rooms. This access into people's lives and souls through the mass media can be used for evil as well as for good, but at the beginning of my career, I didn't see it as evil. I can't say I understood it as an opportunity for "ministry" either. I just saw it as a force multiplier for getting my image and my music out.

The combination of forces—radio, TV, touring, and CBS' marketing of my image—converged like several streams flowing into a mighty river, and the floodgates of fame began to burst open. The first time I walked onto the stage as Collin Raye at a festival in Salt Lake City that year, I was astonished by the cheering crowds. Mine was just one of many other acts on the bill that day, but I was now Collin Raye, the guy with a hit record on the radio, and the Number One music video on TV; the crowd went wild! After I played my forty-five-minute set, the organizers invited me downstairs to sign autographs, and I imagined that a simple task like that wouldn't take very long. I presumed that maybe three or four people would show up. When I got downstairs, however, *six hundred people* were lined up to get my autograph! I signed and signed until my hand was numb and they finally had to make way for the next act.

Steve and I learned a few lessons about country music marketing that day. First, a live performance followed by an autograph signing was a chance to build a fan base. Second, one should always bring something to sell! Both Steve and I had forgotten to bring materials to sell at the event, but we would never make that mistake again. Our learning curve was steep, but we were cruising up it rapidly.

Musically, as touring became our livelihood, the band got *real* good, real fast. One of our more memorable concerts was later that year in Nacogdoches, Texas, where, after performing almost ninety minutes of *our* songs, the audience didn't want the experience to end and brought me back out for four encores, each one with three or four songs, mostly rock 'n' roll covers. They would not let us leave the stage and would have stayed for more, had I not run out of things to play. That was an awesome night.

Versatility and Vocal Cords

CBS sold its record label to Sony that year, and the eventual change in my team of producers would have a detrimental effect on me. But for the moment, my producers saw the value of the star power I was amassing and quickly pushed me to do a second album. We commenced the search for songs and came up with a dozen or so great ones. Honestly, I was so pleased to be following my dream that if someone at that early stage of my career had asked me to cultivate the redneck image and to sing about pickup trucks and beer, I probably would have done it. I knew that I could sing anything they wanted me to sing: in fact, I knew I could sing the phone book and make it sound good. Thankfully, I never became the typical country singer, and there is a good reason for that: Jerry Fuller.

I owe my high level of vocal ability to the best possible mentor I could have had in the early years of my career: my friend Jerry, who "discovered" me in Reno and worked with me on my first album. He trained me, pushed me, and honed my voice to make it what it is today. I learned more about singing from Jerry than from all my other producers combined. He was what I would call a "singer's producer", who would work a singer to death and not let him settle for anything less than perfection. Most people will grudgingly admit that the teachers and coaches who demanded more from them were the ones they appreciated the most later on, and that was certainly true of Jerry. Because of his discipline, later producers would marvel at my vocal quality and my ability to record a song in two or three passes and have it come out great.

Jerry taught me better vocal technique; that is, he helped me to improve my enunciation, pitch, phrasing, and use of emotion in song. These techniques separate the men from the boys in performance, and I became proficient in them as the style and melodic versatility of my music indicate. I think Jerry's greatest gift to my career, however, was his encouraging me to sing in a higher register. He made me realize that I sounded *great* when I sang high. No artist or athlete can appreciate the full range of his own talent; he needs a coach to identify his strengths and to bring them to fuller expression. Jerry was the coach who did that for me. I am so deeply thankful to the Lord for the gift of a good voice and for Jerry's mentoring, which provided the packaging and refining that my voice needed to be of greater quality and service. My voice has not grown deeper or slackened in quality after twenty years of professional performing, as most men's voices do. Amazingly, it has remained virtually unchanged.

As a brief aside, sometime in the late nineties, when my career was already in full gear, I was singing so much and speaking to so many people at the meet and greets that I thought I might be putting too much stress on my vocal cords. I decided to get an analysis from Dr. Robert Ossoff, informally known as the Nashville throat guru, who runs the Vanderbilt Voice Center. During the session he inserted a scope into my throat to get a view of my vocal cords—I could see my own vocal cords on the monitor in front of me. To my astonishment, he held up two fingers to describe the two vocal cords as the prongs of a tuning fork and said, "Only one of yours works." The second vocal cord, he said, was paralyzed. As far as I know, it remains so to this day. He added, "This tells me that you are probably going to lose your voice in a few years." Not good news. Yet my voice today is exactly the same as it was twenty years ago and shows no signs of stopping. Singing is my way of communicating my message to others, and it seems that God wants me to keep doing it. I say that I believe in miracles, in part, because I am living proof of one.

I'm in the Music Business Now

I soon learned that nothing lasts forever. Not long after *All I Can Be* went platinum, I got my first bitter taste of the business part of the record business. After Sony took over my contract, the company made a few personnel changes at the executive level, and Jerry butted heads with the new bosses on issues such as recording venues, songs, and styles. These were fundamental concerns that required a great deal of coordination and agreement on all sides, but there was no agreement between Jerry and Sony, and a civil war was breaking out.

Jerry was a West Coast guy, not a Nashville good ol' boy, and that meant that he too was an outsider. Admittedly, Jerry could sometimes be abrasive and commanding. He was used to being in charge, and he resented what looked like an attempt by Sony to force him out. The hard part for me was finding myself in the middle of warring factions. The conflict escalated and soon reached a breaking point where I was forced to make one of the most difficult decisions of my career. Sony told Steve in effect that they "might not be willing to make my next album, or Collin Raye, a priority", which was no doubt the biggest threat facing us. Sony had made it clear to me that they thought I had a very promising future and that they were fully prepared to put the resources behind me to push me forward. The main artists on Sony's Epic label at the time were Doug Stone and Joe Diffie, both of whom had gotten off to great starts with the label; however, Epic now wanted to make me their top priority—but they wouldn't do it if Jerry Fuller was on board.

Jerry wasn't budging an inch, though. Steve and I talked about what to do, and the potential loss of the Sony contract was the determining factor in our decision. Sony held the purse strings, and they were willing to pull the plug on my whole career because Jerry refused to accept their demands. We decided to separate from Jerry and let the chips fall where they may with him—which they did shortly thereafter. Jerry sued me for breach of contract. This was a classic Nashville business debacle: Sony caused the problem, but I was the one who got sued.

Our original production agreement with Jerry stipulated that he would be entitled to compensation if we chose to terminate the relationship. Jerry stood on it and took us to court. Rather than risk a serious judgment, a heavy payout, and negative publicity, we settled out of court with him, which cost me a great deal. After that, we all went home licking our wounds.

I was less worried about the money than I was about the broken relationship with someone who had played such a significant role in my life. In fact, it took me a while to get over the loss. I loved Jerry and his wife, Annette, and their family. Because loyalty in personal relationships has always been important to me, I felt horrible that a good relationship had ended on such a negative note. Jerry and I eventually got back to friendly, speaking terms when we both sat on the Academy of Country Music board a few years later, but our relationship was never the same. I regret that things between us could not have worked out more amicably.

Celebrity, as I was to learn, is like flypaper—it's sticky and attracts problems. That reality hit me like a ton of bricks after the incident with Jerry: "I'm not just making music", I admitted sadly. "I'm in the music *business* now." It was the first of several lawsuits in my career: my introduction to the cost of doing business in a fallen world—and in Nashville.

In This Life, 1992

For the second album, Sony assigned Garth Fundis to be my new producer, joining my mainstay producer, John Hobbs. Doug Johnson was made my A and R (Artists and Repertoire) liaison. Garth had always impressed me and turned out to be an excellent producer. He had worked with Don Williams and Keith Whitley and was just starting with Trisha Yearwood; I knew he was great in the studio, and I felt confident in his leadership. We decided to name the album *In This Life* after the song of the same name written by Mike Reid, who had an interesting first career as an All-Pro defensive tackle for the Cincinnati Bengals back in the seventies. This talented man was also a concert pianist.

"In This Life" was one of the most beautiful songs I had ever heard, and fortunately Mike and his cowriter, Allen Shamblin, pitched it to us in the nick of time, the night before we started our next recording session. We cut "In This Life" first thing in the morning; that's how convinced we were that it would be a hit. Released soon thereafter as a single, it hit Number One on the charts for three weeks.

Three more songs from *In This Life* did very well, including "That Was a River", which became a Number One hit, and "Somebody Else's Moon", which reached the Top Five. Another fun song, "I Want You Bad (and That Ain't Good)", a straight-up rocker, reached Number Six on the charts. Of concern to me at this time was that I was quickly becoming tagged as a ballad guy, and I didn't like that. I was a showman, a rockin' live performer, and I wanted to release at least *some* singles to radio that would identify me as such. A performer can be only so animated and active on stage doing love songs. I wanted to rock too and put on exciting, memorable live shows. "I Want You Bad" and the video that followed it were my deliberate attempt to get out of the strict ballad identification and showcase that other dimension of my talent. The last thing I wanted was to become the country Perry Como. Ballads were only part of what I did, and I was confident in my versatility as a musician. Thankfully, the audiences seemed to get that message too. *In This Life* went platinum, my second in a row.

Extremes, 1994

The entertainment business never stays still; or rather, it never lets entertainers stay still. The key word is *business*. Records translate into money, big money, and Sony was pushing me to do another album. They wanted to keep the momentum of the first two albums going. I had very much enjoyed making the last record with Garth Fundis; but because of scheduling conflicts, he wasn't able to help me on the next album, and I needed a new production team. My friend John Hobbs, who was always my mainstay on the production team, suggested that we talk to Paul Worley, with whom he had worked on several records for Highway 101, and Pam Tillis. I knew and admired Paul's work and thought he was a good-hearted, soulful guy. When he expressed interest in working with me, I was excited at the prospect. We added production engineer Ed Seay, who had tremendous musical sense. These three men were a formidable team that would, thankfully, stay with me for a few albums.

Now that I had two platinum albums under my belt, I had a little more leeway to determine the course, structure, and content of the third album, and I decided to name it *Extremes* because I wanted it to be an album that explored the extremes of human emotion. All the songs on it were chosen for their high emotional content, as that fit my developing sense of my own mission: to touch people's souls with songs that comforted them and raised their spirits.

The album was one of the most commercial records I ever made and spawned *five* hit songs, three of which went to Number One while two others made it into the Top Five. "That's My Story", which became one of my signature songs, and "My Kind of Girl" were released as singles and performed very well, the latter hitting Number One. They are fast and fun and meant for pure enjoyment. To make the videos for the songs, I chose the talented director Jon Small, who had done a number of big-time videos and had been Billy Joel's first drummer. He grew up with Billy on Long Island and had the accent to boot. He was very good at what he did and would eventually become Garth Brooks' exclusive video director. I was so lucky to get him to do the videos, and they had such great success that I used him for the "One Boy, One Girl" video and at least one other down the road. Both videos were a great deal of fun to make and were extremely well received.

The "love interest" in these two music videos was the actress and songwriter Tammy Hyler. I was dating Tammy at the time, and Jon really liked the fact that she was a current girlfriend. He thought she perfectly fit the part of the wife in the videos.

Tammy was a significant person in my life. She stuck with me through thick and thin for about five years in the mid-nineties at the height of my heyday. She was a stalwart support to me in my musical career, as I was to her. She is one of the funniest people I have ever known and made me laugh every step of the way. Anyone who has seen the videos of those two songs will notice her innate talents for acting and humor. We considered marriage, but she lived in Nashville, while I lived in Texas, and we eventually broke up due to the endless stress of trying to have a long-distance relationship. However, I will be forever grateful for her many significant contributions to my life and career.

Typical of the *Extremes* album was another very touching song called "Man of My Word", which took emotion to the other extreme. It's about a grieving husband who sings to his deceased wife. This song was a Top Five. *Extremes* also included a couple of very powerful ballads: "If I Were You", a gorgeous song written by my producer John Hobbs and Chris Farren that hit Number One; and the deep and somewhat forlorn tune, "Dreamin' My Dreams with You", which was easily my favorite song of my whole early repertoire.

The Impact of "Little Rock"

By far the most significant song on the *Extremes* album was "Little Rock". It was significant because of its social commentary and strong emotional impact. Ironically, it was the song that I was the least comfortable with because I thought it might be too dark for radio. Even though it had a hopeful message, it didn't seem that a song about a recovering alcoholic would appeal to the driving audience that country radio targeted. Fortunately, I was dead wrong about this. It was one of the few instances in my years of working with record executives when they went with a song against my wishes and were, thankfully, right. It hit Number One soon after its release and became a candidate for Song of the Year; the video for it received a nomination for Video of the Year. "Little Rock" was written by the Dallas-based songwriter Tom Douglas and was his very first hit. I am happy to say I had a hand launching his songwriting career. Douglas was a real talent and an awesome human being who later wrote songs for Tim McGraw, Martina McBride, and others.

Sony wanted to release "Little Rock" as a single right after "That's My Story", which had just hit big, and I was nervous that a dark song like this would dampen that success, but to my surprise, "Little Rock" flew up the charts. Part of its appeal was its powerful, well-acted video, directed by friend Sherman Halsey, which told the song's story effectively. I acted the part of the alcoholic dad with a family that suffered terribly from my addiction, and the clever part was the addition of a flashback scene showing me as a little kid whose own dad was a big, scary, abusive drunk—a part that the actor played very well! The image emphasized the intergenerational nature of alcoholism and the cycles of behavior that get passed down in families.

I don't exactly remember whose idea it was, but at the end of the video we appended an 800 helpline number for Al-Anon and Alateen, and amazingly, it caused a minor nuclear reaction in suffering America. Within six weeks of the release of the video, I was told that the toll-free number had received more than a quarter of a million calls for help! That's how powerful the video was. It helped people identify problems in their own situations and gave them the impetus to call for assistance. "That's my dad", "That's my husband", "That's my—" was heard over and over on the phone because we had given people an image that reflected their suffering and some hope that there was something they could do about it.

Prior to "Little Rock", I never thought that country music could engage in social issues successfully, but the response to the song changed my thinking about what country music could accomplish and about my own role in that project. I thought, "Ah, now I see things more clearly. The Lord didn't put me here just to fulfill my personal dream of playing before cheering crowds, being famous, and making money. I'm supposed to be that guy who pushes the dirt and brings things to light. This is how I can give back to Him for all I've received." My new understanding that issues of great importance to people and society could actually be turned into hit songs set the course for future albums. I began consciously looking for songs that had comforting messages for those who needed strength in their suffering. The country music business at the time wasn't known for its depth of concern for humanity, but I knew I could get away with it.

Road Trips, Records, and Routines

By 1994, when *Extremes* became my third platinum album, I was fully committed to the life of touring, performing, and being a country music celebrity, a status that I accepted as part of God's will for my life. I was much more aware of the impact of my gift on others, and I knew that this life was the one I was supposed to be living. I had three albums full of music to play at every concert and was living out my dream.

At this point, I found that I had to strike a delicate balance between studio time and tour time, and I did this, like all popular artists, by fitting record making between road shows. Paul Worley would book studio sessions for me on those days when I was not traveling or at home with the kids, and somehow I recorded all the rest of my albums in this piecemeal fashion. It was tough, but it was the only way to balance all the priorities of a busy life. Only recently, when I recorded *His Love Remains* (2011), did I have an experience of complete focus and total dedication, without interruption, in the making of an album, and because of that, it was the album I recorded in the least amount of time and with the greatest intensity.

My life during the nineties was a constant treadmill; my regular schedule included touring, making records, playing or attending the annual Fan Fair in Nashville—as well as the annual Country Radio Seminar—and countless other charity or industry events. And of course, being at home with the kids was my absolute number-one priority. Routine is always hard work, but in those years, my routine also carried many blessings; it was a source of great productivity as well as stability and predictability for others who were connected to me.

There were also some supremely cool, non-routine moments during that decade, such as meeting some of my personal heroes, traveling to new and unusual places, and performing on stage with some of the greats of the industry. Country music demanded much of me in the nineties but also gave much joy and meaning to me and my family. I hope that I have given as much back.

The universe was filled with immense beauty and grace for me during these beginning years of my career. I was experiencing the grand symphony of life in all its wonder, but more than that, I was living my dream and working hard to impact the world for the better.

7

I Hope You Get What You Want Out of This

The Albums and Songs of Collin Raye

(mid-1990s to 2002)

[B]ut lay up for yourselves treasures in heaven, where neither
moth nor rust consumes and where thieves do not break in
and steal. For where your treasure is, there will your heart be also.

—Mt 6:20–21

I first met Garth Brooks in 1991 at the Grand Ole Opry House, where both of us were performing. Garth is a very smooth but intense guy who has perfected the art of leaving a lasting impression on people. He's an extremely outgoing, personable man, which is one reason he became so popular, and I experienced his gift firsthand. This particular night, before the show, someone introduced me to him backstage, and he shook my hand firmly, looked me straight in the eye, and told me how pleased he was to meet me. Then he inquired about my family and my music and put me so much at ease that I felt as though I had him all to myself for those privileged few moments. At the end of the brief encounter, he said something that has echoed in my mind like a continuous musical refrain throughout the years. He gave me a strangely prophetic challenge about the opportunity I had been given in coming to Nashville. Garth said simply, "I hope you get what you want out of this." I thanked him profusely and rushed off to my next engagement, but I have never stopped pondering those words. Actually, since that encounter I have lived with a subtle anxiety that I would miss "getting what I want" out of the opportunity to be a performer.

I have a similar recurring prophetic dream of standing before the Judgment Seat of God at the end of my life and this time coming face-to-face

113

with Jesus, not Garth Brooks. He looks directly at me as Garth did—although it feels more as if He is looking straight *through* me—and His benevolent voice says, "I allowed you to have your dream, because you wanted it and because I love you. What did you do with that dream?" His tone is not condemnatory, nor is His look in any way harsh, but He's intent on an answer from me. The dream always ends there, with that question, and I know that one day the dream will become a reality.

Prophetic messages like these challenge me to look beyond the superficial dimensions of the entertainment business to find the deeper meaning of my talents and to use them for God's Kingdom. Our beloved Pope John Paul II, would always tell young people that they would never be satisfied with themselves unless they gave their lives away. Self-giving is the only pathway to a meaningful life in this world and is the habit of heart that leads us into the world to come, but it is the opposite of the egocentric grasping we see increasingly around us. Dreaming about accomplishing great and glorious things is not wrong; it is wrong only to keep that dream for oneself alone.

I am at peace about Garth's challenge to "get what I want" out of a high-profile career in music now, as long as "what I want" is what God wants to accomplish through me.

Finding My Musical Purpose

When I first signed with Sony records, I thought that God was allowing me to be with the kids and at the same time to fulfill my musical dreams. I did what I had to do to get a foothold in the business, but deep down I didn't enjoy working the crowds, people pleasing, or playing political games to get ahead in a rough-and-tumble business.

Yet, by the mid-nineties I could see that my music was changing lives. "Maybe this is what my mission is", I would say to myself in my more lucid moments. I was seeing the transforming power of my music on others. I was getting the message that changing lives through music was a mission, *my* mission, and was the reason God allowed me to get on stage. To this day, fans show me pictures of the tombstones of their loved ones engraved with the words "If you get there before I do", and I never cease to marvel at the enduring influence of that tune. "In This Life" became a wildly popular wedding and funeral song. Later, "If I Were You" became my biggest wedding song of all. Music is a powerful influence for good or evil, and I was determined to make it work for the good.

Believing that music can do more than make people *feel good*, I didn't want to waste my talents keeping people focused on the nonessential, shallow things of life. I wanted to tap music's power to raise people's hearts and minds to the "eternal verities", as William Faulkner called them, of truth, beauty, and goodness—the things that connect us to the world beyond. I share the sentiment of George Frideric Handel, who supposedly said about his masterpiece, *Messiah*, "I should be sorry if I only entertained them; I wished to make them better."

I Think about You, 1995

After my third album, I didn't mind being known in Nashville as the guy who sang songs with social messages, but even that came with some risk of alienation in a genre that was increasingly dedicated to songs that celebrate being a partying redneck. It was a risk I was willing to take, as my mission was clearer now and I was more mature in embracing it. Album number four, *I Think about You,* was loaded with socially relevant songs, and deliberately so. It can be seen as the peak album of my career both in terms of positioning (it was the fourth of the seven albums I was to do with Sony, excluding the greatest-hits album) and in terms of my own maturity as an artist (I believe it best expressed my vision for music and my attempt to minister to others through music). Of the eleven songs on the album, five of them reached Top Five on the charts and another one charted high, which is unheard of for an album today, and it became the biggest seller of all the albums that I made. Three of those hit songs went Number One, and, with all that success, I was beginning to think I could do no wrong.

The love song on the album, "One Boy, One Girl", was a Number One hit despite, or possibly because of, a corny line at the end about the boy and girl getting married and having twin babies, one a boy and the other a girl! "Not That Different" was perhaps the most critical song of the whole album. Written by Karen Taylor-Good and her partner, Joie Scott, it was actually a love song about two people who were on the point of breaking up because they didn't think they had very much in common. The lyrics of the chorus show the couple working through their difficulties and finding that they were not as different as they had thought. It struck me as a great message not only about romantic relationships but about human relationships in general. We decided to make the video for "Not That Different" into a commentary on ethnic and social differences—specifically, on racism—much as we had done the "Little Rock" video as a commentary on alcoholism. It was one of the best we ever produced.

My friend Steven Goldman directed the video and took us to New York City to shoot footage of real people who are looked down on by society or treated with less dignity than they deserve: the handicapped, the homeless, and others who are different. The people we filmed on the streets of New York were real people instead of actors. Steven even found an elderly gentleman, a Holocaust survivor who looked as if he were right out of *Schindler's List,* to be part of the video. In one gripping scene, the man looks straight at the camera and hikes up the left sleeve of his jacket to reveal a gruesome concentration camp number tattooed on his arm. It turned out to be an extremely moving video, and as hoped, both the song and video reached Number One.

ACM Video of the Year Award

The title song to the album *I Think about You* was written by Steve Seskin and the great Don Schlitz (who wrote "The Gambler" for Kenny Rogers), and I again had the wonderfully talented Steven Goldman direct production of the video. It was produced by a dream team of talent and turned out to be my ticket to the one major trophy that I ever received from the Academy of Country Music (ACM). *I Think about You* won Video of the Year in 1997, and not the least of my reasons for being proud of it was that Britanny acted in the video with me. I discovered that she was a natural-born actress.

At the time, I was developing a reputation for being the social-message guy, which was a role that fit me like a good suit, and I was inspired to do a song about the exploitation of women. My message was not overtly about sex abuse or trafficking but aimed a more subliminal message at men— in particular, about the way they tend to look at and treat women as sex objects. The message in the refrain was subtle but very clear: when a man looks at a woman impurely, he is looking at "someone else's baby". That was the challenge I wanted to communicate in both the home scenes and the action scenes of the video. Of all my videos, this one took the longest to shoot because I wanted to get that message just right.

To recap it briefly: I acted the part of a vice squad detective who was shown dealing with exploited and abused women in several seedy, inner-city scenes. The viewer gets the impression that this cop has seen it all. Some of the women were prostitutes; others were abused by their deadbeat partners et cetera. The guys who portrayed the dregs of society in the video were all character actors and did a great job of looking and acting like the losers they were supposed to represent. One scene even shows the cops bringing a battered woman to a shelter run by a nun, who is there in her religious habit to meet us at the gate. (She was a real nun, not an actress.)

After the graphic scenes, the video pans to me, the streetwise cop, returning to my existence as a single dad with a preteen daughter at home. I sit at the table, watching her in the background, wondering what will happen to her as she gets older. The scene attempts to tap into a sentiment that would be (and should be) the concern of every real father for his daughter at a vulnerable age. Britanny is washing dishes in the kitchen behind me, looking as cute and innocent as can be, and I am singing:

> When I see a pretty woman walking down the street
> I think about you
> Men look her up and down like she's some kind of treat
> I think about you
> She wouldn't dare talk to a stranger
> always has to be aware of the danger
> it doesn't matter who she is
> I think about ...
> You ... eight years old
> big blue eyes and a heart of gold
> when I look at this world, I think about
> You and I can't help but see
> that every woman used to be
> Somebody's little girl, I think about you.[1]

I loved making that video because it was pure Collin Raye. It was everything I wanted to do with my art, and judging from the massive positive feedback it generated, it seemed to strike a chord in the hearts of the millions who viewed it.

At the Thirty-Second Annual ACM Awards ceremony in 1997, I received the trophy for Video of the Year, and my costar, Britanny, accompanied me. We sat behind Buck Owens, one of my heroes—what a blessing that was! Best of all, I finally got my chance to express before a national audience, and in front of the glitterati of Nashville, all the things I had always wanted to say to them about culture and values, even if only for the sixty seconds they gave me. I meant every word:

> I want to say first of all that I feel so thankful to win this, especially this award, because I feel so strongly about this video. I think it proves once again that country music can be enlightening and potent as well as entertaining.... I want to thank Steven [Goldman] for doing a tremendous job, for taking the vision and turning it into a wonderful reality. I want to thank my family and friends, from Arkansas to Texas to Oregon, and my daughter, Britanny, my costar in the video here tonight with me, to her and Jake, her brother, at home tonight—I love you guys! Thanks for making me so happy! And I want to thank my Lord God in heaven for giving me a wonderful life, a lot of great people in it, and for having so much patience with me.[2]

God was patient with me as I worked to get to the place where I am now, despite the pitfalls of the country music business and my own mistakes. And I am thankful for the wonderful music that so many good people helped me to get onto the airwaves and into people's hearts during all those heady and exciting years.

More Hits and Messages

Three other songs off that album became hits: "On the Verge", "Love Remains", and "What If Jesus Comes Back Like That". "Love Remains", written by Tom Douglas and Jim Dadarrio, was a beautiful story about the power of love to sustain us through the many passages and trials of life. The version of "Love Remains" on this album is a secular song about the power of love with no explicitly religious overtones, but I rerecorded the song in 2011 and added a line at the end that transformed it into a song about the love of God: "Hope lives on ... and *His* love remains." The title of the 2011 album, *His Love Remains*, was taken from that last line; it expresses most perfectly the power of God's love, which sustains us through every difficulty of life.

Finally, "What If Jesus Comes Back Like That" was a surprise hit because we never intended it for release as a single. However, thanks to Blair Garner, host of the LA-based radio show *After Midnight*, who loved the song and played it constantly, it accidentally rose on the charts and took off. It was written by my friend Doug Johnson as a thought-provoking message for Christians, intending to strike at the hypocrisy of those who believe in the Bible but so easily put aside the humility of Christ and look down on others with pharisaical disdain. It posed the challenging questions: What if Jesus returned to the world—today? Would we recognize— or accept—Him in the "distressing disguise" (Mother Teresa's term) of the homeless man, the derelict, and other social misfits who might possibly be the living image of Christ among us? Would Jesus be welcomed if he came back today? Essentially, I saw the song as a musical interpretation of the parable of the sheep and the goats in Matthew 25: "I was hungry and you gave me no food" (v. 42). Given its controversial message, we never would have guessed that this song would make it onto the charts, but God clearly had other plans for it.

The Gift: Collin Raye Christmas, 1996

Sandwiched between two platinum albums, *I Think about You* (1995) and my first of greatest hits (*Direct Hits*, 1997), I had perhaps the most pleasurable recording experience of my entire career—making a Christmas album. My genius producer, John Hobbs, helped me give creative expression to all the Christmas songs that my heart had loved since my childhood, and I was determined that this was going to be a real Christ-centered Christmas album that accurately expressed the content of my personal faith, as opposed to one of those secularized "country Christmas" albums that the Nashville money machine produces in spades. Some of the worst songs produced for those albums are Kenny Chesney's "All I Want for Christmas Is a Real Good Tan" and my friend Joe Diffie's "Leroy the Redneck Reindeer". Christmas is a reminder of the most momentous event in human history—God becoming man. It was my hope to create an album so inspiring that it could eventually be ranked with the Christmas albums of artists such as Bing Crosby and Julie Andrews.

In fact, if I were asked to choose which one of my albums I would like everyone in the world to hear, it would be this Christmas album because it was so special—from the choice of songs, to the musical arrangements, to the recording, to the subsequent performances with a symphony orchestra. I felt it was a gift in every way, which is why I titled it *The Gift*. I added a few nonreligious songs beloved to all Americans, such as "I'll Be Home for Christmas", "Winter Wonderland", and "The Christmas Song", but I excluded all references to the secular icons that distract from the central meaning of Christmas, such as Frosty the Snowman and Santa Claus. All my favorite holy songs of Christmas are there: "The Little Drummer Boy", "O Holy Night", "The First Noel", "Away in a Manger", and "Silent Night", to name a few. Britanny, thirteen at the time, sang the latter two with me as duets; her young, sweet, and pure soprano voice was a perfect counterpart to mine.

The dignity of Christmas merited more serious musical accompaniment than usual. We needed a big orchestra with strings, brass, and woodwinds. John Hobbs hired players from the Nashville Symphony and worked like a master craftsman with his magnificent arrangements to make the traditional Christmas songs burst with life. He also recruited talented musicians such as Larry Cansler and Ron Huff to write the orchestral arrangements. Larry had worked with Kenny Rogers and the First Edition and had created many musical scores for Hollywood movies. Mr. Huff was the maestro of the Nashville Symphony Orchestra at the time. He did the arrangements for "The First Noel" and "O Holy Night", which are easily my favorites on the album. I would like to think that our version of "The First Noel" ranks among the most beautiful renditions of that song I have ever heard, something confirmed time and again by many fans and people in the music business.

The best part of recording this album was being able to work with some of my own musical heroes on several of the songs. The great Johnny Cash with his rich, deep, eminently recognizable voice narrated the opening sequence to "It Could Happen Again", a spectacular song about an event that happened in 1914 during the First World War. The song was written by my then girlfriend, Tammy Hyler, as a tribute to the power of the Prince of Peace over war.

Another unanticipated blessing of this album was the participation of literally *all* the Beach Boys in the recording of "Winter Wonderland". Earlier that year, I had appeared on their collaborative album, *Stars and Stripes*, so they may have been reciprocating, but I believe they really did it as a favor to John Hobbs, who had worked with them for years and who was one of the few people who could bring Brian Wilson, Mike Love, Carl Wilson, Bruce Johnston, and Al Jardine together in one place again. John wrote an awesome vocal arrangement for them to achieve a classic Beach Boys sound. I think my heart stopped for a brief second when I glanced over at the men standing at the microphones in the studio: the legendary Beach Boys themselves, with their bigger-than-life harmonies and personalities, were singing on my record! Working with such rock 'n' roll history on my own album was one of the peak moments of my career. With the exception of recording with my own baby girl, it was the most special of all the many blessings of that album.

The very same week the Beach Boys were in Nashville recording with me, I had the honor of performing live with them during their concert at Fan Fair. I sang "Sloop John B" and "Be True to Your School" right along with Mike Love and Brian Wilson. It was another truly surreal moment of my life. Getting to know the great Carl Wilson during that time may have been the best part of that experience. He died of cancer shortly thereafter, in 1998, but his spirit was so sweet, and to this day he is missed by many.

I don't think I ever sang better on an album than I did on this one. Because of the sacred and sentimental nature of the music, I approached it with a spirit of prayer and preparation that went beyond my normal professional standards. I paid attention to every detail of the music and production; I went to Mass, meditated, prayed Rosaries, and asked that God would make this the best Christmas album ever. God and his musical angels truly anointed this album. To this day people tell me that it is the best Christmas album they own; sometimes they say it is the only one they listen to during the holiday season. I am very proud of that album and will always hold it as my most enjoyable recording experience. I pray that it will continue to open the hearts of many people to the saving grace of Jesus Christ, God made man, for years to come.

The Walls Came Down, 1998

The name of the next record, *The Walls Came Down*, was the title of a song I wrote about the emotional walls that inevitably arise between lovers. *The Walls Came Down* achieved only gold status (half a million records sold), which was impressive but a sign that my platinum days were potentially winding down. I had been with Sony for eight years at that point, and I was still at the peak of my career with this album. The songs were the combination of social commentary, romance, heartbreak, and artistry that were my mark. My song mix often defied simple categorization and reflected my desire never to be a one-dimensional artist. Reviewers described this album with adjectives reflecting a broad range of human emotions and moods, such as refined, laid-back, mellow, confident, romantic, amiable, good-natured, intimate, sentimental, stylish, and theatrical. *The Walls Came Down* was all of the above.

One of the best songs on the album came as a surprise. "I Can Still Feel You" was written by Tammy Hyler after we had suffered a difficult breakup. About six to eight months after that experience, my producer, Paul Worley, wanted me to hear a new song that he thought I would want on the album. After he played it, I commented somewhat sadly, "Boy, that hits close to home." It was only after he saw my reaction that he told me that Tammy had written it, and then I knew that it was about us. Given that Paul and I both thought it would be a hit, recording it was a no-brainer, despite the personal connection I had with the lyrics. Our judgment was absolutely correct; it shortly hit Number One, and I was proud and gratified to stand with Tammy at her first Number One party. In a way, the success of the song brought a bittersweet closure to our very loving and joyful yet turbulent relationship.

Another Number One song on the album was "Someone You Used to Know", a sad song about lost love written by Rory Lee and Timothy Jon Johnson. It was a heart-wrenching ballad that appealed to any forlorn person hurting after a break-up—like myself at that moment. The album had another Top Ten hit—"Anyone Else" written by Radney Foster. My brother, Scotty, and I cowrote "Start Over Georgia", which I hoped would touch those who, like me, were trying to get back to basics—back to the family-values mindset that American culture used to endorse. I am proud of the song, which to me contained some of the deepest sentiments and best lyrics the Wray brothers ever wrote. My favorite line is the opener: "I think I feel like an old beat-up two lane / The one that the state's not about to repair."

Another song of note is "The Eleventh Commandment", written by my dear friend Karen Taylor-Good and Lisa Aschmann; it is a stinging indictment of child abuse in our society. The lyrics are haunting and end up suggesting that "honor thy children" should have been added to the Decalogue, as the eleventh commandment. God gave us ten commandments—and I do not question His wisdom—but artistically, we were making a point about the dignity of children. If that song saved even one child from harm, it was worth the effort.

Thanks to that song, I became an official ambassador for Childhelp USA, an organization that I had supported for years. The video we made for "The Eleventh Commandment" is among my best but was deemed too graphic for CMT, the country music video channel. Yet, to this day, we still get requests for copies of the video from law enforcement and service organizations that use it to educate people about domestic abuse.

There were two other milestone songs on the album. One was called "I Wish I Could". Written by my friend Tom Douglas, it was a subtle yet powerful song about how parents are always afraid for their children. The other milestone was my friend Hugh Prestwood's "April Fool", which was three minutes of absolute poetry.

Ultimately, the album title *The Walls Came Down* was prophetic, for my own relationship with Sony would be tumbling down in the not-too-distant future.

Tracks, 2000

The year 2000 was a prolific, with the release of my sixth studio album, *Tracks,* and two specialty albums. *Tracks* would be my second-to-last album with Sony and achieved only gold status; it was to be my last big-selling record.

As Paul Worley and John Hobbs, longtime friends and producers, were no longer with me, I quickly adjusted to the unique skills of my new producer, Dann Huff, the son of Ron Huff, who had worked with me on the

Christmas album. Dann had been the producer for Faith Hill and had a flair for pop. Faith's crossover into the adult contemporary pop scene was unmatched by any male country artist at the time, but many thought I had the versatility and the ability to do just that. Thus, Dann and I aimed for a pop hit with this album.

Tracks was eclectic in style and weighted toward pop. It still had some good down-home, foot-stomping country rockers, such as "She's All That", which was in the style of my earlier hit "That's My Story". It was also full of the strong ballads "I Want to Be There", "Completely", "She's Gonna Fly", "Landing in Love", and "You Will Always Be Mine". This last ballad had such touching lyrics, for example, "There are moments when I love you beyond the limits of my human heart." We were sure it would end up as a popular wedding song. In typical Collin Raye style, the album also contained a couple of heavy-message songs: "Harder Cards", about real justice for crimes committed, and "Water and Bridges", which was a profoundly hopeful song about post-abortion regret. Both songs were written by the great Craig Wiseman. The album was my usual mix of songs that defied clear categorization.

When "Couldn't Last a Moment" was released as a single, it quickly shot to Number One. Country audiences still can't get enough of those deeply emotive songs depicting the jilted lover singing about his lost love. It was, lyrically, a mirror of "Someone You Used to Know" from the previous album but in a far more pop musical package. Since we were deliberately breaking some new ground on this album, we added a duet with my friend Bobbie Eakes, a soap opera star who had been a regular on *The Bold and Beautiful* and *All My Children*. She has a gorgeous voice. She and I sang a killer love song written by my piano player, Geno LeSage, called "Loving This Way". It was one of the best duets I had ever heard and was a pleasure to perform with Bobbie. I would enjoy touring with Bobbie a lot that year.

Jake the WrestleMania Aficionado

During this most prolific period of my professional life (the mid- to late nineties), I made sure not to put my family life on hold. My son, Jake, was going through his teen years at that time, and I tried to get as much quality father-son time as I could by doing some things that he would love and remember. Jacob had a real passion for professional wrestling, which was a sport I had been interested in since my dad took me to see Ernie Bemis, "Mr. Kleen", wrestle in Portland in the late sixties. Jake watched it on TV a lot, so I thought it would be great to take him to see a live show someday. Our first live wrestling event was the Super Bowl of wrestling, the big pay-per-view event WrestleMania, which in the spring of 1993 took place at Caesar's Palace in Las Vegas. I was able to obtain excellent tickets for the show, and Jake absolutely loved watching the antics of guys such as Hulk Hogan, Lex Luger, Mark "the Undertaker" Calaway, and Bret Hart right there, under the lights. Over the span of about five years, we frequented numerous WrestleManias, Royal Rumbles, and SummerSlams, and Jake became a familiar fixture at these events; but I still wanted more for him, something that went beyond just being a spectator. Steve Cox and I pulled every string to make a connection with someone at the World Wrestling Federation who could get us backstage to meet the wrestlers. When we finally got backstage after two years of trying, Jake was in paradise.

I still believe it's easier to get into the White House than it is to get backstage at one of these events, and there's a valid reason for that: the wrestling profession doesn't want kids behind the scenes because they might see the good guys (the "babyfaces") and the bad guys (the "heels") actually getting along and hanging out together. They want to keep up the well-established illusion of serious conflict between the two sides—and they don't want to disappoint the kids, who might think that it's all fake.

That's another thing I learned about the wrestling profession—you never call pro wrestling "fake". The metal chairs that crash across people's heads are real; the hard tables that break over backs and the body slams to the canvas are all perfectly tangible and real—and so is the pain that wrestlers feel. I've never seen so many guys with scar tissue on their heads and faces. The events are scripted, to be sure, because these wrestlers are entertainers, like professional stuntmen, but they must *never, ever* be called "fake".

To me, pro wrestling is a soap opera for teenage boys and old ladies: 60 percent of the crowd at a wrestling event consists of young males, 30 percent are families, and a good 10 percent are single elderly ladies who get a kick out of the action. It would make for an interesting sociological study.

Because of our backstage access, Jake became a buddy to many of his heroes, such as Bret "the Hitman" Hart, Davey Boy Smith ("the British

Bulldog"), the Undertaker, and Owen Hart, the younger brother of Bret Hart. Owen was Jacob's superhero and one of the best men I've ever known. Jake and Owen bonded for some reason that is unknown to anyone but God. Even though Owen was perfectly cast as a real bad guy in all the fights, Jake loved him, memorized some of his lines, and learned to imitate aspects of his well-crafted "character" that came through in his performances. Owen took to Jake too. He would spend a lot of time with him on our backstage visits and would even call him on his birthday; their friendship lasted for several years. He was a sweetheart of a guy.

Sadly, Owen died tragically in May of 1999 when doing a stunt in the Kemper Arena in Kansas City. A broken rope resulted in an eighty-foot free fall from the top of the arena. His death was a serious blow to Jake—and everyone else in the wrestling world, for that matter. Owen was only thirty-four years old and left behind a wife and two wonderful kids. Jake, Britanny, and I attended the funeral in Calgary, Canada, and Owen's wife, Martha, did me the honor of asking me to sing several songs at the funeral; nothing could have been more difficult—or more special—for me. If I remember correctly, I sang "One Boy, One Girl" in honor of their two kids, "Amazing Grace", and "How Great Thou Art"; I think it was the first time my kids had experienced the death of a loved one, and the loss of their friend was very difficult for them. They really loved and admired Owen.

After Owen's death, we soured on professional wrestling somewhat, although I retained my respect for the men and women of the profession who, in their own way and style, are superb entertainers and often work for very few rewards other than the satisfaction of seeing people smile. The kids and I had a great deal of fun watching professional wrestling all those years, and I got loads of quality father-son time with Jake, as I had wished.

More Sufferings and Surprises along the Way

During the cutting of *Tracks* in 1999, there were several signs that it was time to move out of Texas and closer to the center of my professional universe, Nashville. Since Connie's and Jake's dual health catastrophes in 1985, the kids had been in Greenville, Texas, where they lived with me when I was home and with Connie when I was gone. They had spent a happy and peaceful childhood there, but they were now of high school age, and one day they both came to me and asked me if we could move out of Greenville, where they were unhappy for a variety of reasons, not the least of which were some escalating conflicts they were having with Connie. The request was music to my ears. I saw it as an opportunity to move to another place and to make a better life with the kids. Even though Connie didn't like the idea, she accepted it as something that the kids wanted, and the three of us packed up and moved to a 5,600-square-foot home in Brentwood, Tennessee, an exclusive suburb of Nashville. It was the biggest house we had ever owned. Although we would live in it for only about a year, it holds many wonderful memories for us. Britanny and Jake both enrolled in Brentwood High School in the fall of 1999, Britanny as a junior and Jake as a freshman. Living in Nashville began a new chapter in our lives that would be filled with many challenges. The Chinese have a curious way of cursing a person with the wish, "May you live in interesting times." These were interesting times for us.

The first challenge was the relationship Britanny formed with Charles Matthew Bell, known as Charlie. Britanny had dated Charlie in Greenville, where he had a job as a bartender; he was tall, good-looking, and charming. Charlie was four years older than Britanny, but I did not object to their dating because I initially liked him. For starters, he seemed to have no bad habits, at least not the ones that cause immediate concern: he didn't smoke or do drugs. I was okay with his moving to Nashville so that he and Britanny could be close enough to continue dating because he seemed to be a good influence on Britanny, who had been struggling with certain issues with her mom and having a bit of a tough time in the transition from Texas. I felt that it was okay that he was there.

As time went on, however, Charlie began to remind me of my dad; he had that same restless "malcontent" personality and found it very hard to keep a job. He would work at a department store for a week, have a falling out with someone, and then suddenly decide to quit. Then he worked in a restaurant for a few days, and that would end similarly. I was getting the impression that he was more of a "Good-bye Charlie" than a stable guy. I was monitoring their relationship as it developed and always made sure that there was plenty of adult supervision in our home when I had to leave town; however, I believe that I let him hang around a bit too much and gave them too much freedom and alone time. I know now it was a parental mistake; I was too trusting with teenagers.

Sometime in the beginning of Britanny's junior year, the two were not getting along very well. Charlie left suddenly one day and returned to Texas, and I was relieved that he was gone. Peace was restored, and Britanny went back to her school books and regular routine. Deciding that he didn't like Tennessee very much, Jake moved back to Texas too. I knew that he was still very attached to his grandmother Doris, who had done so much for him, and I thought it best that he should move back if he really wasn't happy in Nashville, although I missed him.

A few months later, at a Sunday evening Mass, when Britanny stood up for the closing prayer she became faint and collapsed back onto the pew. Her head fell back, her eyes rolled upward, and she looked as white as a ghost. This scared me to death. She came around quickly, shook her head, and said in a weak voice, "I don't feel well." She rallied somewhat as soon as we left church, and I took her to Cracker Barrel, where she ate some chicken and dumplings. The meal seemed to make her feel better; however, I made an appointment with our family doctor for the next day

Dr. Jones checked her out and initially thought that she might have an ovarian cyst or something of that nature. I was worried and prayed that she wouldn't have any problem like that. He asked me to wait outside the exam room while he did some more tests, and when he called me back in, I saw Britanny sitting on the chair with her head down, being very somber, which was unusual for her. The doctor had ruled out any cyst or tumor, and that made me very happy, but when I asked what the problem was, he said, "She's pregnant."

"What!" I exclaimed.

Britanny immediately broke down and bawled her eyes out, and my first reaction was to comfort her. Scolding her never crossed my mind. "Oh my gosh, it's okay, baby; it's okay" were all the words I could get out as I sat there and hugged my baby girl. It took me a few minutes to wrap my mind around this astonishing news, but then Britanny said, "It's Charlie's, Dad." My second reaction was, I suppose, a typical fatherly reaction; I said to myself, "Oh boy, I can't wait to get my hands on that Charlie Bell." The thought of a shotgun—as in "shotgun wedding"—came to mind, although I didn't want to force him to marry Britanny, but to keep away from her!

Instead of voicing any threats of violence at a tender moment like that, I said, "But you haven't even seen him for all these months." The pregnancy was undoubtedly the result of an earlier encounter before Charlie took off.

Poor Britanny felt so terrible about the whole incident. She was only seventeen, and it was as much of a shock to her as it was to me. I recalled that my own mom was pregnant at age seventeen with Scotty. It was another of those surreal moments of my life. Britanny and I have always dealt with every good or bad situation as a *united front*, and this time was no exception. I kept assuring her, "It's okay, honey, we can do this", but what I really meant was, "We can do this without Charlie." I asked her to make no rash decisions at that time and assured her that we would work things out. The thought of her getting married to Charlie scared me more than her being pregnant; I didn't want her to compound one bad decision with another.

I truly give that young lady credit for being tough beyond her years and for fully embracing the reality of motherhood at such a young age. She already knew my admiration for motherhood as the most important, most dignified, and toughest job in the world—bar none—and I was deeply gratified that she accepted the gift of motherhood with such maturity. Despite the difficulty of the circumstances, it never crossed her mind *not* to have the baby. It never crossed my mind either. It's easy to say that you favor the right to life when you are not facing a crisis of this proportion. Here we were, getting an opportunity to put that truth into practice. Both Britanny and I saw a new life, despite the less-than-ideal circumstances, as something positive rather than negative; it was not a tragedy. I remember thinking while I was still in the doctor's office, "Well, buddy, you've been talking the talk; now you have to walk the walk." Many people say, "You don't know what you'll do until it happens to you." Now it *was* happening to me, and Britanny and I stepped up to the plate together.

Expecting a child, of course, affects everyone in the family. For my part, I couldn't believe I was going to be a grandfather before age forty! My baby was going to have a baby. I truly think that my *positive* reaction to the whole incident was critical for everyone in the family. I don't take any credit for loving life and babies, but I am aware that mothers and fathers can have an important influence on a whole family when a child is pregnant out of wedlock. They can sway the feelings of all around them for good or for ill, and I hate to think of all the parents who take their pregnant teens to the abortion centers of this land to abort their grandchildren. I believe it is a grave responsibility for everyone—especially for parents— to stand tall in support of life when their kids find themselves in the throes of an unexpected pregnancy. My understanding of God's truth is that every human being will have to give a reckoning of the blood of the inno- cent (cf. Gen 9:5–6; Joel 3:19–21; Prov 6:17).

We got right to work preparing for the arrival of the newest member of our family. The initial shock of it wore off very quickly and then turned to joy when I flew down to Greenville to make the big announcement. Connie surprised me when, before I could even open my mouth, she said, "Britan- ny's pregnant, right?" Mothers are clairvoyant about things like that. She took it all very well, as did her parents, Doris and Gary. Jake was actually excited about the arrival of a new baby, so it seemed that we would all embrace this moment without the divisions that often happen in families on such occasions, and I was grateful to God for that.

His grace was so tangible in those days; He helped us to see everything we needed to see. Britanny was mature enough to recognize her mistake and to take responsibility for it, but we also realized very quickly that God has an incredible way of turning our mistakes around and bringing tre- mendous good out of them. We gave glory to Him for this pregnancy and surrendered all our worries to Him with confidence and even joy. It was amazing how fast He changed what could have been a very desolate situa- tion into a massive experience of joy that was full of peace and anticipation.

Charlie *cried* when he heard the news, not for sorrow, but for happiness. He wanted to get married right away and to make a good start of things, but I was not going to let them move so fast. Seeing only disaster around every corner of that plan, I counseled them to make no decision about marriage until after the birth of the baby, and then we would see how things looked. Prudence is the better part of valor. I give Charlie credit, though, for at least wanting to do the right thing.

Daddy, It's a Little Girl!

Britanny had her first ultrasound when I was still in Greenville giving the news to the family, and I will never forget her phone call from the doctor's office that day. She said with such joy, "Daddy, it's a little girl!" Her words reminded me of her own birth, when the delivery nurse told me and Connie, "It's a little girl!" The circle of life is so beautiful sometimes. We were going to welcome another baby girl into the family, and I couldn't have been happier.

I was very busy touring at that time and was scared to death that I was going to be on the road when Britanny gave birth, but God gave me the grace to be there. I am so grateful that I was with her when she went into labor on June 8, 2001. We brought her to the hospital that day, and when I went to move the car, Charlie called me to come into the delivery room immediately because it looked as if she was going to give birth sooner than we expected. I was surprised that she had gotten to that point so quickly because Britanny's own birth was a long, slow process. Her labor, however, was mercifully quick. In the birthing room, Charlie held one of Britanny's hands, and I held the other, and very soon our little Haley Marie Bell saw the light of day. Oh, the joy of that moment!

In a life of so many wonderful moments, it is hard to say which is the greatest of them all, but the moment my first granddaughter came into the world ranks as one of the best. She went full term and was delivered without a hitch, and she looked absolutely perfect. We basked in the beauty of that radiant little newborn. I was a grandfather now; my baby girl had just had a baby girl, and all was well with the world. Britanny looked so natural and perfect in her new role of motherhood, and that was the first time I really saw how tough she was. She handled labor so well. The next day we drove Haley to her first home on Stonebridge Drive in Franklin, Tennessee, where we had moved by that time, and we began a new era that would forever change me and my family.

Among the many happy consequences of having babies in the family is the infusion of life that they give to their elders. I am a perfect example of how much grandkids energize a granddad, but I have to say that I was also pleasantly surprised at how positively Haley's birth—and four years later, Mattie's—affected Connie. Being a grandmother has definitely brought out the very best in her; in fact, the new life around us opened up a soft side to her that I had not seen in many years. It was apparent that Connie's greatest joy was the time she spent with her granddaughters.

Specialty Albums for Kids and Lovers, 2000

The year 2000 saw the release of my children's album, *Counting Sheep*, and another album of love songs called, creatively, *Love Songs*. Sony in Nashville had a derivative in New York City called Sony Wonder that gave me a very simple assignment: they wanted me to make an album that would help children go to sleep, with music that kids would enjoy but that wouldn't drive their parents crazy (as was the case with so much children's music at the time!). I had no genre restrictions; it didn't have to be country; it didn't have to sound like anything in particular. I just had to be creative, and *Counting Sheep* may be the most creative album I have ever done because it was an incredible mix of beautiful classics along with some fresh, new songs written just for the album. Among the classics were "When You Wish upon a Star" from *Pinocchio* and "Stay Awake" from *Mary Poppins,* which closes the album. My close associate Karen Taylor-Good, who had written so much for me in my heyday, wrote "When You Say Your Prayers", which is a truly gorgeous song, and co-wrote "A Mother and Father's Prayer" with the great Melissa Manchester, who sang that as a duet with me. Her beautiful voice is unmistakable to a wide audience. That song was the single release for the album, which we didn't expect to become a hit on the country charts because it was written for a smaller, select audience.

A creative new songwriter, Robert Ellis Orrall, wrote two awesome songs for this album, the most notable of which was the title song, "Counting Sheep", which sounds very much like a McCartney/Lennon creation, except that it's about kids falling asleep. It's just brilliant. I would also record the ageless, classic Irish lullaby, "Too Ra Loo Ra Loo Ra", which I have always loved since I first heard it sung in *Going My Way* with Barry Fitzgerald and Bing Crosby. In fact, that song had an extraspecial meaning for me since I had often sung it to my Britanny and Jacob when they were little, along with "Hush, Little Baby", and I later sang it to my granddaughter Haley. Whenever she heard me begin to intone, "Too Ra Loo Ra Loo Ra", she would raise her little head and know that Poppy was getting ready to put her to bed.

The children's album was an absolute joy for me to do. It also had more of an impact than I could ever have imagined. It seems that every week when I am touring, many people—sometimes as many as five—come up to tell me stories of raising their kids listening to *Counting Sheep*. That means so much to me and makes the effort worthwhile. I am very proud of that beautiful record.

Love Songs was a compilation of the greatest love songs I had done, and it was wonderful to see them all brought together on one album. Some of them were top singles—"Love Me", "In This Life", "If I Were You". Others were album cuts such as "I Volunteer" and "Survivors". I also recorded a bonus track for this album, the classic Don McLean song "And I Love You So", which is arguably one of the three or four most beautiful love songs of all time. My high-tenor voice was particularly suited to that song, and it was so special to include it on this album.

Two Greatest-Hits Albums, 1997 and 2002

Perhaps it would be best to conclude with a few words about the two composite albums made of my hits over the years. There are few things more satisfying for an artist than to compile a collection of his many hit songs. Such an album is a huge statement to the world that he has reached a level of expertise and fame that comes to very few. It is a sort of unwritten declaration that he has achieved—through talent and hard work—a certain status. But therein also lies the danger for him. The tangible evidence of accomplishment in one's field can be a huge ego trip. Lord knows I have never been free of the inner struggle with vanity, which fame and success make exponentially more difficult to defeat, but I keep trying.

On the positive side, greatest-hits albums are also the gifts that keep on giving because they tend to have a longer listening trajectory than an individual album, which quickly becomes dated. In fact, people may buy several versions of the same album as technology changes. I myself have purchased four or five versions of Elton John's *Greatest Hits* as technology passed through the vinyl, 8-track, cassette, and CD stages. Because the hit songs usually have greater emotional significance for people, these albums become part of our musical collections and stay with us through many years.

Direct Hits was my favorite of the hits albums I did with Sony and was also phenomenally successful, hitting double platinum (two million in sales) since its release in 1997. I personally chose the name *Direct Hits* because of my love for military terminology and history; I thought a clever, military-style name just sounded cool. I had never heard a name like that for a greatest-hits album. I also refused to call it *Greatest Hits* or some other bland title like so many others. My friend Trisha Yearwood once asked me how I came up with such interesting names for my albums, and I was flattered by her question.

Of the fourteen songs on the album, ten of them were my earlier hits; the other four had not been previously released. One of these was "The Gift", written by Jim Brickman, because it is immensely romantic and we thought it would make a good single to release to radio. We also added "Little Red Rodeo", written by Phil Vassar, which I am proud to say was his first cut performed by a major artist. I also included my own version of the song "Open Arms", originally performed by Steve Perry and Journey, as a bonus track for the fans who had watched me do it live. "Open Arms" is one of the most beautiful love songs ever written; it is sad and mellifluous and brought out the best of my high-tenor voice. "The Gift" would reach Number One on the adult contemporary chart, and another song on the album, "What the Heart Wants", reached the top spot in country. "Little Red Rodeo" became a Top Five. I am so proud of this record because it is the compilation of many great accomplishments.

My second greatest-hits album, released in 2002, would get the somewhat lackluster title *Collin Raye: 16 Biggest Hits*. I didn't choose the title this time; the album was put out by Sony after I left. As the legal owners of the recorded masters of the songs I had made in my decade with them, they could continue making money off my name. They already had an established series of biggest-hits albums by other artists, and this album became part of that. I didn't feel slighted by the effort. Underappreciated, yes; but slighted, no.

Faith and Glory

In my hit-making time with Sony, I sold almost eight million albums, with five platinum or multi-platinum albums to my name, two gold albums, sixteen Number One singles, and twenty-four Top Ten songs in a row. Not bad, from a professional point of view. If, because of my vanity at that time, I didn't credit all the glory and honor for those successes to God, I do so now. Experience and maturity have given me a much deeper understanding of Jesus' words to His disciples about any accomplishments we may be tempted to attribute to ourselves: "He who abides in me, and I in him, he it is that bears much fruit, for apart from me you can do nothing" (Jn 15:5). That truth has become abundantly clear to me in recent years.

As I conclude these chapters about some of my greatest musical moments, I am reminded of a question from a viewer that came in a recent interview with Marcus Grodi on EWTN's *The Journey Home* program. The young man asked rather innocently what he had to do to become a star in music! That same concern was once a burning question in my heart too, so I answered him with a few pieces of advice from thirty-plus years of sweat and experience.

I told him that, first and foremost, if he wants to succeed in music, as in life, he must put his faith above all other things. His relationship with God has to rule everything and be number one on his list of priorities, because if he surrenders that, any future success he achieves will be short-lived. I told him that he should define "success" as achieving things of lasting value, and maintaining a strong relationship with God is the one thing in life that will never pass away.

Secondly, I told him that a person with ambition for good things must never allow himself to be seduced by stardom or to be defined by material success. A man whose identity is in ticket or record sales will lose his identity once the sales dry up—which they inevitably do. Though we may think that achieving fame is within our own power, it's really up to God to open the door to success. If God allows us to embrace our dream and to work very hard to achieve it, we must never sell our souls for it. Anyone getting into music today has to examine his motives very deeply and ask himself why he would want to be the next American Idol. The deeper question is whether *God* would want him to be the next American Idol.

Finally, I told the young man that he must truly love music and musical performance; otherwise he will never have the stamina to continue on the arduous pathway to success. Despite the apparent glamour of stardom, the road that leads there is long and lonely and loaded with deadly pitfalls, sheer cliffs at virtually every turn, and more than a few improvised explosive devices planted by treacherous enemies and false friends along the way. The music business is a dirty business, I told him, and if love doesn't motivate him to reach his goals, he will never have the inner strength to get through the politics and the negative influences.

I told him that, ultimately, each of us has to love the level of success that we achieve and be content in the place God puts us. We may want something different from what God shows us to be His will, but that is sinful human nature wanting more than what is good for us.

In these few words of advice, I was essentially retelling the story of my own musical career. It is said that wisdom comes from life experience but that life experience comes only from making mistakes. In that regard, I must have gained great wisdom over the years. Yet, looking back on my heyday, I recognize that any mistakes and failures I experienced were also doorways to greater opportunities, even when they seemed disastrous to me at the time. It is only faith that has made it possible for me to keep success and failure, joy and sorrow—all things—in focus and to give glory to God for all that I have done and all that He has permitted to happen to me.

In the end, my hope for getting what I want out of this career in music, as Garth Brooks had wished for me so many years ago, has been well founded. I cannot change the mistakes I have made along the way; I can only thank God for the great gifts and opportunities that have molded me and prepared me to do His will as best I can every day. I hope above all to give glory to God and to serve His people with my talents. Now I never look back.

8

The Good Ol' Boys of Nashville

Surviving the Country Music Business

(2001–2002)

*For we must all appear before the judgment seat of Christ,
so that each one may receive good or evil, according
to what he has done in the body.*

—2 Cor 5:10

Every man has his Waterloo, as they say, and the record business was mine. After years of sustained success, of platinum records and hit songs, of fame and fortune, my Nashville career went down in flames virtually overnight. I don't hesitate to admit that my own mistakes contributed to my downfall. For a while, I was on the top of my game and at the pinnacle of success, but people usually don't stay on mountain peaks very long. If any measure of vanity made me attribute all that success to myself, I was sorely shaken out of the illusion when my time of being one of the "anointed" was finished.

Yet, as I look back at the disaster of 2001 and 2002, I don't see only destruction: I see grace at work in all things, in the bad as well as the good. It seemed at the time as if Nashville was a dead-end road, but it wasn't. Saint Augustine, the fourth-century convert who later became a bishop, put it so well; he said the three greatest virtues of the Christian life are humility, humility, and humility. It takes a long time for the average person to learn that virtue, and it probably took me longer than most; but humility has made it possible for me to see God's gentle hand guiding my life through all its ups and downs.

Humanitarian of the Year Award

The year 2001 started out well at least. In the spring, I received a momentous award from the Country Radio Broadcasters Association. This group holds an annual convention and gives out its Humanitarian Artist of the Year Award to the country artist who did the most for charity in the previous year. Their ceremony didn't have as high a profile as the CMA/ACM awards, but it was perhaps more significant for that reason. The radio programmers are the hardworking and fairly nonpolitical gatekeepers of the airwaves that broadcast country music to the average person. They know who is who in Nashville, and I believe they give out awards based on merit, not on politics.

The Humanitarian Artist Award is presented each year by the person who won it the year before, and so my friend Clint Black presented me with this great honor. The following year I presented it to Kix Brooks and Ronnie Dunn. These guys were big acts—people I respected—and I was proud to be counted among them.

Supporting worthy organizations was one way I could use my celebrity status for good. Charities get a real boost when someone in public life draws attention to them, and during the year for which I won the award, I had worked with the Tennessee Task Force against Domestic Violence, Childhelp USA, Al Anon, and Alateen. In previous years I had worked with other charities that have been close to my heart, particularly Catholic Relief Services and the Special Olympics. I count the Humanitarian Artist of the Year Award to be one of the most gratifying honors I have ever received and am thankful to God for it.

With Catholic Relief Services in Kosovo and Macedonia

By the late nineties I had been a donor to Catholic Relief Services (CRS) for many years, and I jumped at the chance to do more for the organization when CRS asked me to go with them to Kosovo and Macedonia. The trip took place just two weeks after the end of the Kosovo War in June 1999. As this was my first visit to a war-ravaged country, the devastation I saw there made a deep impression. By the time I arrived on the scene, the whole region was divided into sectors that were controlled by different peacekeeping units from countries such as Germany, Ireland, and the United States. We stayed in Skopje, the largest town and capital city of Macedonia, and spent the next several days traveling around in armored vehicles, visiting various CRS-run refugee camps. CRS didn't assign me a specific task; they wanted me only to be a benevolent presence, which was a natural fit for me. I played with the kids, shook hands, and sang to people everywhere I went.

One camp was memorable for a number of reasons: above all, it was run by a twenty-two-year-old American, who had an impressive ability to manage what was, in reality, a small city. He did an amazing job keeping everything in order with the help of a cadre of highly dedicated CRS volunteers. The camp was built to hold four thousand refugees but was overrun with twelve thousand souls by the end of the war—and there were beautiful children everywhere. As I walked through the camp, I started talking to the kids, joking around, and slapping hands with them, and I soon found myself surrounded by about seventy-five kids who were all smiles and looked at me with such innocent curiosity in their faces. Kids are kids, no matter what the culture, and it was a joy to win them over and to relieve some of their distress.

The next day, the CRS people took me to a school that had just reopened, and I found myself in front of a class of Albanian school kids who were all orphans. Every one of them had lost his parents in the war. Furthermore, not a single student spoke or understood English. When someone handed me a guitar and asked me to play a song, I had no idea how I was supposed to reach them. I fell back on my default position for such situations: "When in doubt, sing a Beatles song!" I began to strum and to sing, "When I find myself in times of trouble / Mother Mary comes to me / speaking words of wisdom ..." By the time I got to the refrain, "Let it be, let it be", literally *all* the kids in the classroom were singing along with me in heavily accented English. They all knew the words and the tune because they had heard it often on the radio. It was an amazing experience of the power of music. A bunch of kids who had looked rather glum when I walked in the room were all smiles and hanging all over me by the time we were done. If I ever meet Paul McCartney, I'm going to tell him how his song inspired so many kids that day—and at least one American country singer as well.

My favorite group of peacekeeping soldiers was the Irish contingent because they were the friendliest; in fact, I had a chance to sing for them one day as we visited the town near Pristina, the capital city of Kosovo, where they were stationed. Needless to say, there was no language barrier with the Irish. When we arrived there, the CRS people asked me to sing a few songs for the troops. The first song that came to mind was the famous "Danny Boy", which I sang with the greatest of feeling for those valiant soldiers. To a man, they all sang along and soon began to weep and hug each other. They couldn't help remembering their beloved homeland, which they missed as they answered the call of humanitarian duty.

I am so grateful for the experience of being a musical missionary to many needy people at that time and place. Catholic Relief Services gave me a great gift by bringing me to a country where I could do some good for a little while, and I will never forget the people I met on that trip or the power of simple music on the lonely and suffering. I would do it again in a heartbeat.

Terror and Politics Back Home

My departure from the Nashville limelight came shortly after the terrorist attack on September 11, 2001. I was not in the United States when the Twin Towers came down. I had gone to Switzerland with my band to be the headline act for the Gstaad Summer Music Festival, which I had first played in 1993 with Emmylou Harris. This time I closed the show after performances by Sara Evans and Gary Allan, and when the festival was finished, I had planned to do some vacationing in Europe with Jake.

We were scheduled to take a morning flight back to the United States on September 12. On our way to Zurich the day before, our driver was listening to the radio when a French-speaking newscaster began saying something that was incomprehensible to me but with emotion that was unmistakable: something terrible had just happened. In broken English our driver translated, "Plane heet Vorl Trade Zenter. Plane heet Vorl Trade Zenter." He repeated this ominous message several times, and I presumed that some plane—a little Cessna maybe—had crashed into one of the Towers and that the intensity of the newscaster was just hype. After we arrived at the Zurich Airport Hilton, however, my stage manager, Kurt Fetty, ran into the hotel and immediately came back out, exclaiming, "We're under attack! We're under attack!"

Announcing catastrophic news seems to make people repeat themselves, but I guess repetition is part of the shocked reaction to situations that people find hard to fathom. This news was almost too horrible to believe. Our nation had sustained its first foreign attack on our soil since Pearl Harbor; in fact, the whole Western world had been thrown into a full-scale red alert that immediately shut down airports and might eventually lead to war. That *was* hard to believe.

"Who could have attacked us?" I asked Kurt. "The Russians? Who could possibly do this?" I thought he was talking about a military attack, and I was trying to figure out how that could have happened. Kurt didn't know, but he had seen on the TV monitor in the hotel lobby that one of the World Trade Center towers was burning. A jetliner had crashed into its top floors, he said, and no planes would be leaving Zurich that afternoon or evening. He had no more information than that. Looking back on it now, it must have been just minutes after the American Airlines plane hit Tower One of the World Trade Center (8:50 A.M., eastern standard time.) *CNN* was already displaying the title "America under Attack".

We found ourselves in the lobby full of people standing around the TV monitor, watching the dreadful news unfold on the *CNN World* channel. We witnessed, live, the second airplane hit Tower Two. Within an hour we saw Tower One, and then Tower Two, disintegrate before our very eyes. Nothing can describe the appalling chill I felt from knowing that so many lives were being lost at that very instant while we were powerless to do anything about it. Worse yet was seeing the desperate people jumping from the buildings and their bodies landing on the pavement nearly a thousand feet below. *CNN* in America quickly scuttled those gut-wrenching scenes, but we continued to see them in Switzerland *as they were happening*.

The only comforting thought at that moment was the realization that Jake and Kurt and I were among a large group of Americans who were all in the same situation. There was solidarity in our exile: we were all far away from home, missing loved ones, frightened of the unknown, and mourning together this horrible deed done to our beloved nation. We spent the next five days at the Hilton with our compatriots while the airports remained closed. The hotel was kind enough to cancel all incoming reservations so that the stranded Americans could stay there until they could fly home.

My son was with me, and I thank God for that, but Britanny and Haley were back in America. Because the phone lines were overloaded, it took me quite a while to reach them. Even though I knew they were not in the state where the attacks took place, I was still frantic until I could talk to Britanny. The worst part of the early moments of the crisis was being unsure about its duration and extent. By the second day, I knew that Britanny and Haley were safe, in contrast to a world that had just become much less so.

One of the redeeming aspects of our week of exile was that Jake and I had more father-son quality time than we had anticipated. As we were waiting for the next available flight to the States, we could not leave the hotel much; but fortunately, Jake had brought with him a small, portable DVD player and three DVDs with episodes of the *Andy Griffith Show*. We watched the shows over and over, and those wholesome American programs gave us some comfort and peace amid all the stress. We appreciated our culture and nation as we never had before. Meanwhile, we kept an eye on *CNN* and called home daily to make sure that Britanny and Haley were okay. We did no further tourist activities; those last days in Zurich became a time of mourning and prayer—with good old Andy Taylor and Barney Fife to keep us company.

When we finally did get on a plane back to the States, the first city we landed in was Chicago; and honestly, I was never so happy to be back in our native land. We weren't yet in Greenville, Texas, where the girls were, but I knew we were *home*.

My Final Record with Sony: Can't Back Down, 2002

It wasn't long after my return to the United States that I began to work on what would be my last album for Sony. Rounding out my long list of producers was the extremely talented James Stroud, who was an institution in Nashville at the time, and still is. Although he was the head of another label, DreamWorks, he had the freedom to freelance and agreed to work with me on a new album. I was elated. He was one of the most successful producers in town and had been instrumental in the careers of Clint Black and Tim McGraw; he had produced big hits for them and for many others. He had the reputation of being a great song man and of knowing what it takes to make a successful album. That was my goal for this next album since the previous one, *Tracks*, had not done as well as we had hoped. We were looking to get back to platinum. James and I had known one another for a few years and possessed a mutual respect for each other's gifts. I couldn't wait to get into the studio with him. Little did I know that *Can't Back Down,* my seventh studio album, would be my sayonara to Sony.

My good-bye to Sony resulted from decisions made by its executives. Allen Butler, the head of Sony Music Nashville (SMN), had, in my view, a more devastating influence on my professional life than any other man. With Tim DuBois, president of Arista Records, Butler had been vice president of radio promotion at Arista in the early nineties, when Alan Jackson and Brooks and Dunn were exploding. SMN hired Butler as general manager and then made him president/CEO in 1997. He was in charge of all Sony labels, including Epic (my label), Columbia, and Monument, which had just signed the Dixie Chicks.

As I found out later, Butler was feeling heat from the mother ship in New York to get better numbers. His response to this pressure was to insert himself into the production operations of the individual artists, including the recording process and the delicate work of A and R. He did not have expertise in these areas, but he did have power; and he asserted his authority to a degree that, in my view, had a catastrophic effect on two of my albums.

Butler wanted to make the final decision about which singles would be released to radio—but he didn't seem to trust the professional judgment of the people who were producing the albums. This was no small issue. Today, most people purchase music on the Internet as individual songs rather than as albums. Prior to the iTunes era, singles were released for radio broadcast in order to sell not only the singles but also the albums of which they were part. Choosing songs for radio was one of the most challenging parts of promoting an album and absolutely essential to its success. Picking the right singles required a comprehensive understanding of the charts, a feel for the current musical preferences of a particular artist's audience, and a perception of "what will work"—the special talent that comes from being blessed with "good ears". Allen Butler did not appear to have all of these qualifications.

While making my previous album, Tracks, Butler and I clashed over his choice of radio releases. Before Butler got involved with those selections, my production team released the single "Couldn't Last a Moment" early in 2000. The song hit Number One in a very short time, which promised good sales for the album. When the album went out the following May, our plan was to release the upbeat rocker "She's All That" as a summer single to keep the momentum going. Butler, though, nixed that and moved up the breakup ballad with Bobbie Eakes, "Tired of Loving This Way", which was originally intended for release before Christmas.

The conventional wisdom in country music is that summertime singles need to be lighthearted and fun; the time to release something sad is during the winter months. The fate of "Tired of Loving This Way" seemed to verify this: once the single was released, it had the predicted effect of stopping the album's momentum. In all probability, our original plan would have provided me with three consecutive hit songs and given Bobbie her first hit album. Tracks might even have achieved platinum status. Instead, the disappointing sales of Tracks not only failed to reach platinum level but destroyed Bobbie Eakes' chances at a recording career.

Butler and I also disagreed over the single releases for my 2002 album, Can't Back Down. James and I worked well together on the recordings, and we had an arsenal of good songs; I felt in my bones that this album was going to be one of my best. Yet, after Butler heard the songs, he said he was "not sure he heard a single" among them. As I was heavily invested in this album, and very excited about the songs, I couldn't believe it. "Are you kidding me?" I said, adding that every song was a good one and that some were absolutely great. Butler remained unmoved and insisted that we cut three more songs, and he was the boss. Both James and I were irritated with his decision, but we cut the songs anyway. Ultimately—as we suspected—none of the three made it onto the album.

The quarrel over a single did not end there. James and I had cut a sweet little song with a good message entitled "Ain't Nobody Gonna Take That from Me", which I liked a lot but knew wasn't a radio song. It was good album filler, but no more. Yet, out of all the songs we had lined up, Butler decided to release this one as the first single. Needless to say, James and

I strongly objected; any of the other songs on the album would have been better. I particularly favored the killer ballad "It Could Be That Easy", which I had imagined could turn out to be a career song for me on the level of "Love, Me". When Butler did not see its potential as a single, I suggested the beautiful "One Desire" and a few other up-tempo songs that were sure to be hits, but Butler rejected these also and stood his ground on "Ain't Nobody" despite strong objections from James and me.

As far as I could tell, Butler was basing his judgment on his own polling system. He had taken the whole Sony staff on a corporate retreat and had asked them to vote on potential singles. Not surprisingly, all the employees agreed with their boss' choices. Asking subordinates (from mail room workers on up) to choose songs that experts in the business often deliberate on for long hours was a popular, but not necessarily reliable, way to determine the best singles to release.

In my decade of wrangling with Sony executives about singles and albums, I was not always correct on what worked and what didn't work, but I was right about 80 percent of the time. In this case, I knew I was right on a fundamental matter, but it made no difference because Butler pulled rank and went with his favorite song for the single. Sony released "Ain't Nobody" to radio, and it was a total flop—as predicted.

The Relationship with Sony Deteriorates

To an outsider, a dispute over a song may seem petty, but to people in the recording business, it can be a matter of life and death for projects and careers. The question of which single to release isn't just a matter of personal taste or preference. An artist's integrity and reputation can often ride on decisions like these, and mine certainly did in this situation.

The dispute over the single was the straw that broke the camel's back. Tensions had been building with the label, but up to this point I had been able to manage them; this, however, was the second major blow to my recording career in a short time, and I wanted out. Though I still owed Sony two records on my eight-album contract (Can't Back Down wasn't released yet, just the failed single), I had been approached by a couple of other major labels that wanted me to leave Sony and sign with them. The other deals looked promising. Steve, my manager, even brought in a powerful music business attorney to see if they could force a "coup" and get me out of the contract, but Butler vetoed every request to cut me loose. I told him, "Allen, you're obviously sick of us; just let us go to another label that will get behind me and give me a push." His response was an emphatic, "No! No! No!"

This was strange to me. As much as I was tired of Sony, it seemed Sony, or at least Butler, was also tired of me and no longer appreciated what I had to offer. On top of that, their attention was now shifting to the Dixie Chicks, who were starting to explode and were making Sony a great deal of money. Yet Butler refused to release me to go to another label. What sense did that make? Steve and I both continued to persist in asking for my release until it finally looked like Allen agreed. In one meeting with Steve, he shouted out in frustration, "Okay, we'll let Collin Raye go!", and we believed that he meant it. That was our first mistake. We didn't ask him then and there to put the permission in writing while he was still in the mood, and that was our second mistake.

On the basis of his presumed verbal permission to leave, Steve and I started shopping my talents and *Can't Back Down* to other labels. A few days later, Steve got a shocking e-mail from Butler announcing Sony's release date for *Can't Back Down*. We were astonished that Sony was not letting me go with the songs of my unreleased album. In so doing, Sony short-circuited my chance of working with another label. Worse yet, they were not releasing another single to drive sales of the album. In an e-mail to Steve, Butler wrote, "There's not going to be another single." Since album sales depend upon the release of successful singles, I believed then and I believe now that Sony was killing this album. What other reason could they have had for putting out an album with no fanfare, no money for promotions, and no singles to drive it? These decisions almost guaranteed the album wouldn't sell well. It seemed Sony didn't intend to make any money on it, which, given the corporate appetite for profit, didn't make any sense to me at all. And how could they not know that this would stop my career cold? I felt as if I was on the receiving end of spite.

The failure of this album did a great deal of damage to my reputation. Then, following this humiliation, Nashville threw me a few fast balls that I was unable to hit. Given the principle of "three strikes, you're out", my future didn't look good.

Strike One: Whispers on Music Row

Soon after the release of the album, it was painful for me to hear from a very powerful, well-connected attorney that a strong whispering campaign against me was underway among the elites in Nashville. The attorney told me that apparently some of the people involved in the *Can't Back Down* fiasco had made a few discreet phone calls to the heads of other labels in Nashville for the purpose of getting me blacklisted. This was confirmed by some contacts I had at Sony and throughout Music Row. The substance of the rumor going around was "You can't work with Collin. He's hard to work with." After my name got on the good ol' boys' blacklist, no one would have me; the movers and shakers in Nashville were able to make sure that no other major label would sign me. It's scary how a few actions removed from the public view can do so much damage.

Sadly, many went along with the whispering campaign because they presumed my own record label was telling the truth, but others went along with it because perception is reality in that town. The two failed albums in a row added to the insinuation that I was "hard to work with". This became my reality. My career never recovered from this blow. My hit-making days were over; I never charted a Top Ten after that.

Strike Two: Woman Scorned Element

To make matters worse, even James Stroud at DreamWorks, the man who had produced *Can't Back Down* for me, began acting aloof, refusing to return phone calls, and looking through me at events as if I were a ghost. I was totally unnerved by his behavior because we had been working so well together up to that point. This situation was not the result of anything Sony had done, however, but was brought about by a completely unexpected development.

Strike two came when James began to date an ex-girlfriend of mine as we were making the record. She was involved in the production of the album, and close proximity in the studio led the two of them to start showing interest in each other. Within a very short time, they were dating. I liked them both very much and didn't feel at all threatened by their relationship; however, I don't think my ex-girlfriend wanted me to be happy about it!

The dynamic between them and me changed drastically; I felt as though they were snubbing me. I admit that I reacted poorly to this treatment. There were several times when I acted rashly, which didn't help the situation. Most notably, I left the woman in question a number of angry and hurtful voicemails. This was wrong of me and only threw fuel on the fire of that smoldering relationship.

In the space of a few weeks, my association with another very powerful man in Nashville ended badly and cost me a great deal professionally. If I had entertained any hopes of being picked up by his label, DreamWorks, all such hopes were dashed to pieces by the breakdown of these relationships. The whole situation became a massive train wreck caused by pride, jealousy, and anger, together with a lot of miscommunication. I could have handled my end of it in a much better way, and I regret that I didn't. I believe the person I am today would have behaved differently.

Strike Three: The Cost of Cutting Loose

Meanwhile, I hadn't yet gotten free from my contract with Sony. I still owed them one record on the eight-album contract, and, as I was about to learn, Sony was not going to release me from this obligation for nothing. I had worked hard and completed seven studio records for them with a greatest-hits album and two specialty albums added to the mix. I sold nearly eight million albums and made them many millions of dollars over the course of a decade, but all that was not going to cancel my debt for one more album. Recording companies often cut performers loose from their contracts. I based my hope on that common practice and miscalculated the role that politics and money played in Nashville—and that was my third strike.

I also owed Sony something more. The company had given me a "bonus" of a million dollars after my fourth platinum album, but it wasn't a bonus in the traditional sense; it was an advance against future album sales. It was dressed up to look like an athlete's signing bonus, complete with a party for me with all the bells and whistles, which also provided a great public-relations story, but it was not a simple cash payout. This "bonus" was set up so that Sony was able to recuperate their "investment" in me by recovering a certain percentage of the advance each time a new album was released. If I left Sony without making all of the albums stipulated in my contract, I would have to pay Sony whatever amount of the advance they had not yet recovered. My overly trusting nature at the time of the signing would come back to haunt me. Once we reached a point of irreconcilable differences, the result was that I had to pay back a great deal of money.

The price Sony demanded of me to break my contract was about three hundred thousand dollars. There was no way I had that kind of money; in fact, the prospect of paying that amount led me into bankruptcy. Financial problems were just one of the many cascading effects of such a deal gone bad.

The Truth

Although I can see my Nashville breakup with greater clarity as time goes by, there are moments when I shrink back in horror at how the whole drama played out. It didn't have to end that way. My hit-making career shouldn't have been destroyed by human pettiness or vendetta, but it was, and I am still saddened by how it ended so quickly and catastrophically. Anyone whose reputation and career have been destroyed by a conflict with a powerful personality will be able to understand the pain that I have experienced. The even deeper wound is the one that was caused by the harm done to my family.

Many people in the intervening years have asked me what happened to my Sony deal and why I stopped making hits. People wondered where I went after 2002. One reason I am writing this book is to give an account of what happened in Nashville; I've been silent about the injustice for far too long. Whenever I am asked to speak about it, I try to recount the situation fairly, taking ownership of my own responsibility for the breakup, but it has been difficult to tell the whole story. Now I have been able to express the full truth, or at least as much of it as I can see. In the end, I was not the only one to leave Sony. By May 2003 Allen Butler and two of his vice presidents were also no longer at the company.

Deeper Meaning

I was still reeling from my own personal upheaval when, in 2003, we were made aware of a mysterious illness afflicting my granddaughter that would demand a great deal of my attention and resources. Life became increasingly difficult for us, and I wonder if, in the grand scheme of God's plan for me, my breakup with Nashville gave me the freedom to be available to my family when they needed me most.

As for those who have treated me unjustly, I must forgive them as I have been forgiven. By the power of God's grace, I have been able to forgive them—from the heart—and that alone has allowed me to move on and to deal with some of the rather serious consequences of my departure from Nashville. The older I get and the more I suffer, the more perspective I gain about the reality of human sinfulness, a reality that I must confront in myself above all every day. When someone intentionally harms you, it takes a good amount of time and a whole lot of grace to forgive him and to let go of the hurt. I take comfort in knowing that in some mysterious way God brings good out of it.

These days I am much more willing to participate in God's process of mending fences where they can be mended and to look to the future without holding on to the past. The Sony chapter is behind me now, and the rest of my life is ahead of me. I can even say that I am grateful for both the good times and the bad in the record business. Without the bad, I may never have made any progress in overcoming my tendency to pride and vainglory, parts of my human nature that I will struggle with until my last day. I understand why the Church calls this ongoing process conversion and redemption.

A New Symphony

The famous Catholic televangelist of the 1950s and '60s, the late Archbishop Fulton J. Sheen, used a perceptive analogy to describe redemption. He compared God's creation to a great symphony orchestra with many instruments tuned just perfectly to play in harmony. God wrote the perfect piece of music and left it in the hands of a flawed human conductor, Adam. The piece started well but ended on a sour note when sin entered the world. What did the divine Composer do? He took the final sour note and made it the first note of a new symphony! That was Sheen's masterful explanation of the *New* Adam, Jesus Christ.

Despite the negatives, there were many sublime and wondrous experiences on the journey from Texarkana to Oregon, through Reno and LA, to realize my dream of making hit records in Nashville. I'm sad to say that my hit-making days ended on such a sour note, but with reflection I can see its redemptive value. A perfect little child by the name of Haley was the note that Jesus plucked out of my old sour symphony and made the first note of a new symphony. From her sufferings, I would learn once again how to be faithful to God's original score.

9

Haley

God's Holy Gift to Us

(2003–2007)

For this reason I bow my knees before the Father,
from whom every family in heaven and on earth is named.

—Eph 3:14–15

Everyone's life is a roller coaster in some fashion, and in the five years following my separation from the good graces of Nashville, I felt as if I were riding the Cyclone at Coney Island. The downs were really down: a death and another car accident in my family, bankruptcy, another move, and a change of managers. But the ups were incredibly blessed: my family grew by two beautiful granddaughters, and I produced two new albums with some friends who wanted to help me keep my career going and to see me succeed.

The peak of the roller-coaster ride was that beautiful, precious, little grandchild named Haley, who was born two years before I left Nashville and who was to give all of us such joy and peace in a very turbulent time. In these years we began to see unmistakable evidence that she was affected by some neurological problem that was a mystery even to the smartest minds in medicine, but Haley was the absolute pinnacle of innocent love and trust that transformed all the adults around her. As for me personally, she helped me to grow in trust in God at a time when I was becoming jaded by the world. Everyone says that children are weak, but I discovered that they are incredibly strong. I once heard a beautiful saying: "A soul can be healed by spending time in the presence of a child." It sure can!

Aftermath of the Nashville Breakup

The first and most immediate consequence of the Nashville breakup was bankruptcy. Even before I broke with Sony, I had to face the stark fact of declining income. After Sony demanded the three hundred thousand dollars for an incomplete contract, my financial manager, Chuck Flood, warned me that I could not meet my financial obligations if I maintained the standard of living I had been enjoying since the mid-nineties. We had always lived within our means, but our means were now significantly reduced. We were rapidly approaching the point where my debt would become unmanageable unless we downsized.

I do admit that I was my own worst enemy in some ways; my lack of business acumen led to a whole range of problems that I had to resolve quickly. For example, I had signed bus leases that obliged me to pay the bus companies even when we were home. I also had put my band and crew members on salary instead of paying them on a contract basis, which meant I had to keep paying them even when we weren't working. The system functioned well when the money was rolling in, but it was untenable during the hard times. Somehow I had to lighten the load of these touring costs.

Declaring bankruptcy was contrary to everything I believed about personal responsibility, but my business manager tried to convince me otherwise. He insisted that bankruptcy was a responsible act to preserve my business and family from financial catastrophe. I finally gave in to his counsel. I declared bankruptcy and began to work my way back to financial solvency.

Third Radical Change in my Life

Despite the darkness of this period, there remained one steady beacon of light that was a source of joy for all of us: Haley. One look at her soft little face always dispelled any depression or anxiety that I may have been feeling. When we baptized her two months after her birth in the Cathedral of the Incarnation in downtown Nashville, like a magnet she had drawn many of the most significant people in our lives to that joyous celebration. Haley was baptized in the very same gown that her own mother had been baptized in eighteen years earlier. For Haley's godparents, Britanny made an excellent choice in Jack and Lisa Parris, the parents of a wonderful Catholic family in Greenville, Texas.

Despite Haley's sustained screaming throughout the ceremony, Father Armor soldiered on and made that little angel a child of God in the waters of the baptismal font. The video of the baptism shows Father performing the actions and mouthing the words, but the only audible sounds are the screams echoing off the hard walls of that huge cathedral!

Haley occasioned the third radical change in my life: this time it was *grand-fatherhood*. Most grandfathers don't have the joy of seeing a grandchild grow and develop before their very eyes on a daily basis. I am so thankful that God allowed me to witness my granddaughter's early development before we knew about her neurological problems. Soon after Haley's birth, I had made a decision to homeschool Britanny and Jake, and my most precious image of that period is of our little newborn baby on top of the dining room table while her mom and uncle were taking their final exams.

Britanny and Charlie planned to get married, and I was torn between supporting Britanny, who thought marriage would be best for her new family, and trusting my instincts, which told me that she and Charlie lacked the full knowledge and maturity needed for a marriage to last the test of time. Respect for my daughter's decision eventually prevailed, and I reluctantly supported them a few months later when they got married.

The Most Beautiful Bride

Having accepted their decision to marry, I decided to put aside my misgivings about the future and throw myself into helping Britanny prepare for her wedding. My only daughter wanted to get married, and it was going to be the best wedding we could pull off. We were a team, as usual, and I didn't just provide the funding—as fathers are supposed to do—I worked with her on all the details of the ceremony and reception; she consulted me on virtually everything. The price of flowers alone was outrageous, and that's putting it mildly. Charlie and Britanny were to be married in our home parish, Saint William in Greenville, the church where both of my kids had received first Holy Communion and confirmation. They attended the parish's marriage preparation classes, and soon the day of the wedding arrived, May 18, 2001.

As I walked my baby girl down the aisle, she looked so confident and beautiful in her wedding dress. I think it was one of the proudest moments of my life. With each step (which I wished had been ten times longer), I couldn't help but flash back to the little girl I had taught to ride a bike, to the ballerina whose recitals I attended when she was five, to the cute voice on the other end of the phone during daily calls from Reno, and to all the fun times we had on our many vacations. Nostalgia overwhelmed me. All of a sudden, my baby girl was a wife and a mom with a year-old baby girl of her own. It was such an emotional walk. And yes, I did—I cried.

The reception took place at the magnificent Wyndham Anatole in Dallas later that evening; it capped off a very good day. The beautiful event was attended by all the family and friends who meant the most to us, and I feel we did everything right for such a special occasion. The speeches were good, the food was great, and the music by the jazz combo we had hired was excellent.

At one point the band asked me to come up on stage with them to sing "New York, New York", and I couldn't have been more delighted. As I began singing, little Haley spotted her Poppy in the front and ambled away from her Mama and across the dance floor to see me. When she got to me, she put her arms in the air the way little kids do when they want to be picked up, and I reached down with one hand and scooped her up while singing Sinatra into the microphone in my other hand. Haley absolutely stole the show that night as she sat on my arm and stared with those huge brown eyes, wide open in utter amazement at the singing, as if no one else but her Poppy were in the room. Who could have imagined the suffering ahead for this little picture of innocence?

Brittany and Charlie's marriage was blessed with a second beautiful child, Mattie, who came into the world on February 11, 2004. I was ecstatic when I heard that Britanny was pregnant again. I was so glad to see our family growing and my daughter developing into such a great mom. Among the many talents my daughter has, her greatest gift is motherhood. She was undoubtedly put on this earth to be a mother, and I often tell her that.

Death of a Granddad

Connie's parents, Doris and Gary Parker, had been such a marvelous influence on my kids in their formative years and did a very good job of keeping up with all the goings-on in the family. They were particularly delighted with their new *great-grandbaby* and came to see us in Nashville while Charlie and Britanny were still living with me. During the visit, we noticed that Gary was feeling very ill most of the time. In fact, he generally stayed up in Jake's room and isolated himself, which was unusual for him. Doris took him to a doctor, who said that Gary looked as though he had a bad chest cold that would clear up and gave him some medication. We did not worry very much about it after that, although the deep, nagging cough wasn't going away and Gary just stayed in bed.

One Sunday as we were on our way to Mass, we got a call from Charlie before we were even halfway down our street. "Come back. We can't wake Grandpa up." He was frantic. We rushed back home, and when I ran upstairs, I saw Charlie administering CPR and doing his best to revive Gary, who was lying on the bed looking upward with his arms out, as if he had tried to get up and had fallen back in that position. We immediately called the paramedics, who told us to get him off the bed and onto the floor and continue CPR. We did so, but it was clear that Gary had already left this world. Doris was standing in the corner crying, but to her credit she remained fairly composed throughout the whole ordeal. I think her strength helped us all to manage the tragic loss of Gary that had abruptly shattered our little world.

Britanny and Jake went up to Gary a few times, shaking him and saying, "Wake up, Grandpa, wake up!", but it wasn't to be. This was the first time they had seen a dead person, which was doubly shocking because it was their beloved grandfather. When the paramedics arrived, they confirmed within a few minutes that Gary had expired. They put his body into a bag and onto a stretcher, which they carried down the stairs and out the front door to the ambulance. The scene brought back memories of Connie and Jake both lying in the hospital a heartbeat away from death, and I was reminded of the incredible fragility of life: "My God," I thought, "one minute you're alive, and the next minute you're dead."

At the funeral, Doris asked me to sing "In the Garden" and "How Great Thou Art", which I struggled to do because I had laryngitis from all the crying during the past few days. I squeaked out probably the most pitiful versions I have ever sung of these two wonderful songs, but I'm sure God honored my efforts because my heart was in the right place.

Gary is sorely missed by all of us, and we pray that he will come fully into God's Kingdom. He wasn't a churchgoer, but he was a good man; and I pray that God will count that, with all of our prayers, in his favor. He raised a daughter and three sons and was an absolutely wonderful grandfather. He always treated me like a son.

The One That Got Away

In the summer of 2000, I met Jennifer Poage, who was the secretary to my financial manager, Chuck Flood. In time we took a liking to one another and had become very close by mid-2001. She was a very significant person in my life for a number of years, and I really loved her. I know she loved me too. She was demur and sweet-natured and lovely, which contrasted with all that I was, but somehow our personalities meshed well. We were a good fit. I had hopes that one day we would get married.

One of the reasons we got along so well was that we were both single parents; there was never a time when I had to explain to her my love for my children or the sacrifices I had to make for them. She understood that perfectly. Her son, Noah, was about Haley's age, and I became something of a father figure to him, a role I truly enjoyed. In fact, Haley was quite attached to Noah too but had trouble pronouncing his name; she called him "Woah."

Jenn and I stayed together for about four years, and she very patiently and generously walked with us through many of the ups and downs I have described in this chapter. Sometime in late 2005 we split apart, and I take full blame for the breakup. My vanity asserted itself many times throughout the course of the relationship, as did my hot temper and self-righteousness in arguments, my independent spirit, and my inability to close the deal with marriage. It sounds trite to say that I took her for granted, but I did, and I am embarrassed by it now. Moving from Nashville to Texas a few years later was the death of our relationship, but I have only myself to blame for losing the one that got away.

Memories of Innocence

Prior to Mattie's birth, Britanny and Charlie moved back to Greenville to be closer to both families, and I stayed in Nashville. As being apart from them was *killing* me, I regularly made the ten-hour drive down to Texas. I slept on their couch in their little apartment but had the joy of being awakened every day by little Haley waddling up and tapping me on the face saying "Poppy, Poppy" in her diminutive voice. It seems that all I did while I was there was sit in her little room and play with her on the floor. I am so thankful to God that He allowed me to be around in those days of innocence when her little body and personality were developing so beautifully. That was a blessed time because we didn't know yet that she was sick. There were no signs of the disease at all in these early years.

I can say without prejudice that Haley was the most beautiful child I ever laid eyes on. She had huge brown eyes, soft blondish-brown hair, and a perfect little face. She was anointed in every way, and she brought so much peace and joy to us just by her presence in our lives. I couldn't help but wear a smile whenever I was around her. In those first three years of her life, she hadn't developed the ability to speak other than one word at a time, but she knew who everyone was and was as active and curious as all kids are. The very presence of that little child around had a kind of calming effect, which was perhaps preparing us for the next few ups and downs of the roller coaster.

As she grew, Haley developed what I can only call a mystical sensitivity, which may have been a spiritual gift or just one of those fruits of innocence that God gives to children. She seemed to sense things that adults were unaware of. Oftentimes when I was holding her in my arms, she would point at the crucifix on the wall and say, "Ju-Ju", meaning Jesus. I would say, "That's Jesus! That's Jesus!", and she would point again, wanting me to bring her closer to Him. When she got to the crucifix, she would bend forward and kiss His feet. It was an amazing thing to see. No one taught her to do that. She had an innate sensitivity to religious symbols.

Something similar would happen when we were driving with her in the car. She would sense or immediately spot churches, whether Protestant or Catholic, when we were still far away from them or even at times when they were totally *out of view*. From her little car seat in the back of the car she would ring out, "Ju-Ju!", and point in the direction of a church before we even saw it. Every now and then, when we presumed she had mistakenly pointed to some other type of building, we found out that there *was* a church on the next block! We were amazed at this gift and wondered how she could know about these things that adults couldn't see until we were upon them. Her spiritual sensitivity was utterly uncanny and remains a mystery to us, whose souls lack the purity of a little child.

I am glad that I put a high priority on taking family vacations in these years, as I had done when Britanny and Jake were young, and some of those trips were the source of our happiest memories of Haley. I can still remember Haley learning to walk on my tour bus as we drove to California. It was so cute to see Britanny gently guiding Haley's wobbly steps down the aisle of the bus. What a precious image! From a vacation to Hawaii I have memories of Haley and me floating in the pool together and playing in the sand on the beach.

Other memories are of Haley's Uncle Jake reading books to her, especially one called *I'll Love You Forever*. I can hardly hold back a tear when I think of the two of them sitting on the couch reading that story. I am so proud of Jake for giving so generously of himself to his little niece. He also knew to emphasize those special lines in the book that she especially loved, and it was so delightful to see her smile while she still could. Then there are the hours and hours we spent together watching her favorite television show, *Barney and Friends*. She called that famous purple dinosaur, "Bob-ba". She couldn't get enough of his show, which is so entertaining and sweet. She also liked *The Wiggles* but not as much as she liked Barney—no one else ever achieved Barney's status in her eyes.

Something's Wrong, but We Don't Know What It Is

In 2004 we began to notice signs that Haley was physically regressing. Earlier that year, when Mattie was born, she was walking up and down the hospital corridor, sporting her "I'm a Big Sister" T-shirt, but soon after that she began to lose her ability to walk. She had a curious habit of tucking her little stick legs underneath her and would usually sit back down anytime we helped her to stand up, which we did every chance we could. Charlie thought we were spoiling her because we were carrying her so much, but I was sure there was something more to it. She also drooled a lot and had a hard time swallowing.

Her gradual loss of the ability to articulate words was one of the most difficult deteriorations to witness. Nothing could stop her long slide downward into silence, and I was frustrated at being unable to help her communicate more. Around the ages of two and three, she could say words such as *ju* for "juice", *Ju-Ju* for "Jesus", and *Poppy* for me, but she could speak only one word at a time, never a complete sentence. She would say "Ah do" when she meant "yes". After age five, however, she couldn't speak at all: making the sound "Mmm-mmm" was her sole means of communicating.

The neurologist at the Scottish Rite Children's Hospital in Dallas examined her and admitted that there were definite signs of some neurological disorder, but he was baffled as to what caused it. He uttered what would become the distressing refrain of all the medical personnel we consulted over the next several years: "We know there's *something* wrong, but we don't know what it is." That year we took her to Phoenix Children's Hospital and Dallas Children's Hospital and always got the same answer, "We just don't know." That certainly shook us up. It's easier to face an enemy you can see than one who is hiding in the bushes. Our search for the answer to that mystery would cost us intense emotional stress and many thousands of dollars over the next few years, but at this stage, we were just content to help this precious little child have a "normal" life to the extent that that was possible.

All the School She Needed

Charlie and Britanny thought that it would be good to put Haley in preschool, but I had mixed emotions about the whole idea because I thought it would be too overwhelming for her. They sent her to the L. P. Waters School in Greenville, Texas, because it catered to a whole range of children whose special needs put them out of the mainstream.

I remember how cute she was the day we enrolled her in the school. The teacher made all the kids sit on their own square mats on the floor, and Haley went over and kneeled on hers. Each child was given a piece of paper, and Haley held hers while looking around the room with her beautiful brown eyes. When the teacher asked, "Now does everyone have their paper?", Haley lifted her paper up like the perfect little student that she was!

Later that semester, I went to pick her up at school and found her kneeling next to a talkative little boy. Looking up with her expressionless little face, she pointed at me and said, "Poppy", signaling to her loquacious friend that it was time for her to go.

Her year at L. P. Waters turned out to be an endearing experience for all of us. My initial mixed feelings about it were won over by the way all the adults and kids catered to Haley and took such good care of her. Above all, Haley really enjoyed going to school, and that was the most important thing. It would be her only year of formal schooling, but as we always said: "It was all the school she needed."

One of the greatest moments of my life—and I'm sure Britanny would say the same—was Haley's graduation from preschool later that year. In the bleachers prior to the ceremony, we could spot our little angel easily on the other side of the gym because she was the smallest child sitting among all the other students. She looked adorable in her bright blue graduation gown. We laughed so hard when we saw a little boy put his arm around her and kiss her for no other reason than that he loved her. Everyone, from teachers to students, was always so sweet to her at that school. The greatest moment of the day, however, was when Haley was presented with her diploma. By that time, she had lost the ability to walk on her own but could feebly move her legs and walk if someone held her arms above her and walked with her. She was the first to be called to get her diploma, and there was not a dry eye in the house as one of her teachers walked with her step-by-wobbly-step across the stage. The whole gymnasium erupted in applause, which showed that all the parents, teachers, and families there appreciated her heroic act of crossing the finish line of preschool. It was immensely heartwarming that they, too, recognized the dignity of the child we had cared for and loved for six years.

Soon thereafter, she began to regress more dramatically. She got to the point where she didn't want to walk, or couldn't, and was confined to a little stroller. In the stroller she kept her arms in front of her chest with her little hands balled up into fists and her thumbs sticking out between her index and middle fingers. That was the position her hands and arms stayed in for virtually the rest of her life. I loved to pick her up and hold her, but I have to admit that it was heartbreaking to see this innocent child gradually lose all of her basic motor functions. She was completely relied on us for every aspect of her physical care, and all she could give back to us—literally—was her dependence. Her vulnerability made us love her even more, if that were possible.

Even though Haley lost her ability to walk, she still loved to move. Jake and I would take turns pushing her around the house in that little stroller and stopping to play hide-and-seek, a game all little kids love and the one Haley loved the most. Another simple enjoyment was inventing sweet nicknames for her. Jake called her Bear Bug, and Britanny called her Angel May (an affectionate name she got from the little girl in *To Kill a Mockingbird*). We all delighted in using these and other baby names such as Geezy and Sussa, which mean absolutely nothing, of course, but were terms of endearment.

The Kid Who Cheated Death Twice

Jake was a big part of Haley's life. He had graduated from high school by now and decided that he was going to do something with his life. He had always had it in his heart to be an actor, and despite my gentle fatherly warnings about the challenges of trying to make it to Hollywood, he thought it was his time to branch out and to do something he wanted to do. I couldn't blame him—after all, I had done the same thing when I was his age—and I supported him on his first big move away from home. Connie chafed at the idea of his pursuing an acting career, but I reminded her that she had been overwhelmingly in favor of my going into music when I was his age. She and Jake had suffered together from the very beginning and had bonded through their ordeal. As it turned out, there was more to her mother's intuition than I gave her credit for at the time.

Jake chose an acting school in Austin, Texas, which was about a three-and-a-half-hour drive from where we lived. He was never a great driver, due to the injuries he sustained at birth, but I had bought him a nice, sturdy used car and trusted that all would be okay with his driving. I felt better knowing that he would not be alone, as a lot of his friends from our home area went to the nearby Texas State University. Once Jake had gotten settled, I went down to visit him every other week or so and stayed with him and his friend Sean in their apartment for a weekend or a few days. I made sure everything was okay and gave him a little money and did all the things a dad is supposed to do for his son in college.

Then one day I had a serious scare. I was driving home from the Dallas airport after a trip, and I noticed that there were six or seven missed calls from Jake's friend Matt. But he left no message. I called him back immediately, and sounding shaken he said, "Jake's been run over by a car." The news sent a jolt through me like a thousand volts of electricity.

I picked up Connie, and it wasn't until we arrived at the hospital three and a half hours later that we got the full horror story of Jake's accident from his friends. And what a mess it was. Jake had gone to a bowling alley to celebrate a friend's birthday. When it was over, he was pulling out of the parking lot onto the four-lane road to go home and apparently misjudged the speed of the car coming toward him. The girl driving the car saw him a split second too late and hit the back end of his car, spinning it around and pushing it into the middle of the road, facing the opposite direction. Jake was okay at that point but got out to survey the damage. He must have been so flustered at being hit that he didn't think to look both ways before crossing the street to check on the poor girl in the other car. Then the unthinkable happened: he was hit again—not the *car* this time, but *him*. The driver of a Ford Escort coming down the highway at fifty-five miles per hour didn't see Jake until it was too late.

The impact of the Escort was brutal. The bumper clipped Jake's knees and flipped him up on the hood, where his face hit the windshield. Because of the speed of the car, Jake's body was thrown sixty feet when the driver slammed on his brakes. To make matters worse, Jake landed face down on the pavement. Several witnesses called 911, and soon the paramedics arrived. A trauma helicopter took him to an Austin hospital, where they rushed him into surgery to save his legs. That was when Matt was frantically trying to contact me.

After the surgery, I cringed when I saw Jake's face all bloody and scratched up with road rash. My poor boy was awake, and when he saw me and Connie, he started to sob. A dam of emotion—from all the shock and trauma he had just sustained—broke wide open. I lightly kissed his head and assured him in my most fatherly way, "It's okay, bud, it's okay. Everything's gonna be all right."

The rest of the family came to see him in the hospital, including Mattie, who was an infant, and Haley, who leaned over and hugged her "J.J.", as she always called him. I think that was the best comfort he could have had at that time. Once again I found myself keeping vigil at the bedside of a loved one in a hospital. I stayed with Jake almost the whole time he was there, except when I needed to take a day or two to do a show. Afterward I came right back to Austin to be with him.

Even though he was down and out for a while, Jake quickly got back to his normal, wonderful self, cracking jokes all the time and worrying about everyone else. I was very proud to see that sweet young man handling his own personal crisis very well.

The damage to his body, however, was extensive: his right leg was broken clean through in two places, and his left leg was partially fractured. Both legs needed rods. His hip was injured, and his right ankle was so seriously broken that the doctors thought he wouldn't walk again without a severe limp. I don't throw around the word *miracle* too easily, but clearly my son's recovery from that accident was a complete miracle. Even though his face had hit the windshield and he had landed on it after being thrown sixty feet, he had suffered no brain injury whatsoever—not even a concussion. Jake seems to have a miraculous streak running through him: he overcame near-impossible odds as a baby, and, for a second time in his young life, he survived a life-threatening incident with unexplainable durability.

When I went to look at the scene of the accident about a week later, the outline of Jake's body was still painted on the road, and I thought, "Wow, that's my son." It defied imagination that he even survived a trauma like that. I was overwhelmed with the thought of it. The accident was so horrific that everyone who saw it happen assumed he was dead; in fact, employees at the bowling alley had asked some of Jake's friends, "Who's that kid who got killed?" As I looked at that outline, I shook my head and recalled the little baby who had toughed out his first year of life hooked up to machines in Reno. It wasn't hard for me to see that Jake was meant to be here; he was placed on this earth for some good reason besides his innate goodness and awesome personality. "God just loves that boy", I said as I pondered it all.

Jake stayed in the hospital for two or three more weeks and then transferred to Baylor University Rehab in Dallas for a few weeks of intense physical therapy to get him walking again. Today the miracle boy shows hardly any signs of that traumatic event: he has no scars on his face, no brain damage, no limp, and no memory of the accident at all. He's the kid who cheated death twice—few people can claim that.

Twenty Years and Change, 2005 and Fearless, 2006

Throughout this string of family crises, the roller coaster took a few turns upward as well. I was very eager to produce another album to let everyone know that I was still around. I teamed up with my old pianist, Geno LeSage, to produce two albums in two years with the independent, fledgling label Asperion. We cut *Twenty Years and Change* in 2005 and *Fearless* in 2006. It was a risk to go with a minor label because they didn't have the resources to put a great deal behind promotion. At this time country music was changing, and the new reality was that artists basically had to *buy* their way onto the radio waves; as a result, it was becoming increasingly more expensive to get singles to radio. This label didn't have those resources, but because of my established reputation we had good hopes for the success of the albums and decided to take the risk anyway.

Twenty Years and Change has so many good songs on it. It was intended to be a very commercial effort with a lot of great up-tempo songs and some cool covers. For example, I did an exceptional cover of the eighties' classic pop song "The Search Is Over", which I had always loved. It was performed originally by the band Survivor, and like "Open Arms" on the *Direct Hits* album a few years before, it was a showcase for my strong, high voice. I also cowrote with Melissa Manchester "All I Can Do Is Love You", which is an absolutely beautiful song.

Fearless was an interesting venture into alternative music and was a quirky, eclectic mix of songs primarily because it wasn't originally intended for an American audience. In fact, if I had known it would work its way back onto the domestic scene, I would have recorded a few of the songs very differently, such as the Latin-sounding version of Sinatra's "My Way". There was also a strange song called "The Airport", which was done exclusively for eastern-European audiences. My manager, Steve, and I had maintained a connection with Stan Cornelius, who had gotten me and the Wray Brothers our first national record deal with Mercury/Polygram back in 1985. Stan's wife was Russian and had contacts in Moscow. He seemed to think that they could get us into the national Russian chain store (their version of Walmart) and sell tons of records. After cutting the record, Steve spent two weeks in Russia trying to cultivate the deal, but it just never blossomed. As fate would have it, *Fearless* eventually was released to an

American market, and I am always surprised when fans bring copies of it for me to autograph at concerts. Inevitably they find it on the Internet, and some of them say they like *Fearless* better than *Twenty Years and Change*. The moral of the story is that an artist never knows what his fans will like or choose. What is certain, though, is that neither of these two albums is boring!

The greatest song on the *Fearless* album is "Lady", which was written by me and my brother, Scotty. We hoped it would make a great wedding song and named it with that in mind, but it was originally written for and about my granddaughter Haley. The original title was "Baby", and the original lyrics describe how we sat and watched TV together:

> Baby, sitting by me on the sofa watching TV
> With the sound all the way down
> How could a man like me
> Be so in love with this baby?

I changed the word *baby* to *lady* to make it a couples' song. It was a great song on an album that didn't get a chance. I hope that someday I'll be able to do this one over again or that some younger artist will take the songs and rerecord them for a modern American audience.

Under New Management

A later consequence of my Nashville breakup was an unexpected change in the relationship I had with my longtime manager, Steve Cox. Steve was so special to me; in fact, he had been like a father figure for many years. To this day I revere him as the greatest man I know and a model for my life. He was one of the few who had seen me at *all* my worst moments and still stuck by me. After the Nashville breakup, however, it seemed that his priorities were more focused on matters back in Reno, while my priorities were focused on getting my career back in gear. This disconnect between us in matters of business led me to make one of the most gut-wrenching decisions of my life—I decided to let Steve go as my manager.

What a horrible experience it was. The decision initially hit him very hard, and it must have seemed like some sort of a divorce since we had been together for so long; but in classic Steve Cox fashion, he recuperated quickly and told me that he wished me well and would do anything he could possibly do to help me if I needed him in the future. What a great man. I will be forever grateful for his friendship and the way he handled this difficult bump in the road.

I didn't know it at the time, but there would still be a few more bumps to negotiate on the highway leading out of good-ol'-boy-ville.

Following Steve's departure, thankfully, I had a safety net. The remarkable Ken Kragen soon stepped into the manager spot after the *Fearless* project unraveled. Ken had been a recognized icon in the entertainment business since the sixties, when he managed the Smothers Brothers. He was also Kenny Rogers' manager during his heyday in the seventies, eighties, and nineties and did the same for Lionel Richie. More recently, he had become the manager for Trisha Yearwood and Travis Tritt. This seasoned pro seemed like a good fit for me. Ken was recognized as one of the greatest promoters in the business. His brainchild and biggest claim to fame was the 1985 "We Are the World" tour de force that raised over sixty million dollars for African hunger relief. Michael Jackson and Lionel Richie co-wrote the song, and later, the Live Aid concerts helped to corral every major pop and rock personality on the planet in support of the campaign.

I had met Ken numerous times in the nineties, and we both liked each other. He had dropped hints several times that he would be open to managing me, and when I finally needed a manager, he agreed to take me on. I was grateful that a man with his credentials would work with me, and I needed the clout that he brought to the ticket.

When Ken took over, he had some very good ideas for moving my career forward. He immediately steered me in the direction of doing songs focused on the military because he knew that this was a favorite theme of mine. I am fiercely patriotic, and we felt that the military was an important, ongoing issue in the life of our country in the wake of 9/11; we believed that the fans would resonate with music directed toward that subject.

A Deal with Time-Life

Ken's great network of entertainment contacts helped me to get another record deal with Time-Life, although significantly scaled back from what I had with Sony. Michael Curtis, a longtime producer from Muscle Shoals,

Alabama, with whom I had worked on a Civil War documentary a few years earlier, and Teddy Gentry, the bass player for the group Alabama, wanted to work with me on another album, and I was very excited about that. Alabama has always been one of my favorite acts. All the guys in the band are solid, strong family men—every last one of them—and I have the utmost respect for them both personally and professionally. I had had numerous previous contacts with Gentry, and I knew that he and Randy Owen of Alabama always respected my work and always rooted for me. I even got to sing one of their signature songs, "Tennessee River", on stage with them earlier in my career, and it was a total blast! It seemed that they had always tried to help the industry take more notice of me. I'll never forget Randy's and Teddy's kindness.

Their idea was first to do songs that we could get to radio in order to reinvent a radio presence for me. That was critical to success and would get me back in the loop. Even with all my wounds, I was still alive. I still had my voice, which God had enabled to remain literally unchanged and melodious throughout this long period, and I had a lot of song left in me. I was lucky to be working with a quality team like Teddy Gentry and Michael Curtis.

I spent a lot of time in Muscle Shoals recording the album. We called it *Never Going Back* after a real cool song that Britanny and I wrote with the help of our friend Troy Powers. It included a few rock/contemporary-pop covers such as "Without You", recorded by Harry Nilsson in 1970 and Mariah Carey in the following decades. The incomparable Susan Ashton sang it with me as a duet. We also did an up-tempo version of "Stuck in the Middle", originally done by Gerry Rafferty and Stealers Wheel in the early seventies. This album was also the most explicitly religious album I had ever done up to that point, including spiritual songs such as "The Cross", "The Only Jesus", and "I Love You This Much", all dealing with the theme of applying Christian faith and values to the many challenges of life.

By far, my favorite song on the album was "She's with Me", a song I wrote as a tribute to Haley to express how much I loved her and how proud I was of her for going through all her trials so heroically. I wrote it in a flash of inspiration when I was on a plane, and, in the course of about forty-five minutes, the Lord gave me the entire song, fully formed and perfect. It said all I wanted it to say. I take no credit for the song because I am not talented enough to write a song that quickly and perfectly. It had to have come from another Source.

When *Never Going Back* was finally released two years later, it didn't do as well as I had hoped. It didn't get the push it deserved from Time-Life for various reasons. Yet, it is a wonderful album.

Selected Hits, 2007

A third greatest-hits album, *Selected Hits*, released in 2007, was less than a full-scale album in the classic sense but was intended as a new concept in selling music; it was a six-song collection, of which four hits were recorded at a live performance in Salt Lake City, with the addition of two new releases to keep the audience aware of my ongoing productivity as a musician. I added my own recorded message as a seventh track on the album to personalize it. Incidentally, it is the only one of my albums that has a picture of me in a full smile on the cover!

The two new releases on *Selected Hits* were "A Soldier's Prayer" and "Quitters". The former was an encouraging song for soldiers and their families with a strong message of faith. "Quitters" was a remake of a George Canyon song that was *overpowering* to me when I first heard it. It tells the incredible story of a handicapped young man who struggles daily to overcome his limitations but refuses to give up on life or get beaten down by his disability. It is fundamentally a message of courage and hope with some inspiring lyrics for those who face any kind of hardship in life. One of the blessings of that song was that Haley and Mattie got to make cameo appearances in the video. Haley was in her wheelchair, which, I believe, heightened the effect of the song's meaning. Words can't express my joy at seeing those precious, perfect, angelic grandbabies of mine on film. In fact, I will be forever grateful to the Utah-based health and wellness company USANA, which produced the video and later helped me to do the video for "She's with Me".

The Weight of the World

Looking back on this period following the Nashville breakup, I wonder how we survived this roller-coaster ride. The calamities and difficult decisions that took place were remarkable—bankruptcy, death, accidents, relationship ruptures, and other failures—and these were only a prelude to the greater hardships that were to come in the following years. Yet, there was one constant source of inspiration through it all: little Haley.

I never knew that a suffering child could teach me so much or touch my heart so deeply. She was a gift in every way. To this day, I can never think about her without sheer delight in my heart. Her most important lessons for me were straight from the pages of the Gospels: childlike dependence on God our loving Father and absolute trust. She showed us what trust is supposed to *look* like. Even as her problems got more serious, her sufferings became a sort of living testimony to these truths and transformed all of us into better people; her helplessness became our strength, her needs were our joys, and her dependence our freedom. We gave her the best of everything we had.

Above all, Haley modeled for me the virtues of simplicity and humility during a very complicated time for our family. I needed to learn those particular virtues after being at the height of popularity and fame for a decade or more, and I had the best of teachers. Even though she couldn't speak, her life resounded with a wisdom that can't be learned from a book or a lecture.

Looking back, it's easy to see how God's hand was still guiding me. One thing that has come clearly into focus with hindsight is the question of my availability to my family during the years they needed me the most. Had I stayed at the top of the charts with all the demands that come with that life, I could not have given them as much as they needed at the time. The separation from the Nashville powers that be was harsh, but it would have been impossible for me to meet the demands of both family and fame if I had stayed. I can only praise God for His incredible timing. It's as if it was all planned.

Life was burdensome after such a drastic change in my career, but it was made bearable because of a weak little baby who was strong enough to lift the weight of the world off my shoulders.

10

God Said No to Everything We Asked

Praise Him Anyway

(2008–April 3, 2010)

Be still, and know that I am God.

—Ps 46:10

During our long struggle with Haley's illness, we would often hear sympathetic comments from people who would look at Haley and say, "Oh, that's so sad" or "Isn't it hard?" Some people even had facial expressions that clearly communicated, "Gosh, I'm glad that's not me." I'm sure that most people didn't mean any harm in reacting the way they did, but my response, in thought or word, was always straight from the heart: "Yes, of course it's hard, but you don't know how *blessed* we are to have this little saint in our presence. She's the most perfect human being I've ever known. She never sinned or even thought about anything bad. She's so perfect and pure; and when she leaves this earth, I know she will go straight to heaven. There will be no stop-off point for her."

Whenever Haley would be with us in public, it was such an honor to act as her liaison, so to speak. When it seemed that others were uncomfortable around her, I would say to them, "It's okay. She's with me." Truthfully, I wanted her, in turn, to be *my* advocate when I need it the most. One day it occurred to me that such a concept could be made into a song. In the lyrics of "She's with Me", I imagine what it might be like on that day when I am standing at the gates of heaven receiving my just judgment for all my sins—it's a frightening thought. As I am being turned away from the gates, I hear the little voice of my baby granddaughter ring out loud and strong saying, "It's okay, Lord. You can let him in—*he's with me*."

Hospitals and Healers but No Improvement

By late 2007, Haley was seven years old. Soon after her heartwarming and memorable performance at her preschool graduation she completely lost her ability to walk. As she regressed, she used to sit on her knees with her legs splayed-out in a sort of W position, but then she was unable to do that too. By this time she was on a feeding tube for nourishment and could barely even swallow water. In essence, Haley was hardly mobile at all, and that was so distressing for us; despite her decline, though, we did what we could to make her feel happy and loved.

A delightful memory of that time was playing one of her favorite games called You Better Not Hit Me. It was simple: either Jake or I would put our face close up to hers and look very serious and say to her, "You better not hit me, Bear Bug. You better not hit me!" At that challenge she would slowly raise her little arm up—oh, it seemed like it would take her five minutes to get it up!—and barely tap the face in front of her with her little fist. We would make a show of it and fall back dramatically and pretend she had socked us into the next room. Sometimes we could discern a laugh even though it became more difficult for her to show any expression on her face with the progression of the mysterious disease. She still loved watching her Barney, of course, but, all in all, we knew she was getting worse—and that caused us no little distress.

During this time, we were doing everything humanly possible to seek medical help. Her main hospitals were Children's Hospital and Scottish Rite Hospital in Dallas, which were working with her consistently, and we also sought help at the Mayo Clinic in Minnesota, at Saint Joseph's Children's Hospital in Phoenix, and at Johns Hopkins in Baltimore. They all performed their tests and, as was almost predictable by now, all the tests came back negative. No one could find *anything*. Yet, we still believed she was going to be okay. We clung to hope as families always do in desperate situations.

In the course of a few months, we redoubled our efforts to find help for her. That was when a friend helped us get into Phoenix Children's Hospital and another hospital in Phoenix that specialized in neurological disorders, but the story was always the same: *nothing*. After all the strikeouts at hospitals, we tried the holistic healing route. I wasn't sure what this form of healing entailed, but I researched a technique called craniosacral therapy and found a lady in Dallas who did this type of treatment. Haley seemed to feel better when she went there, but the therapy's ultimate effectiveness was doubtful as there was no improvement in her overall condition. We tried a couple more alternative therapies, but, ultimately, no form of healing seemed to work. We always ended up back at square one.

A Curse and a Blessing

During Haley's decline I still had to work to pay the bills, which meant being on the road a good portion of every month, but I always felt so bad to leave her. Then I had other matters of a professional nature that added to the pain.

In 2009 my manager, Ken, wanted to reduce his workload and asked if I would hire Pat Melfi in Utah as a comanager. I knew Melfi because he had promoted a number of my concerts in the western states, but it was largely on the basis of Ken's recommendation that I agreed to hire Melfi as a manager, splitting commissions between the two of them.

Melfi organized what is called a "combo tour", a series of shows in which two big-time acts perform together on stage in order to increase the appeal of each. He put me together with Restless Heart, a band I respected. They had an impressive string of hits in the eighties and nineties, and their sound and harmonies very much resembled that of the Eagles. Together, we had close to fifty Top Ten hits to our names. I was initially very excited about the arrangement because the combination of the two acts would widen our appeal and get us into new venues.

However, Melfi and our booking agent, Steve Lassiter, had booked our combo performances at my own regular venues, which were new to Restless Heart, but not at any venues that were new to me. As a result, my income was cut in half, because the venues believed they were getting a two-for-one deal, an arrangement I was not aware of until it was too late to change it. A 50-percent decrease in income was not my idea of success, nor could I afford it at this time.

At some point, without my knowing it, Melfi asked Time-Life to pay him, beyond what they were to pay me, a percentage of the royalties on the sales of my album *Never Going Back*. Time-Life refused and eventually decided not to spend any significant amount of money or effort on the record's promotion. I couldn't help but conclude that Melfi's request had something to do with this decision.

Adding it all up, it seemed to me that Melfi was working every angle to drum up more business for himself, no matter the cost to me. When I confronted him on these points, he denied doing anything that might have harmed me, but I could no longer trust that his decisions would be in my best interest.

One good thing Melfi did for me was to hire Melanie Anne Shore as my pianist. Mel, as she is known, was a piano prodigy and a remarkable musician in every way. Her perfect pitch, amazing musical ear, and hand skills on the keys were noticeably far and above any I had ever encountered before, with the possible exception of John Hobbs, who worked with me on six albums. She had a strong background in classical, jazz, and R and B, and held degrees in jazz studies and jazz composition. I was impressed with her from the start.

More important than Mel's credentials were her musical surety and multi-genre ability and understanding. She could look at a piece of music for the first time—or even hear it for the first time—and master it effortlessly. Her talent was simply amazing. In fact, Mel came into my life at a very good time, when touring was becoming a real drudgery; her abilities lifted me up and inspired me to fall in love with musical performance all over again. I am a far better and more rounded musician because of the time I spent with her as my musical partner.

Mel accompanied me through the next three difficult years, and I was blessed she was there. Doing concerts all over the U.S., Canada, and Ireland, we fit together so well, onstage and off, it should have come as no surprise to me when before too long we realized that we had feelings for each other. The term "soul mate" is thrown around a lot these days, but I felt like she was quickly becoming that to me. Our personalities and musical compatibility were striking; she was the perfect Robin to my Batman. Our relationship always remained proper, yet she became a strong emotional helpmate to me, and I to her.

One Last Hospital

Sometime in 2007 I met the famous six-term Utah senator, Orrin Hatch, who I think is such a great man, a great statesman, and a truly benevolent soul. In the course of our conversation, he asked me about my family, and that gave me the chance to explain the situation with Haley, in which he expressed great interest. I told him how desperate we felt after trying so many hospitals and other paths to healing, all of which had failed to produce even the most minimal results. He suggested that we take her to Primary Care Children's Hospital in Salt Lake City, which he said was a first-class place that would give her the best, state-of-the-art treatment. To my surprise, he also offered to talk to them himself and give us a direct, personal recommendation. That was like striking gold. The hospital indicated that if we could move to Utah, they would work with us intensely and indefinitely and do everything they possibly could for Haley. It looked like our absolute best chance for a medical solution. I was so grateful, and will ever remain grateful, to Senator Hatch for such an act of perfect charity in our time of need.

I was also very happy to be going back to live in a western state because it seemed that Haley always did better in the cooler, fresher environments of the west. In Texas I was always allergic to something, and Haley was too; she always seemed more alive on our western trips. On top of that, we all loved the landscape and the mountains of Utah, and many of my best concert experiences had taken place there. For some reason, the people in Utah always responded to my music a bit more intensely and always came out in droves to see the show. So for these many reasons, we decided to make the move.

When we got to Riverton, Utah, a suburb of Salt Lake City, we placed a call to a friend of mine who, as a Mormon bishop, would be able to send us a couple of strong backs to help us unload all our furniture from the big truck into the house. To our surprise, fifteen young men from their teens to their mid-thirties showed up that Saturday morning and proceeded to move every stick of furniture and set the rooms up in the house and even to connect a couple of our electronic devices that needed installation. They accomplished their task in barely an hour and absolutely refused to take money, food, or even a drink of water. And they did it all with such natural smiles and joy. They were just the nicest people. How impressed we were that these young men would spend a Saturday morning doing such a work of charity for total strangers. Even though my faith and theirs differ doctrinally, I don't think there are any kinder, more loving, and Christian-acting people as a whole than Mormons. That applied to several of our neighbors during those years as well.

Further Stress

I'm sad to say that Britanny and Charlie's marriage, which had started on such a joyous note with their wedding, ended in divorce after a few years. All my misgivings about Charlie were confirmed in the first few years of their marriage, and the breakup only added to the stress of Haley's desperate medical condition. The divorce was bad enough, but on top of it Charlie and his new wife, Kristin, then added to the financial and emotional stress by trying to prevent us from moving to Utah to seek the treatment that Haley needed. We couldn't pass up this new opportunity for medical treatment, for goodness' sake, and we couldn't access that care in Texas, but Charlie and Kristin must not have seen it that way. Their legal action was completely unnecessary because we were committed to making sure they could see the girls on a regular basis and to covering the cost for these visits.

The legal rigmarole lasted a whole year, and the only effect of it was to enrich two sets of lawyers. I believe a Christian experiences the truest test of his faith when God asks him to "love his enemies". For a while there, I felt that Charlie was my enemy, and humanly speaking, I could not love him without the help of God's grace. I am happy to say that his family and ours are friends again, and that we love Haley and Mattie's two little half-brothers, Brooks and Bentley, as if they were my own grandsons.

Britanny stayed very strong during the whole year of legal wrangling, but I knew it took its toll on her too. She was getting hardened against Charlie and against life in general. More than once I heard her say, "Isn't Haley's condition enough? Can't everyone just leave us alone?" I am so proud of her, though, for getting through it and finding forgiveness for them in her heart. As in all things, we stood together through this dark time.

No More Hope for a Medical Solution

By the end of that year, there still weren't any breakthroughs for Haley. The staff at Primary Care Children's Hospital in Utah couldn't have been more loving and gracious and generous. I simply cannot say enough good things about them. Dr. James Bale was the head of the neurology department at the hospital and a truly wonderful man, but after a full year of working with Haley, he came to us with tears in his eyes and said the saddest words I think we have ever heard: "We are so sorry. After all this, we still don't know what she has. All we know is that whatever she has, it's getting worse. She's deteriorating." The finality of that news hit Britanny like a ton of bricks. It was the same verdict we had received from every other healthcare provider, and now we found ourselves at *another* full stop. We had invested everything in this one option, which seemed so perfect, but all hope for a medical solution now seemed gone. If *they* couldn't find out what the problem was, no one could. We were all just devastated.

From that point on, Britanny wanted to move back home to Texas. She wanted to live closer to family and to work out a peaceful arrangement with Charlie. She needed to minimize the stress we had been under for several years, especially during the past year, by getting back to basics and living more simply. Soon thereafter, she returned to Greenville and downsized again to a three-bedroom duplex.

The house in Utah I put up for sale; all my worldly belongings I put in storage. I bounced back and forth between Salt Lake City and Greenville—with road dates in between—for most of 2008 through 2010. Even for someone as used to travel as I was, it was a difficult existence. However, I was with Britanny, Haley, Mattie, and Jake as much as humanly possible, and that made it all worthwhile.

Refusal to Give Up

After returning from Utah, Haley began to show serious signs of slipping. She was totally immobile now, and we held her and cuddled with her a lot, even though she really didn't like to be held very much at this stage. In fact, just picking her up was difficult because her little nine-year-old body now weighed more than seventy pounds due to tube feeding that saturated the tissues and kept her nourished. It was increasingly difficult to move her or to put her into the bathtub for bathing. Also, she had developed a strange curvature of the spine; her torso remained straight but her hips shifted towards the left into a position that looked painful to us. The doctor told us, however, that her body had done that on its own, for comfort, and that it probably wasn't bothering her. This disease was a mystery through and through.

She was also contracting pneumonia a lot more frequently, something on the order of a full week out of every month or so. She had a heavy, often violent cough, and we needed to suction out her upper respiratory tract about every fifteen minutes. Making sure she did not choke required constant vigilance. All facial expressions disappeared, and she never smiled now, not even when watching Barney. We would put her in a position on the bed where she could see the television, and she would watch with interest for a while; but before long, she would just stare at the wall blankly with no attention to the TV. Increasingly there was nothing we could do for her except love her and care for her. She was almost totally unresponsive to any of our words, actions, or touches, and she was totally dependent upon others for every need.

On the positive side, for several months a visiting nurse named Courtney came several mornings a week to give Britanny a break so that she could attend a little more to Mattie's needs. Courtney is one of my favorite people in the world; she was so generous and helpful to us during that whole ordeal. She became like a member of the family. We will always be deeply grateful for her sharing the burden of care. Little Mattie was in kindergarten at Bowie Elementary in Greenville, the same school that Britanny and Jake had attended when they were kids. Mattie was an excellent student with a perfect-conduct record. Every day after school, she would come bounding home, all smiles and pure joy. She was a consolation in an otherwise desolate situation.

One More Ace to Play

Haley was a joy to us too, but our love for her was mixed with pain, worry, and dread. Her situation seemed only to worsen, no matter what we did, but we refused to give up on that precious little girl. As she declined throughout 2009, I still had one more ace up my sleeve: the Upledger Clinic in Palm Beach Gardens, Florida. It had been recommended by several people as the mecca of craniosacral therapy, which Haley had gone through for several months with a private practitioner in Texas. That work had had some positive effect on her, even if temporary, so we hoped that the premier center for this type of therapy would bring a reversal of her condition. I knew it was a long shot; yet, at this point, I could leave no stone unturned. I was sure it could do no harm.

The Upledger Clinic agreed to work with Haley in February 2010, but then we were faced with a problem of another sort. Haley was becoming more difficult to move, so getting her to Florida was a real challenge. Knowing that travel by commercial airliners was extremely difficlt because of the cramped space, my manager at the time, Dave Fowler, got a friend to lend us a private jet, fuel included, to fly us to Florida for the therapy. I will always be deeply indebted to Dave, to Steve Williams, who lent us the plane, and to the pilot who got us to Florida and back. He was one of the many angels who came to our aid in our time of need.

We spent the better part of two weeks at the clinic, but I didn't mind the cost. It was really the last thing I could do to help Haley. The sessions were conducted twice a day by two women therapists who were kind and intuitive about their patient. They immediately sensed that Haley was afraid of this new place and wanted eye contact with her Poppy at all times in order to maintain her comfort level. I stayed with her every waking moment. The therapists laid her out on a massage table and lightly laid their hands on various parts of her body that were afflicted. The concept of the therapy is that light touch, properly placed, activates the body's own healing capabilities. The touch is supposed to stimulate the membranes and fluids that surround the brain and spinal cord to improve the functioning of the whole central nervous system.

Eventually Haley became more relaxed as the sessions continued, and I do believe that there was at least one positive benefit from those two weeks: her hip displacement straightened out. We were pleased about that, of course, yet it fell far short of what we were hoping for as a result. By the grace of God and the kindness of some wonderful people, we were able to say that we had tried everything we could possibly do to help her.

The Last Time I Saw Her Awake

When we returned from the Upledger Clinic, Haley fell into a routine that was pretty stable but hard on Britanny. Someone had to be up all night suctioning out her little throat every few minutes to prevent choking, and most of that difficult task fell to Britanny although I helped her with it when I was home. In the morning, there would be a lot of maintenance things to do, such as changing Haley's diaper, feeding her through the feeding tube, and bathing her (every other day). Although she disliked baths, she loved when we wrapped her up in three warm towels after a bath and held her close. They were her "swaddling clothes", and she felt safest in that position. Even though she was nine years old, she was like a baby. When Haley was wrapped up, I used to sing the "Baby Bunting" lullaby, which my mom sang to me when I was a kid, and she seemed to like that very much. Making her as comfortable and happy as possible was all we could do in what would be her last weeks. Haley had no desire to do anything but lie on the bed with the TV on. I insisted that we take her out in the car to see things once in a while because I didn't want her to languish, but she really didn't like going out. She just wanted to lie in that bed.

In reality, as much as she had deteriorated, we still had no idea that she was so close to dying. Maybe it was denial or wishful thinking on our part. She was almost ten, and I thought we wouldn't have to worry about losing her for a few more years. But God had other plans.

I vividly remember the last time I saw Haley coherent. It was in late March 2010. I had to go on the road for three nights of shows in the Midwest. As always, I would have much preferred to stay with Haley and the girls, but I still had to work to pay the bills. The morning I got up to go to the airport, I kissed our baby girl and told her how much I loved her, and Courtney, who was there that morning, responded in a child's voice, as if for Haley, saying, "We love you too, Poppy!" Haley looked at me with those big, brown, puppy-dog eyes, and I assured her that I would be right back. It was a bittersweet departure, one of the many that I reluctantly had to make from her and the family in those days, but little did I know that it would be the last time I would see her awake.

Another Palm Sunday Catastrophe

Melanie and my guitar player Chris accompanied me on the Midwest trip, as well as my manager, Dave, and his brother Jonathan. The morning after our last show, we were in the van driving to the Kansas City airport to fly back to our respective homes. About half an hour into the drive, I received a text message from Courtney that just said, "Call ASAP." Courtney never called or texted me for anything, and I dreaded the thought of what she had to say. I knew it wasn't good. I called her immediately, and she answered crying and so distraught that it took me a few seconds to understand what she was saying. One phrase, however, was clear enough: "She stopped breathing." As she calmed down, she went on to explain that the EMTs had come, restored Haley's pulse, and then flown her to Dallas Children's Hospital. She told me they were all heading there immediately. I asked to talk to Britanny, but she was so upset and crying so hard that there was little I could say to make her feel better.

Back in Greenville, it had started like any other morning. Britanny had suctioned out Haley, who then closed her eyes and looked relaxed as if she were going back to sleep. That was a good thing because Haley seemed to enjoy sleeping. Britanny left the room for no more than a few minutes to start a DVD for Mattie in the living room, but when she walked back by the bedroom door, she looked in and feared Haley was gone.

Britanny went into immediate red alert, frantically trying to wake her up, and when that didn't work, she began administering CPR as well as she knew how. Hearing the commotion, Mattie came into the room and started pleading with her sister, "Wake up, Haley, wake up", but to no avail. Mattie was five years old at the time, and the poor child had to see her own sister on the brink of death. Britanny called Charlie and managed the crisis as well as she could until someone could get there to help her. I believe it was Charlie who called 911 on his way to the apartment. Luckily the EMTs were only about a minute down the road and arrived before Charlie did. They immediately took over the CPR. They were eventually able to restore her pulse, but by that time Haley had been without oxygen for close to fifteen minutes; it was very likely that her brain had been seriously damaged. They flew her to Dallas Children's Hospital, which was our home away from home for so many years.

That hour-and-a-half drive to the airport was the longest ride I have ever taken. I can't imagine feeling any more helpless than I did then. I cried out loud to God in anguish, and I didn't care if anyone else heard my pleas. I repeated over and over again, "Lord God, in Christ Jesus' Name, please, don't let this end today! Please, don't take her! Please, let me get there, Lord, before You take her. Please, don't let her die without her Poppy being there. Please, don't let Britanny have to go through this without her Daddy being there. Please, don't let the next time I see her be at the funeral home, please, no, not today. Please, Lord!" I have never prayed so deeply or desperately as I did at that moment.

Mel was supposed to fly to Utah that day but changed her schedule and accompanied me to Texas. Jonathan was able to get us on an earlier flight, yet I have no memory of the flight at all or even of being on that plane. When the plane touched down a few minutes early at Dallas' Love Field, I breathed a sigh of relief and thanked God. Mel and I immediately hopped in a cab, which drove straight down Stemmons Freeway and got us to the hospital in record time. Haley and the rest of the family had arrived there about two hours earlier. Connie and Doris arrived not too long after that. I knew Children's Hospital fairly well by now and went straight to where I knew they would be. When the elevator got to the correct floor, we made a beeline through the waiting room and were buzzed through the double doors into the intensive care unit, where I saw Britanny and Charlie talking to the doctor. Britanny had a stunned, numb look on her face as if she was there but not there, and Charlie looked as though he had been crying. I immediately hugged Britanny, and when she felt my arms around her, she broke down weeping. I tried to listen to what the doctor was saying, but I was so caught up in the emotion of the moment that virtually nothing of what I heard registered.

When the doctor was finished, we went over and peered at Haley through the window of an isolation room. I could see her little body dressed in a hospital gown and lying on a bed under some kind of oxygen tent. She was motionless except for the up-and-down rhythm of her chest from the respirator that was breathing for her. It was excruciating for me to see our precious, sweet little baby with her angelic face and beautiful, thick, brown hair, lying there unconscious. We were utterly helpless to do anything for her. As initially they didn't let us in to see her, our only response was to watch and pray, watch and pray. Sometime later the nurses let us go into the room, but they made us put on masks and gloves to protect her from the possibility of infection. Thus commenced the toughest week of our lives; these would be the last six days of Haley's earthly life.

Haley was alive but unconscious. The doctors said she was in a coma, but I doubted it. I had seen a full-blown coma twenty-five years earlier with Connie, and Haley didn't look like that. In Connie's case there was absolutely no reaction to any stimuli at all, no opening of the eyes, no movements of limbs, no signs of life other than the faint blips that were registering on the monitors. But Haley would open her eyes at times and look around, at no one in particular, and even raised her arm at least once. To me, these signs meant that she wasn't fully comatose. I was the eternal optimist who thought at some point she was going to come out of this—in fact, I had seen Connie come out of what I considered to be a worse situation.

The Hardest Week of Our Lives

While the days of that week all run together in my mind now, there were two issues in the hospital that stand out for me. The first issue was the visitors. Without being uncharitable, I was less than pleased at the number of people coming to the hospital who had very little to do with the family previously and who had given little or no support to Britanny during the many long years she had taken care of this sick child. Except for the home healthcare nurses who helped us at different times, it was basically Grandma Doris and I who were Britanny's sole means of support in taking care of little Haley. Why were all these people showing up now, when none of them had even come by to read a book to Haley when she was better? I appreciated their sentiments of sympathy, but why was it that those of us who had stood by her for so long had to leave Haley's room so that those who were total strangers to her could go in and stare at her for a few minutes? It didn't make sense to me, and it bothered me. The one bright light among the visitors was Mattie, who was staying with Charlie's sister for most of that week. Children lighten the atmosphere wherever they go, and Mattie certainly brought great joy to all of us in the ICU every time she came.

Connie stayed with us during most of the six days and provided perhaps the only comic relief we had all week. Charlie's mother had brought her preacher to the room, I presume, for the purpose of consoling us, but his awkward and ill-timed words had the opposite effect. He started by saying, "Well, you know that there is a Hereafter." He paused and then continued, "She's probably gonna go to a better place." His little sermon was Basic Christianity101, and we did feel as though it was an unnecessary intrusion into our private moments with Haley. I *wanted* to say, as politely as possible, "We appreciate it, brother, but we're way ahead of you"; however, before I could get it out, Connie chimed in: "Mister, you need to just go ahead and leave. We're fine. We don't need any further explanation." I was never so thankful for Connie's legendary bluntness than at that moment! The minister meant to help, no doubt, but it felt like an intrusion into our dwindling time with Haley.

The most serious issue I had to confront that week, however, was the intensive care doctor assigned to Haley. From the time we walked into the hospital she was saying, "Well, sometime this week we will have a big decision to make", and other similarly callous statements. The more she pressed the point, the more she gave us the impression that she was just trying to free up a bed for someone else. I found her bedside manner to be atrocious and offensive. This woman was trying to talk Britanny and Charlie into a decision to turn off the life support, but it was too soon for that. She studiously avoided eye contact with me, but my fatherly instincts took over; and I intervened to relieve the obvious pressure she was putting on them. I looked straight at her and said, "Wait a minute. Stop talking like that. Stop saying that to my daughter. You don't know Haley. You don't know what she is feeling inside. We can't make that call." The fact of the matter was that Haley *had just gotten there*, and this doctor was already talking about terminating her.

She shot right back at me with an ugly attitude that could have come from a Nazi propaganda film: "What do you want to save her life for? To go back to the quality of life she had before she came in here?" Granted, Haley was in distress, but at that point there was no good medical or ethical reason to take her off life support. Also I was still hopeful that she was going to get better. If I had caved into that same kind of pressure from the neurologist twenty-five years ago, we wouldn't have seen the miracle of Connie's total recovery. *I* still believed in miracles even if the doctor didn't. It was so unfortunate that, after so many wonderful doctors and nurses throughout the course of Haley's illness, we had to have this cold, callous, calculating servant of the culture of death at the end.

I also thought a great deal about the coincidence that all of this was happening during Holy Week. Twice in my life the most catastrophic things that had ever happened to me took place in the holiest week of our faith, and I thought it meaningful that our family's life-and-death crises happened in such a grace-filled time. In my heart of hearts, I imagined that God would perform some *big* miracle, the one we had been praying for these many lonely years, on Holy Thursday or Good Friday, or maybe even on Easter morning. I couldn't help but be hopeful for a Lazarus moment. Yet, on the other hand, if the unthinkable happened, it would be during the very days in which we commemorate Christ's Passion and Resurrection.

God was certainly testing our faith that week. In reality, Haley's *whole life* was a faith-tester for me and my family. I never doubted God's existence or His ultimate goodness, but I admit that I did get mad at Him and question His motives for brief moments because there was so much I just didn't understand. I was filled with so many why questions: Why couldn't He even answer one little prayer for her recovery? Why couldn't He do something to let us know He was there? Why did we have to go through all this with absolutely nothing to show for it, only to be brought to this point that we had dreaded for so long? Why hadn't He shown up? Where was He when we needed Him the most? Once again, these were the anguished cries of a father and grandfather who had accompanied an innocent, suffering child through years of a debilitating illness. It seemed that our faithfulness had just led us to this point of extreme pain and loss. To make matters worse, we tried to get a Catholic chaplain or a priest from a local parish to give Haley the sacrament of the anointing of the sick, but there was never a priest available to administer the final sacrament to her. We just wanted to see her get better—but God said no to everything we asked.

If She Goes, I'm Done

I was very glad that the hospital agreed to do one more MRI on her brain to see if it showed any improvement from when she entered the hospital. If the MRI showed that she was better, we could move forward with some kind of treatment; if not, we would deal with it. So they scheduled the procedure for the next morning, and we spent the night with Haley, as we had all week. I stayed close to her and kissed her a lot, stroked her little legs and talked to her in hopes that she could hear what we were saying. After Connie came out of her coma, she told me that she *could* hear a lot of what people were saying in the room during those nine long weeks, and I remember her asking me a lot of questions afterward to clarify what she thought she had heard. She was, in fact, quite accurate in repeating most of what was said while she was in the coma. Presuming that was the case with Haley too, we just spent the night speaking to her and doing as much as we could to show her our love and affection. During that night, out of the blue, her left arm shot up in the air very high and remained there for about a minute or so and then slowly dropped back down to the bed. I have no idea what caused it, but it was probably a freak reaction of her nervous system rather than an indication of any improvement in her condition as we had hoped.

I think my knees were bruised from all the prayer I offered in what was to be our own Garden of Gethsemane. One thought kept running through my mind that night. I kept saying to myself, "If she goes, I'm done." I had invested so much of my life and energy in helping her to get better that it was hard for me to imagine what would be left of me if she left us. I couldn't envision myself or my life post-Haley. All I knew was that everything would be radically changed to the point where I didn't even think that I could sing anymore. Life after Haley seemed a total mass of darkness and confusion. I resolved to leave the question in God's hands because I simply couldn't make sense of anything beyond the present moment.

Our meeting with the radiologist after the MRI in the morning was the final blow to our hope for Haley's recovery. The scan indicated a further shrinkage of her brain by about a third from the scan of five days earlier, and he told us that there was *hardly anything left* of her brain. Britanny didn't look at me at all but asked him tersely, "Well, is that it?" And the radiologist said, "Yes, I'm sorry." It was the last time we would hear a doctor say that there was nothing else he could do. Britanny walked back into Haley's room, and the radiologist walked away, and I was left standing there by myself in a kind of total isolation, both physically and mentally.

There is no adequate way to describe the sensation that came over me at that moment, but for the first time in my life, I felt myself *quit* something. I felt God strongly saying to me: "Be still. Get out of my way. I've got this. Just step out of my way." It was as simple and clear as that. It dawned on me, all of a sudden, that perhaps I had been in His way all this time. I knew that, as the patriarch of the family, I had done everything possible to find a healing remedy for my beloved grandbaby because I believed He wanted me to do that. Personally, I needed to rest clear in my conscience that I had done all that was humanly possible to help her. But God was telling me that it was time to look at things differently. *Now* was the time for me to let go. That night He said, "Back off", and I did.

Standing in that corridor in my isolation and pain, I prayed, "Lord, I give up. I give this to You. You're telling me to give up, and so ... I give up." I think it must have been the humblest prayer I have ever uttered; perhaps it was like the prayer His Son prayed in a garden: "Not my will, but yours, be done" (Lk 22:42).

Britanny and Charlie had already decided to take Haley off the respirator, and I got on board with them after the devastating news from the radiologist. At least the family was in agreement on a fundamental matter. There were no further ethical issues for us to debate because we are not morally obligated to use extraordinary means to preserve life when the dying process is so progressed. We reasoned that if Haley could breathe on her own without the respirator then perhaps that would be a good and hopeful sign, but if she couldn't, then it would essentially be the end. We decided that evening that the medical personnel would take her off the machine the following day. There was nothing more to discuss.

Britanny and I were concerned about the effect of all this stress on Mattie. No child should have to see her sister die like that. Since there was nothing that anyone could do before the next day, we decided it would be best to take her out to get her mind off the situation for a while. On top of that, it happened to be Mel's birthday that day. While Britanny stayed with Haley, Mel and I took Mattie to Medieval Times, a dinner theater not far from the hospital. That evening we tried our best to look like we were having fun with the paper crowns and medieval-style dining; but our hearts were certainly heavy anticipating the momentous trial we would have to endure the next day.

When we arrived at the hospital the following morning we saw that the nurses had placed a portable curtain wall around the entrance to the room, which was a sobering and ominous sign that they were preparing for her death. I asked the doctor about what would happen to Haley when they took the tubes out: "She won't know this or feel anything, right?" The doctor's answer was categorical: "No, she won't feel anything. She will have no recognition of what is happening."

I only thought, "You'd better be telling the truth." I didn't want Haley to experience *any* distress or pain in her last moments if this was really going to lead to her death. The doctor then gave the official word to the medical technician, who carefully pulled the tubes out of her.

Immediately her little body arched upward and she gasped for air, and I thought, "Oh Lord, what have we done? Why did we agree to this?" but I soon realized that what I saw was the involuntary reaction of the body to the withdrawal of the tubes and the inflow of air from the environment after the machine was disconnected. It was a normal, expected reaction, if normal was even possible at that moment. However, in about two minutes or so she settled down and her breathing became rhythmic. Then she breathed on her own for approximately forty minutes.

During that interval, the room filled up with people, mostly Charlie's family and other visitors, and the presence of so many people at such a private moment for the family was truly disturbing to me. No one stepped out voluntarily to leave us in peace. I would never have intruded like that on another family's final moments with a beloved child, and I wondered why everyone else didn't have that same sensitivity. After a little while, I asked the main nurse to clear the room and let only the immediate family members be there alone with our Angel May, and she agreed totally and did as I requested. Mel, however, stayed in the room with us.

Britanny climbed into bed with Haley and held her, and I remained very close to the bed, doing whatever I could to have tangible contact with her in those last moments. After Britanny got up again, and I wanted to pick Haley up and hold her, but Charlie discouraged it, saying he thought that it might "compromise her breathing". I didn't insist at that delicate moment, but I felt very sad that I had missed my last opportunity to hold her.

Thirty minutes or so into the ordeal, Haley's breathing became more labored. Courtney, our home healthcare nurse, then came into the room with her husband and two sons. Not in the mood for conversation, I just prayed and prayed. I kept stroking her and staying as near as I could to assure her that her Poppy was at her side to the very end. Britanny had climbed back into bed with her and, at one point in the midst of the talking, took a quick breath and said plainly, "She's gone." Haley had finally stopped breathing—and this time, it was final.

We all broke into uncontrollable sobbing, and I immediately went over to Britanny and hugged her and held her for a long time. In addition to my own grief at losing my baby granddaughter, my heart was truly broken *for her*; no mother should ever have to see her child die. Everyone hugged Britanny after that, and Mel crossed the room and hugged Connie. Though Haley was now gone, we hovered over her little body for a long time, kissing her and touching her. We had just watched our little baby girl die a devastating death without being able to help her, and our continued contact with her was our way, at least initially, to stay connected to her.

It was heartbreaking to see that little lifeless body start to degenerate from the skin tones of life to the gradual grays and blues of death. Slowly the body lost its heat and began to feel cold and clammy. Charlie reached over and closed her big, beautiful brown eyes that had been wide open when she passed away. I continued to kiss her, but it was obvious that the body was getting cold. Soon the coroner came and used his stethoscope to determine that there was no heartbeat and wrote something in a book to make it official: my daughter's firstborn baby girl was gone.

Haley died on the morning of April 3, 2010. She left us after nine years, nine months, and twenty-seven days of earthly life. Our lives will never be the same.

A Miracle at the Passing

For reasons that only He understands, God kept a discreet and dreadful silence in the face of all our prayers for Haley's survival or health. In His mercy, however, He did answer the prayers we prayed *for ourselves*. He actually took Haley on Palm Sunday but gave us a grace period of those final six days so that we could say good-bye. He knew how much we needed that, and He especially knew how much it would haunt me if I had not been there when she passed away. I believe that she had one foot in heaven all week. Even though she was unable to communicate with us, she would be able to hear us and feel our hugs, kisses, and love for the final six days of her life, and we had the immense consolation of being able to tell her and to show her just how much we loved her.

But then, as if He wanted the final word, God showed us something that can be described only as astonishing. I believe it was His way of telling us that He was actually present to us the whole time and that all of this was His doing. In fact, everyone in the room, including the nurses, saw what happened next, as clear as day.

As soon as we stopped hugging each other and crying at Haley's loss, two symptoms of the disease and one topical blemish disappeared from her face entirely. The first symptom was the eczema or rough skin on her forehead that wasn't very visible but could easily be felt. The other symptom was the prominent, dark veins in her eyelids, which is common with a neurological disease. These had been there for the last couple of years. There was also a line of sticky residue under her nose and across her cheeks from the medical tape that had secured the tubes while she was intubated. As I was kissing her forehead after she passed, I suddenly realized that her skin had the downy feel of a baby's skin. I kissed it again just to be sure, and there was no doubt whatsoever that it was silky smooth, like Mattie's skin. The prominent veins in her eyelids had also completely vanished, and her eyelids now appeared perfectly soft and clear. More amazingly, there wasn't a mark or a trace of the stickiness from the medical tape on her face at all. It was astounding! Her face was so perfect, so heavenly serene and beautiful, with no trace of sickness whatsoever. She simply looked asleep. The only sign of death that remained was a *slight* ashen color that still lingered.

I immediately called to Britanny, "Baby, look at her forehead!" which drew everyone's attention to it. One of the nurses gasped, "Wow, I've never seen that before!" Everyone in the room saw it and can testify that I wasn't dreaming. There was no scientific or medical explanation for how all those marks had disappeared like that. I took that as God's way of saying, "You see? I was here. I got her. I came myself [or sent someone very important] to take this baby home. Rest assured—*she's with me*." Days later in the funeral home, the eczema on her forehead and the pronounced veins in her eyelids were visible again on her body, but we were given a grace, a blessed shaft of pure light from beyond that told us that she was indeed in a better place. He was letting us know that He did indeed answer our prayers, just not the way we wanted.

We stayed so long with her that afternoon that the medical personnel were giving us subtle hints that they needed to come in and do their work. Eventually, we had to leave. Someone walked Britanny out, and I stayed a little longer with my arm around our holy child's head. I really didn't want to let go, but I knew I had arrived at the inevitable point of separation. I tried to convince myself that I was supposed to leave, that I had to get up and walk out, but the emotions weren't in it. Leaving her in that hospital room was the hardest thing I have ever faced. It felt as if I were standing with my parachute at the open door of an airplane flying at ten thousand feet and debating with myself whether I should jump. Finally, I shook my head because I couldn't think about it anymore—I had to jump—at which point I got up, kissed her one more time on her precious forehead, spun around, and walked out. I have never done anything so difficult in my life. I felt the utter *finality* of everything in that single moment.

Outside the room, Britanny was there clutching to her chest the plastic bag containing a few of Haley's personal effects—including the gown she was wearing at the time she passed—and I remember taking her by the arm, with Mel on the other side, and walking her through those double doors and into the elevator. How heart-wrenching that departure was for her too; we came into the hospital as a family with our baby girl, and now we were departing in grief without her. I barely remember the walk to the car and the good-byes we said to the others that night. The short car ride to the hotel was practically silent. What was there to say, after all? I was so distraught, so very distraught, at all that had just transpired, but the only thing I could think of now was how to make this experience more bearable for my Britanny. She was a bereaved mother and was taking it hard. Mel helped me to take her to the hotel room, where she went straight to the bed and lay down, still clutching the plastic bag. We didn't say much that evening either. I remember going to get her a glass of wine to calm her, but everything else about that night is a blur.

There are no words for the loss of a child; all the consulting, all the pleading, bargaining, and praying, all the hugs and sympathies were finally over. Haley was in the direct presence of Almighty God; we were absolutely sure about that.

A Grandfather's Love

I can testify very personally that the loss of Haley opened up a font of wisdom and love that matured me beyond any other experience of life. Families may plan for hurricanes or tornadoes, but no one ever plans for a personal disaster like this, and I was no exception. I believe that anyone who accompanies a loved one through such a traumatic event must figure out *how* to respond, but the real sacrifice is that—no matter what he does—there is never a perfect solution.

My first way of meeting this crisis was to tell God that I would do anything, anything at all, to take her suffering away. I would have gladly taken her sufferings upon myself in a heartbeat or even *exchanged my life for hers* at any point in her illness if that would have been possible. But God said no. I couldn't bargain my way out of the problem.

Then I strove to fix the problem and to put an end to her suffering—by any means necessary—but everywhere we turned, the answer was always "We can't help you." It was immensely difficult for me to admit that all the resources and talents at my disposal could do absolutely nothing to make my little grandbaby better. I had to learn the deeper lesson behind the mystery of God's refusals, and it led me to the understanding that there are certain things in this world that just cannot be fixed. That was a hard lesson to learn. Real love isn't about *fixing* people. It's more about *being with* people in their brokenness that cannot be fixed this side of heaven. In our own case, when all attempts to find a solution for Haley's illness ultimately failed, the only thing we could do was simply to *be* with her. I finally had to *surrender*, to cede control of a situation that was beyond me. Earth has so much sorrow that only heaven can heal.

Saint Paul's beautiful passage about love in 1 Corinthians 13 says that love "does not insist on its own way" (v. 5), a message that Haley's illness brought home to me in a new way. For a very long time, I wanted to keep Haley with us indefinitely, even in her handicapped state, but that would have been to condemn her to a life of suffering that God didn't will for her. He clearly wanted her with Him, free of the sorrows of this earthly life. Haley is now in the place of ultimate joy and constant happiness—much better than anything we could have provided for her here on earth—and it would be the most unloving act to want her back from that place of bliss just for *me*. I learned, as if in a new way, that selfless love is always about *the other*, not about me.

The little miracle after Haley's passing taught me that death never has the final word for us who are believers. Love truly reaches beyond the grave to a place where every sorrow will be consoled. If the transformation of her countenance into such radiant beauty after she died was not a sign of victory over death, then nothing was. The miracle was not only a message that she was home with God; it was a sign of the power of our love to overcome her death, just as the crucifix that Haley kissed so devoutly is a sign that God's love will conquer *all* death in the end.

The last word is always God's, and that word is always *love* for those who strive to be faithful and true to Him. That's why we praise Him for all things, even the loss of our beloved Angel May.

11

His Love Remains

Resurrection

(Easter 2010 to the Present)

As for me and my house, we will serve the LORD.

—Josh 24:15

Although the week following Haley's death was agonizing, I didn't want it to end because her interment meant the final parting. We eventually had to meet with the funeral director of Coker-Mathews Funeral Home in Greenville—it was a painful inevitability—but her funeral became yet another rite of passage for our family, the definitive good-bye to her earthly life.

We were unprepared for the onslaught of details that had to be arranged. Nevertheless, we proceeded carefully and tried to make our decisions reflect our respect for the incredible child we had lost. We chose Rest Haven Cemetery in Rockwall, Texas, which was near enough to our home so that we could visit her grave regularly, and we wanted her to be laid to rest in a mausoleum because neither Britanny nor I felt comfortable with putting her in the ground. We chose a beautiful space in the cemetery's mausoleum and purchased a niche with a black marble cover in a safe little corner. As we wished no fanfare at all, we decided to go with a simple service in the funeral home followed by a graveside service, and a very kind permanent deacon from the parish, Lee Davis, officiated at both.

Dreading the thought of seeing her body for the last time in the casket on the day of the funeral, we asked to help prepare her for burial the day

197

before the service, after the embalming process. Seeing her that day in the preparation room was one of the most difficult but also strangely consoling moments I have ever experienced. I will never forget it as long as I live. When Britanny, Mel, and I got to the funeral home, one of the directors led us down the hallway to the preparation room in the back. As we came around the corner, we saw the stainless steel table used for embalming bodies—and there she was. Our baby girl was laid out on that table, covered by a cloth.

It was an utterly surreal experience to look down upon a child I loved so very much and to see her in death. My first impressions were very uncomfortable. Her head was propped up on what looked like a block of wood, which was too high for a child's head and had the effect of pushing her chin too far down. The rough skin on her forehead and the dark veins in her eyelids that had disappeared just after her death had reappeared, but I wasn't surprised about that. God had granted us a window into eternity for a brief second with that little miracle when she died, and we didn't expect it to be permanent. Still, we were hoping to experience something of the serenity of that moment, but peace evaded us that day. I saw the precious hair that I had stroked and washed all those many years; it still looked and smelled the same, but there was no life in it now. They had put makeup on her and had doctored her body to look a little better, but I found it very hard to discern how the doctoring made much of a difference. The soul had left the body, and there was nothing in this world that could even come close to restoring the beauty of the actual living child we had known and loved for more than nine years.

None of that, however, stopped Britanny and me from kissing that beloved girl as if she were still with us for a while longer. We knew that she wasn't there, but that beautiful little shell was the closest thing we had to her, and we thanked God that we had the chance to accompany her body in death before having to see her lying in the casket. Britanny was unsatisfied with the way her hair was arranged, and we talked about braiding it. At this, Mel volunteered for that honor, which was a very sweet thing for her to do. She braided Haley's hair in a beautiful lattice pattern that looked very professional and dignified for burial.

We also bought a white Communion dress to put on her since she had never been able to receive her first Holy Communion in life. We felt that a

Communion dress was a perfect way for her to meet her Bridegroom at the gates of heaven and walk with Him down that long glorious aisle into the sanctuary of her final home. She would make her first Holy Communion in the presence of Christ Himself. Britanny's last motherly touch was a lavender sweater with long sleeves for her thin little arms. It was open and didn't cover up the beautiful Communion dress. When it was all in place, Haley looked just perfect. Those many details of preparation were all so significant because of their "earthly finality". I don't remember the exact time we left the funeral home that day; I only know it killed me to leave her again.

A Very Consoling Service

We had put out the word that we didn't want the funeral to be a public event, because it was certain that many well-wishers would come simply because it was for Collin Raye's granddaughter; the last thing we wanted was any media or a spectacle. Haley's life had been private and exclusive to us, so we *tried* to limit attendance to immediate family members. As it turned out, quite a few extended family members came to the funeral, including many members of Charlie's family; my brother, Scotty; his daughter, Sarah; and her mother, Cathy. Some other close friends who had played a significant role in our journey also came. My dear friend Jennifer Poage came with her twin sister, Jessica, and her son, Noah, who was Haley's age and had grown up with her in her better years. I hadn't seen him for several years, and he looked so much older now. I was delighted to see Dr. Howard Queller, my physician and dear friend, and his wife, Dee. I didn't even know that they had heard about Haley's death, but I felt honored that they came. Connie was there, of course, and her three brothers and their families came as well. Her brother Mike, in particular, had always had a heart for what we were going through with Haley and always asked to help where he could. I think he appreciated our desperate situation more than most, and I was gratified that he was there.

We made sure to get to the funeral home early that day in order to spend some time with Haley. It was evident to us that we had made the right decision to see her the day before the funeral because now we were emotionally prepared to see her in the casket. Even then, she was a heartrending sight to behold. She was laid out in the beautiful Communion dress and lavender sweater that we had dressed her in the day before, and of course, we immediately went up to her and kissed her and wept over her, as any family would. When Deacon Davis arrived, the funeral director asked all the guests to find their seats, except for the immediate family members, who were to walk in with the deacon. After we had processed down the short aisle of the room, we took our place in the front pew: Charlie sat at the end, then Britanny, with Mattie in between them. Then came Noah, Mel, Jake, and I. Connie sat in the row behind us next to Doris and her brothers' families, and I sat there with my arm around Noah and held on to him and thought about how good it was to have Haley's first friend by my side at that moment.

God surely sent Deacon Davis to us that day. In addition to the many beautiful things he said about the Resurrection of Jesus, he brought the truth of God's mercy to us in words I will never forget: "Often when people die, we hope that they go to heaven. In the case of a small child like this, however, I think it's a pretty safe bet." It was the perfect thing to say! I know that the Church doesn't declare at funerals that any deceased person is in heaven, but the deacon gave us a common-sense faith message that resonated in our hearts without being dogmatic: for someone as innocent of sin as Haley was, heaven certainly was a "safe bet". What a beautiful and comforting way to eulogize a child, especially our baby girl. I have always claimed that Haley was sinless because she had no capacity to commit a sin after baptism. Even if she could have committed one, I believe that she would have been purified of sin by all her suffering.

Golden Slumbers

After Deacon Davis had spoken, Melanie, the consummate artist, played a medley of songs on the piano that she and I had chosen. I didn't sing at this funeral for obvious emotional reasons, but I asked her to play several of Haley's favorites, especially the Irish lullaby "Too Ra Loo Ra Loo Ra", which I had often sung to her to put her to sleep. She started with an absolutely gorgeous rendition of "Danny Boy" and then played my favorite Beatles song, "Golden Slumbers" from the *Abbey Road* album, because of its poignant words and timeless melody:

> Once there was a way
> To get back home.
> Sleep, pretty darling,
> Do not cry
> And I will sing a lullaby.
> Golden slumbers,
> Fill your eyes.
> Smiles await you when you rise.[1]

That song always breaks my heart. I can't listen to it without crying or thinking of Haley. Then, after a moment of the "I Love You" song from the Barney TV show, we decided to end with one of the classic Christian anthems of our age, "How Great Thou Art". Mel's playing was so stirring, perfect, and beautiful that everyone in the place was deeply moved, even if they had never known Haley personally. I was so grateful for her talents at that moment.

Jake then got up to read a nice little eulogy about his niece, and I thought he did a very fine job of honoring her. I followed him with a speech that I ad-libbed because I had no way of preparing what I was going to say. I have spent most of my life ad-libbing on stage anyway, so it was familiar to me, but now I wanted to let the Spirit speak through me for Haley's sake. I'm sure it wasn't anywhere near good enough to honor Haley's sweet memory, and I hardly remember anything I said other than thanking everyone for being there. The whole experience was so emotionally difficult for me; I was just trying to get through it. When I had finally said all I needed to say, I sat down, and Deacon Davis concluded the service with that beautiful prayer to the angels and saints that touched my heart so deeply. How consoling it was to imagine that the holy angels would be Haley's escort to the gates of heaven and that all of God's redeemed would be waiting to greet her when she arrived. I truly wished that I could have gone with her.

Before the heartrending moment when the funeral director closed the casket, I remember looking one last time at the three photos we had placed in the casket as sentimental reminders of those who loved her the most: one picture of her mom and her; another picture of me holding her in the swimming pool; and a third picture of her sister and her standing side by side, looking beyond adorable, as only little girls can. The thought of never being able to hold her again in this life was breaking my heart as I looked at her angelic face with eyes closed in death; yet, clutched in both of her tiny hands, previously so paralyzed by the disease, were signs of our faith and hope: the rosaries that we often prayed for her. Britanny's was in her right hand, mine in her left. The strings of simple beads with a crucifix at the end were witnesses to the world that awaits us where we would someday all be together again.

The Sealed Tomb

When I was finally able to tear myself away from the closed casket, I went out and joined the kids in the car. I rode with them those long, somber miles to Rest Haven Cemetery. Deacon Davis accompanied us on the ride, and eventually we found ourselves seated under a tent in front of the black marble mausoleum, looking at the open niche where Haley's casket was soon to be interred. It was a warm spring day, and the air was bright with sun, but our hearts were heavy with the feeling of loss and the anticipation of the interment. We had asked four people to be the pallbearers for the casket, which was a great honor for all of them: Jake and Courtney, as well as Britanny's best friend from childhood, Jennifer Hobbs, and Connie's brother, Uncle Mike. As they drew the beautiful white casket out of the hearse and placed it on the low framework in front of the mausoleum, the group of about twenty guests became totally silent.

Deacon Davis connected with our grief once again and said, "One of the most difficult things for families to go through is interment, because it's so final." That was certainly an understatement. He read a Scripture passage and made some further remarks at the graveside, which were wonderfully consoling. Then he sprinkled the casket with holy water and finished the service with the Lord's Prayer and the final commendation. The whole ceremony lasted about five minutes, but that was fitting. It was not a time for many words. The blessings and the ritual actions of the Church were sufficient to help us get through it. The funeral director then asked the pallbearers to take up the casket again and place it gently in the niche that had been prepared for it—a task they accomplished with great solemnity.

Most graveside ceremonies that I have attended conclude at the point of the last blessing, but ours didn't finish there because we wanted to see the sealing of the casket in its final place of rest. It was very important to us that Haley's remains be safe and secure in the mausoleum. I understand why families leave the gravesite before the covering of the grave, but we were going to stay put until we saw Haley's niche closed. We stood there and watched a little longer as the cemetery workers lifted the square cement cover with the black marble fascia piece and place it over the niche opening to seal it for good. The beautiful polished marble would remain unmarked until the new plate bearing her name would be attached to it in a month or so.

The silence at that place was penetrating. The unobtrusive sounds of nature, normally in the background, were so evident to our heightened senses at that moment and somehow seemed to augment the atmosphere of prayer and peace that surrounded us when the tomb was finally sealed. The chirping of a few little birds and even the slight breeze that came around the mausoleum walls all entered the prayer that ascended like incense.

Eventually, there was no more reason for us to remain there. The extended family members and well-wishers we didn't know well wandered off, somewhat reluctantly, unsure about how to make such an experience end on a positive note. Jennifer, Noah, and Jessica had to catch a plane that afternoon, so we said our teary-eyed good-byes to them and saw them off with many thanks and blessings. Those who remained made plans to go as a group for lunch to a local restaurant.

As we drove out of the cemetery, I remember looking at all the graves of those who have preceded us in death and reflecting that nine years before, I had been with Britanny when we learned of Haley's existence; now her earthly life was finished. It dawned on me that our family, as we knew it, would never be complete again this side of heaven. We wait in hope for a great family reunion in the perfect world to come.

The Mystery of Holy Week

Mercy overflowed in many ways during the weeks of our loss and mourning. My friend Governor Mike Huckabee performed an unexpected act of graciousness the weekend of the funeral: he used the closing segment of his Saturday Fox News show to announce Haley's passing and to ask for prayers for our family. He had interviewed me a few weeks earlier to talk about Haley's sickness, and in that same segment I got to sing "She's with Me" to a national audience. Yet, this final tribute following her death was so special to us. I will never forget Governor Huckabee's great kindness.

God's mercy has surrounded us from the very beginning, though it was difficult to recognize at times in its various disguises. When I look backward from this vantage point, however, I am amazed at how every significant moment of my family's spiritual life is bound up with the divine mysteries that we celebrate in His Church. Britanny and I were baptized on Easter Sunday 1983; Connie and Jake experienced their life-and-death crisis on Palm Sunday 1985; Haley was first taken on Palm Sunday and died on Holy Saturday 2010. To our utter amazement, April 3 was not only the day that Haley died; it was also the day that Britanny and I were baptized. Three generations of our family's spiritual life had thus come full circle, and nothing of this was planned by us. God did it all.

A month or so later, on Mother's Day, when the new plate was installed on the niche, we received an unexpected spiritual consolation. While Britanny was bending down in front of the mausoleum, taking pictures of the new plate, she saw a shadow of a little girl on the black marble of the mausoleum. It was uncanny, mysterious, and beautiful, and Britanny felt deep joy and peace in its presence. She also took a photo of the shadow on the wall, and it came out clearly in the developed picture.

After Britanny told me about the experience, I decided to go back with Jake to the cemetery the next day to see whether the shadow could have been caused by some natural phenomenon, such as the sun shining behind Britanny or some other object. Although we went at the same time of day, we saw no shadow. It was just a grace, and we accepted it with deepest gratitude.

I don't honestly know how my Britanny has endured all the loss and suffering that have been thrust upon her in the last several years. Even though I might be accused of fatherly bias, I have to say that I stand in awe-filled admiration of her. She is the strongest person I know. She not only held up through years of difficult responsibilities and sacrifices for her sick child, but accepted her loss with the deepest of faith. Her faith was tested, to be sure, and there were many moments of doubt and weakness, but she passed the test with flying colors and is such a mature, faith-filled young woman. I am so proud of her. She is the best of mothers and such a model for our little Mattie, who we hope will someday grow up to be just like her mom.

Mattie, for her part, remains the one constant bright spot in so much desolation. Her presence has helped Britanny and me to survive, both physically and emotionally, the loss of Haley. I remember looking at Mattie at one point during the whole ordeal of Haley's dying process and marveling at what a fine, strong, and resilient child she is. Her maturity and strength in the face of her sister's death, I believe, can be attributed only to God's working in her life.

I recall one sweet incident in church, when Mattie was little, that made us all laugh but also showed her spiritual sensitivity. The priest was walking to the back of church to give Holy Communion to a handicapped person, and as he approached, Mattie was staring intently at him. When he was six or seven feet away from us, she casually waved her hand and said, "Hi, Jesus." Her greeting echoed throughout the still church, and many hushed giggles of parishioners broke the reverent silence of the moment. Truly, we must become like children to enter the Kingdom (cf. Mt 18:3).

God sure knew what He was doing in giving us Mattie. She fills us up and helps us to maintain a good, positive outlook on life with solid hope for the future. Every time I hear her rush into a room and ask me in her cute, enthusiastic voice, "Hey, Poppy, guess what?" my heart is uplifted and my grief consoled. I always say that being a grandparent is the payoff for doing something right as a parent.

Beaten Down but Undefeated

We were mentally and emotionally exhausted after the ordeal of Haley's death. I knew that we eventually would have to move Britanny and Mattie out of the little duplex in Greenville because it held too many memories for us. The good memories of Haley would be a constant reminder of her loss, and the bad ones would just be painful. For the first few days after the funeral, we tried to resume our lives and kept the door to Haley's bedroom closed because the memories were still too fresh and painful. A little later, I began to go into her room alone. I would fall on the bed, bury my face in her pillow to drink in the scents of the living Haley that I wanted to remain with me, and cry my heart out. After a short period of mourning, we moved to a little house in Rockwall, the town where Haley is buried. We set up in the new house a room for Haley, which was a way to memorialize her and to help us feel close to her. For a time it was source of consolation.

Mattie was six years old when we moved to Rockwall, and Britanny enrolled her in the local Dorris Jones Elementary School, where she seemed to flourish as she began the first grade. We watched carefully to see how Mattie would deal with the loss of her sister, but she exhibited few signs of intense grief. Kids are like that; they tend to grieve in short bursts for a while and then move on.

For my part, although I was grieving deep inside, I also had a responsibility to my loved ones. Actually, remaining strong for them and doing everything I could do to make their lives happy and healthy was one of the ways I coped with my own loss. Speaking publicly about the loveliness of Haley's life as well as the process of writing this book have been other helpful means of coping for me.

A New Type of Advocacy

There was one other very significant point of light for me at that time. About five days after Haley's funeral, I was scheduled to go to Indianapolis to open a show that was a fundraiser for the Terri Schiavo Life and Hope Network. Terri was the innocent, handicapped young lady from Clearwater, Florida, who was targeted by euthanasia activists and starved to death by a court order in 2005. Her case made international news, and her family responded to the grave injustice of her death by establishing a charitable foundation in her memory. It was amazing, in God's divine plans, that within a week of the death of my granddaughter, I was scheduled to sing for an organization dedicated to the memory of a handicapped woman whose life symbolized the struggle of the culture of life against the culture of death in our country. Apparently, God was not wasting any time in putting me to work in the service of a truly important cause.

In normal circumstances, I would have been eager to do the show, but I was coming off a devastating week and was apprehensive about it. My manager, Dave, asked me, "Are you sure you can do this?" I didn't know if I could, but I told him I would try. My better self wanted to prove that I could be useful for some cause outside of me, so I went with Mel and a guitarist to Indianapolis that week to fulfill my commitment. I remember the sheer willpower it took to go on stage for that event. As I walked toward the lights, I had to give reassurance to my own fragile nature: "Well, here goes—I hope I can do this!" Thankfully, my music flowed that night. Although I honestly can't recall very much of the performance, I do remember being satisfied afterward that I could make a difference for such wonderful people and their precious cause of life. I proved—mostly to myself—that I could still do my job even while I was reeling from grief.

I chose to cancel the meet and greet before the show due to my frail emotional state. Randy Travis, who followed me that night, was kind enough to add another thirty photos with fans to his meet and greet backstage, and I was grateful. I also decided not to meet Terri's family at that time—her valiant mother, Mary Schindler, and siblings, Bobby Schindler and Suzanne Vitadamo—as such an emotional connection with those who had tragically lost a loved one seemed too much for me right then. I was not sure I could get through such a monumental meeting without breaking down. I would meet them at a later event and express my great admiration for what they do. I so respect and appreciate their mission of fighting euthanasia, one of the many growing problems in our country today.

That night I reconnected with John Condit, an executive from the Atlanta-based Cox Media Group, who had brought me to Dayton, Ohio, a decade earlier for a charity concert to benefit cystic fibrosis. He reminded me backstage that he had given me a beautiful white marble statue of Saint Michael the Archangel, which I had cherished since then and which to this day sits on a coffee table in my house. Saint Michael, as we pray, *defends us in battle*, and I believe he has strengthened me and defended me over the last decade in so many of my personal and spiritual battles. The idea for such a providential gift came from John's sister, Jenn Giroux, who asked me to record my album *His Love Remains* when I returned to Dayton in 2011 to perform at another cystic fibrosis event, this time with KC and the Sunshine Band. Jenn later became my manger in 2013.

Because John and Jenn had earned my trust and friendship, they were instrumental in getting me to serve as the national spokesman for the Life and Hope Network. In that capacity I was an advocate for handicapped who are threatened by the same kind of euthanasia proponents that I had dealt with twice in my life. I did many interviews for radio and television

(Fox News, EWTN, and Glenn Beck) and was featured in numerous publications (*National Review Online*, *Music Row*, *Catholic Digest*, *St. Anthony Messenger Press*, and *Celebrate Life*, published by the American Life League). I also did a number of public appearances. After Haley's death, I discovered that I was able to speak with authority about end-of-life issues and about the pain of losing a child because I had personally fought those same life-and-death battles in my own family.

I remained a spokesman for Terri's Network for a good while and am so grateful for the exposure I got while bringing attention to such a beautiful ministry. In November of 2012, with Jenn's and John's help, Britanny and I started our own effort to advocate for disabled children—the Haley Bell Blesséd Chair Foundation, a charitable organization that provides wheelchairs for families with special-needs children who cannot afford the expense. The cause of helping needy children and protecting the disabled is so joyful, because it is one very tangible way that I continue to honor Haley's life and death—and I love every minute of the work.

It was on November 1, the day we officially launched our foundation, that we received some glorious news: Riverton High School in Riverton, Utah—the very place where we lived during the year of Haley's treatment—chose the Haley Bell Blesséd Chair Foundation as the beneficiary of their annual Silver Rush 2012. This is an annual effort in which these selfless kids spend the entire month of December performing acts of service to raise money for a charity of their choice. We will be forever grateful to these amazing students, especially Katie Borgmeier and our dear friend Suzie Evans, for their incredible generosity to this cause. In one month they raised over $107,000 for our foundation!

His Love Remains

I truly thought that when Haley died, I would be useless, finished with music, and possibly unable to continue to take care of my family as I had been doing. That's how much her death affected me. I was numb. I was like a rudderless ship floating out on the open sea. I didn't know where the tides of life would take me or where I would end up. I knew only that life would never be the same. Thankfully, God saw far beyond my limited view of what lies ahead and used His creative powers to fashion a new life for me.

He wasn't done with me yet. There was more to my life's story than even I was aware of, and He would show me how I could still make a difference in the world. In fact, I have come to learn that His ability to bring life out of death and joy out of sorrow is essentially an experience of resurrection.

Today, if anyone were to ask me what my ultimate goal in life is, I would have to say, very simply, that it is getting to heaven to be with our Haley and Jesus for all eternity. There is nothing of greater importance to me. Haley's passing changed the way I value things. Much of what I used to think was important has no significance to me anymore. At one time, I thought the height of achievement was to make hit records in Nashville and then to use my celebrity to further the good causes of organizations that were having a positive impact on the world. I still believe in the importance of such sponsorships, of course, but my view of how to change the world is different: we can really change the world only one heart at a time. It is my hope that in praising God with my voice, I might bring people closer to God and heaven, and in some cases bring people *back to God.*

That was my real motive in making *His Love Remains* in 2011. It is the one album of my whole long career that expresses my deepest sentiments and beliefs so perfectly. Two wonderful ladies, Marie Bellet and Andrea Thomas, sang duets with me, and I am so grateful that they offered their talents and beautiful voices in this effort. It seems God has really blessed this album. Since its release, I have been receiving a growing number of invitations to give my witness and to perform concerts for religious events and churches. In addition to my regular country music appeal, I now hope also to be known as a Catholic/Christian artist and to use my talents for God's glory.

Mel also contributed to *His Love Remains*, and it pains me to add that in the midst of grieving for Haley and learning to create a "new normal" my relationship with her became another casualty. I will not explain further because I don't really know what happened—I'm still as perplexed by it now as I was then. My best summation is that people walk on different places along the life journey that we all share. Some walks are accelerated by circumstances beyond our control, while others move more slowly. It takes a lot of living to learn to see the beautiful forest, for what it truly is, and not to be overwhelmed by each tree that gets in the way or perhaps has fallen. In the aftermath of our breakup, I realized I possessed love unconditional, because of choosing it to be so. I had always known unconditional love for my children and grandchildren, which is natural and automatic and, for me, profound and sacred. Yet my love for Melanie was different—this time I had grown spiritually and emotionally enough to choose to love, in spite of broken-heartedness, hurt pride, and confusion. I consider that a sign of Christian maturity.

God loves us unconditionally, even when we offend Him, ignore Him, betray Him, and turn our backs on Him. He does it because He chooses to, even though it's not easy. That's the absolute definition of true love. How blessed we are to have such a God! Perhaps Almighty God will even bring about the moment, someday, when I can make music with my Mellie one more time. His holy will be done, in all things.

12

Looking Upward

Pure Grace

*For this reason I remind you to rekindle the gift of God that
is within you ... for God did not give us a spirit of timidity
but a spirit of power and love and self-control.*

—2 Tim 1:6–7

Years ago, when I met Garth Brooks in the Grand Ole Opry, he told me
that he hoped I would "get what I want out of this", but at that time I
really didn't know what I wanted from my career. I had already achieved
my immediate goals of proving to myself that I could make hit records in
Nashville and get back to my kids in Texas, but after that, I had no carefully thought-out plan for future success like the ones many of my contem-
poraries had. I wound up succeeding in music by the grace of God, and
because I was good at it; my only plan was to do more of the same.

I'm Done Doing It My Way

After years of success and failure, joy and pain, I have finally found what
I *really* want out of life, and it's not the celebrity lifestyle. That life is not
nearly enough to satisfy the deepest longings of my heart. In essence, I
want only what God wants, and I am willing to let Him show me that now.
It's really that simple, but it took decades for me to figure it out. For His
own reasons, He brought me into the limelight in 1991, and I tried to serve
His Kingdom and use my celebrity status for many good causes. Yet I was
probably an obstacle to Him more than I care to admit. I was headstrong

211

about most things and wanted to do everything *my way*. I guess that's why I once recorded Sinatra's "My Way". It could have been my spiritual theme song for most of my life up to that point.

Now, however, I just want to get out of His way and let Him use me for whatever He wills. I do what I can to discern His will, but frankly His will is sometimes mysterious and difficult to understand. I can't expect to know it perfectly all the time because, on a faith walk, the way is often obscure beyond the next step. These days I like to take life, as the Gospels recommend, one day at a time. My ultimate goal is to make Him smile and to be His instrument, or weapon, or olive branch, as He sees fit, and I trust that He will use me for His purposes. Since Haley died, I've been able to surrender to Him more fully my personality, my history, my future, and my voice—all the things that He has given me—for His glory, and I have promised to let Him determine the agenda. Life is much more peaceful that way.

While I am grateful for all the years I spent as one of the Nashville elite, I have a better view of Nashville from a distance. I can see the forest for the trees now. I don't get too bent out of shape about its defects anymore. I've seen the ugly side of the music business, and I've experienced its sublime joy. I accomplished even more than I had expected in my career, including singing with some of the greats, such as Dolly Parton, Kenny Rogers, and Glen Campbell. I received recognition and respect from my childhood heroes Johnny Cash and Waylon Jennings. I met three of the Eagles and sang on stage with one of them. I even got to pretend to be a Beach Boy a couple of times. When my brother, Scotty, brags a little about being part of one of the hottest acts in Nashville, I just shake my head and smile because I know what it looks like on the other side of fame. At the same time, I am extremely happy that my brother is doing what he has always wanted to do. It's amazing how beautiful the forest can be when you step back and look at the trees from a distance.

A New Mission

As far as my singing career goes, it continues to be swept up in a new and fascinating mission that really began with my album *His Love Remains*. It is a mission that would have been impossible without the experience of Haley's passing. On a weekly—sometimes a daily—basis, the Lord uses me and my story to give suffering people strength and to draw them closer to Him. Some people hear my story and say to themselves, "He survived what we're living through right now. And he's still smiling and funny and performing on stage. We can survive too!" My story gives them hope, and that fills me with the greatest joy. I can attribute that result only to the Holy Spirit moving in their hearts.

Above all, I would be remiss if I did not mention the blessing I receive in meeting parents who bring their special-needs children, big and small, to see me after the shows. They come in wheelchairs and strollers, carried in arms or walking haltingly. When I am with such a child, for a moment I feel as if I am with Haley again, and I know that the child and his parents appreciate the instant rapport between us as much as I do. Naturally, we bond instantly because of our mutual experiences. It's just a joy for me to love them, to kiss them, to talk with them, and to take pictures with them. When I see a mother or a father crying at these moments, I know the Holy Spirit is at work. He is the One who fills hearts with consolation. My work feels more like ministry now than ever before.

I attribute my advocacy on behalf of those special children directly to Haley's intercession for me in heaven. Were I to act as a functionary or a detached professional musician singing for people, making my money and going home, I would betray my calling. Rather, I'm a father and a grand-father who is available to them, who understands their needs intimately, and who shares with them the burden of their suffering, even if for just a short while. It seems that, in the aftermath of Haley's death, my musical career has come full circle too. Touching people's lives like this is what I have always wanted to do; it is the fulfillment of my *real* dream. Through loss and grief, I finally got what Garth wished for me.

Now, instead of using my celebrity status for His Kingdom, God is using my *suffering* by allowing me to touch one soul, one precious life at a time, through music and a special ministry of encouragement. I believe that the deep joy I feel and the profound impact of this outreach to suffering people is due to my greater desire to live in conformity to His will. I always hoped He would use me for something significant, but I'm not sure I always listened to what He had to say. I would often tell Him, "Lord, please use me however You want", but now when I say that, I really mean it. I want that to be my theme song for the rest of my life.

A Simple Wish

If I could offer a simple wish at the end of this book, I would appeal to people's basic humanity and ask that all my readers find in their hearts a profound concern for those who suffer, especially those who have lost a child. There is no loss like that in the world. I've seen my daughter's deep sadness when people, even those close to the family, either downplay the importance of those anniversaries or somewhat apathetically forget them, consistently failing even to ask how she is doing. I don't mean this as a judgment on others because I know that people cannot share our grief in the same way that we experience it. I wish only to highlight the need for a greater sensitivity to the grief of others. The simple act of remembering a bereaved mother on special days such as Mother's Day, her child's birthday, and the anniversary of her child's death has an enormous resonance in her heart and helps her fondly recall the sweet memories of her child and ignite her hope to be with that child one day in heaven. It is understandable that most people feel uncomfortable with such a tender subject and choose to avoid the awkwardness that comes with asking about a deceased loved one; however, such simple gestures of concern go a long way to consoling a grieving mother's heart.

It's no surprise that those caring for special-needs children or those who have lost children tend to have the greatest compassion for us. At one of my events after Haley died, I met an absolutely wonderful lady whose granddaughter, Lauren, suffers from a condition similar to Haley's. Sherry Helton sends a text message to us every third or fourth day to see how we are doing and to give us encouragement. Her messages are like drinks of water for thirsty souls. Likewise, our friends Lola and Clyde Van Dalsem, who recently lost their grandson Aiden, send regular messages that console us and assure us that we are not alone in our grief. I cannot express how grateful I am for such sensitive and compassionate souls.

I am sure that dear little Haley has preceded us to our place of destiny, heaven. Having someone you know and love so well on the other side makes you eager to go there and be with her, even to the point of losing all fear of death. Yet we all have our appointed hour to be reunited with God and our loved ones in His Kingdom, and we must be patient until that time arrives. It's my purpose now to do as much as I can to please God in this life and to be fully ready to meet Haley when my time comes.

Family Matters

About a year ago, I was finally able to get all my furniture and personal items out of storage in Utah and moved with Britanny and Mattie to Nashville, where we live a quiet, modest life when I am not touring. I still travel a lot to do shows all over the country, of course, because that's my source of income for my family. Mattie is entering the fourth grade at the time of this writing and growing in grace and favor before our eyes every day. My son, Jake, lives in Texas, close to his mom and grandma and works hard at his job, which keeps him busy and happy. In his late twenties, he's still single and hoping to find the right young lady, but that is all in God's plans, of course, not ours. Connie is still going strong and entered the Catholic Church independently of me back in the mid-nineties. I was very happy about her conversion; the Church Militant is perfect for her. She's a born fighter! Sadly, we lost Connie's mother, Doris, in 2013.

My brother, Scotty, tours with Miranda Lambert and is healthier and happier than I have ever seen him. He is part of a big act in the business right now, and that is an exciting place to be—for a while at least. My brother will always be my brother, and I will always love him, but our opinions differ on just about every subject. I don't see him often, but every time I do, I am reminded of how different we are. He still has a rebel streak, but he has lost his edginess. And for that I am grateful.

My Mama is in her mid-seventies and resides in a long-term care facility in Texas, where Scotty and I visit her whenever we can. It is sad to see her mind being gradually lost to dementia when she is still very physically healthy. I'm sure the years of prescription drugs exacerbated the problem. She has missed most of our adult lives and virtually all of her grandchildren's and great grandchildren's lives, but I love her more now than I probably have since I was a kid, and I know I owe her so much. She was the best of mothers to her two sons, and I trust that God will treat her mercifully in her declining years.

I see Dad about once a year, and last summer I had the joy of seeing him at the Collinfest in Arkansas, where I had perhaps the most enjoyable conversation I have ever had with him. We talked for a while about my career, and he was obviously very moved and concerned about how Haley's death has affected me. He also gave a nice little hug to his great-granddaughter,

Mattie, who was with me, and that was such a joy to see. I was very proud of him. He is eighty years old, but he has all his faculties and takes good care of himself and seems strong. I pray that I may age as gracefully as he has.

Speaking of family, or in this case, my musical family, I recently attended the funeral of my old friend, musical director, and pianist for twenty years, Geno LeSage. Geno rode the highways with me from the beginning of my recording career through its heyday, and beyond. He lost his life while heroically saving a woman from drowning in 2013. Geno was a very courageous and deliberate man, and his actions certainly don't surprise me, but his passing was a shock to us all and a reminder of the fragility of life. His musical and personal contributions to my career were significant to my success, and I will miss him greatly.

Almost four years after Haley's passing, I still deal with the periodic waves of sadness over her loss. Nonetheless, I get up *happy* every day, and I have learned to overcome these feelings of sadness with the willpower and the personality God has given me. Every day is a new day with a new sense of purpose. The only thing that keeps me focused on earth now is having someone here to care for in a fatherly way. Haley's sister, Mattie; her mother, Britanny; and her Uncle Jake fit that bill abundantly, and they care for me too. My family and I just keep looking upward. Yes, we have suffered deeply. Yes, we have been beaten down and have experienced profound loss. We still grieve, but we remain in His love and—by the grace of God—undefeated.

Pure Grace

Haley's death was blessed in a way that can be seen only with the eyes of faith. It reminds me of the line at the end of Norman Maclean's 1976 novel, *A River Runs through It*, where, reflecting on the death of his brother, he says, "Eventually, all things merge into one, and a river runs through it." I have always understood that to mean that there is one power in life that ties everything together into one lump sum and unifies us, a power that has the force of a sweet-flowing river. That river where "all things merge into one" is grace. It is not an exaggeration to say that the death of my nine-year-old grandchild from an unknown neurological disease became a *river of grace* that helped me to tie all things in my life together, to reevaluate them, and to find meaning in all of them.

I look back to that moment when we closed the casket, and I see it as the ultimate defining moment of my life. From that moment on, I had only one source of strength, and all my stubborn self-reliance fell away. I've learned to distinguish when I need to dig in and to fight for what I believe from when I need to get on my knees and to pray for mercy. I still struggle daily with certain elements of my unredeemed nature, but God has given me the weapons to fight, and it's a battle worth fighting every day of my life until the Lord calls me. In the end, I guess I have inched a little closer to the ideals of my hero Atticus Finch. I'm on that pathway to integrity, and I don't intend to get off.

Although I deeply repent of all the sins and mistakes I have made over the course of a tumultuous life—too many to mention—I don't lament those things now as I used to. They've been transformed. It's futile for me to say that I would have done things differently because it was precisely God's mercy flowing through those human weaknesses and mistakes that brought me to where I am today. I am able to throw my entire history of human weakness into the deluge of God's grace that engulfs me and ask the Lord for the strength and wisdom to turn all my mistakes in relationships, business failures, and errors of judgment into occasions of grace for others. These human failings all look different from the perspective of eternity, and it is my granddaughter Haley who has given me that gift. She has taught me that life itself is a source of joy and a gift to be given. *All is grace*, and I am content now to allow that river to flow powerfully through me and over me and in me, and to carry me through the rest of my life, doing good for others as God wills. It is a river of amazing grace welling up and gently brimming over in a radiant tide of goodness and joy; and the river runs heavenward.

In the end, I believe the ultimate goal of writing one's life story is to attempt to identify, or to define, one's true identity—who one really is and how he sees himself. For me, that's easy. Regardless of all the adventures, escapades, accomplishments, successes, and failures, my first and best destiny is to be a father and a grandfather. That has always been and still is exactly who I am. The other night, at Mattie's request, we broke out some old VHS tapes containing precious footage of Britanny and Jacob as small children. It was a joy to watch Mattie giggle and smile as she watched her Mommy and Uncle J.J. playing and enjoying themselves as kids. It soon dawned on me that my daily life hasn't changed that much in twenty to twenty-five years. What I do now is what I did then: I dedicate myself to my kids and grandkids with total commitment. I play hard in their world and love every minute of it. I try my best to be a great playmate at anything from baseball to Barbies, all the while making up story lines to serve as a backdrop to our many adventures. The only thing that has changed over the years has been my playmate. Precious little Mattie—our daily source of joy—takes the spot once occupied by her mom and uncle, and the skills that I employ with her are skills that I have honed over a lifetime, from the innocent days spent with my first baby girl, Britanny, and my little man, Jacob, to the present day. I taught her mom to ride a bike and two decades later I also taught her to ride a bike. How fortunate I am! Life comes around full circle, and for me, what a beautiful circle it is.

If I may impart some words of wisdom to any young fathers reading these pages, I say this: throughout your life, and most certainly at the end of it, you will not be sustained by any success or triumphs you may have experienced in your professional life. Money and glory are most definitely fleeting, and even praise from your peers is only of relative value and soon becomes outdated. What does last, however, is blind trust in God's perfect plan, and the sweet satisfaction of knowing that you were there with your children, in their world, as much as humanly possible, affirming them and uplifting them in the absolute, guaranteed assurance that nothing on earth means anywhere near as much to you as they do. Not even close. Strive for that and make that your identity. That's real; that lasts; that is what truly matters.

I'm part-time Collin Raye, but full-time Poppy. What a joy and blessing it is to know that I have given the best of myself to my children and grand-children and that by doing so I have been able to make them happy. That is true satisfaction; that is real success. I thank Almighty God for that reality in my life, daily.

To say that I've learned not to take my name, talents, and successes too seriously is an understatement. I not only enjoy poking fun at myself, but also enjoy Mattie's consistent, obvious indifference to the worldly reality of who her Poppy is to many other people. She is not the least bit impressed

with my stage persona or abilities. She couldn't care less about the acco-
lades hanging on the wall or displayed in my office. She just wants to play
with and be with her Poppy. I love it! I love her, and my Britanny and
Jacob, as well as our Haley, already a resident in the heavenly Kingdom
of God. With the psalmist I say, "My cup runneth over" (Ps 23:5, KJV). I
cannot grasp why He should, but God must think a lot of me ... of us ...
of everyone.

That's the real beauty of it all—everyone on earth is deeply loved.
Everyone on earth is also challenged and called by Him, but as our Lord
said, anyone who wishes to come after Him must deny himself and take up
his cross. It takes humility to hear that call, to follow it. My time-honored,
favorite saying applies here: There are two kinds of people in the world—
those who have been humbled and those who will be. But you know what?
That's okay. There's a lot to be said for thinking on your knees.

Undefeated

Darkened souls surround me; it's crazy
Nothing of this world will ever save me.
Wage it alone and start to come undone.
Then you arrive and lift me. We fight as one.

You fill my cup, when I'm used up and poured out, so depleted.
You are my light, you make things right, so I stand Undefeated ...
  Undefeated.

I know I so often doubt you,
But you don't turn away, when I'm about to.
My anger builds within and crowds me out.
Then you let go the mercy, I can't live without.

When war comes round, you stand my ground, as I fall, so mistreated.
You heal these wounds; unseal my tomb; and I rise Undefeated.
You fill my cup, when I'm used up and poured out, so depleted.
You are my light, you make things right, so I stand Undefeated.

So many lies live, on this earth. Only through your truth, I can discern.

You fill my cup, when I'm used up and poured out; so depleted.
You are my light, you make things right, so I stand Undefeated.
When war comes round, you stand my ground, as I fall, so mistreated.
Through so much rain, you keep me sane, and I remain Undefeated ...
  Undefeated.

You heal these wounds; unseal my tomb; and I'll rise Undefeated.

(Britanny Bell and Collin Raye, from the album *His Love Remains*)

Acknowledgments

[to come]

Notes

Introduction

Funeral prayer from International Commission on English in the Liturgy, *Order of Christian Funerals* (New York: Catholic Book, 1989), 162.

Chapter 5

1. Kipling Moore, "Something about a Truck", from the album *Up All Night* (Nashville: MCA, 2012).

2. Josh Kear, Mark Irwin, and Chris Tompkins, "Redneck Crazy", from the album *Redneck Crazy* (Nashville: Columbia, 2013).

3. Luke Bryan, Rachel Thibodeau, and Jason Sever, "Buzzkill", from the album *Spring Break: Here to Party* (Nashville: Capitol, 2013).

4. Carson Chamberlain, Ashley Glenn Gorley, and Wade Kirby, "All over the Road", from the album *All over the Road* (Nashville: Mercury, 2012).

5. Rodney Clawson, Christopher Tompkins, and Josh Kear, "Drunk on You", from the album *Drunk on You* (Nashville: Capitol, 2012).

6. Natalie Hemby, Shane McAnally, and Luke Laird, "Downtown", from the album *Golden* (Nashville: Capitol, 2013).

7. Luke Laird, Michael P. Heeney, and Eric Church, "Drink in My Hand", from the album *Chief* (Nashville: EMI, 2011).

Chapter 7

1. Don Schlitz and Steve Seskind, "I Think about You", from the album *I Think about You* (New York: Epic Records, 1995).

2. Transcript from YouTube video, 1:16, of Collin Raye's speech at the Thirty-Second Annual ACM Awards ceremony, 1997, posted by AwardsShowNetwork, January 21, 2011, http://www.youtube.com/watch?v=ybqjR_OSFXI, accessed 8/27/2012.

Chapter 11

1. Paul McCartney, "Golden Slumbers", from the album *Abbey Road* (Hollywood: Apple Records, 1969).

Index

[to come]

[Photo of Collin at November 1, 2012, launch
of the Haley Bell Blesséd Chair Foundation
OR photo of Haley **(to come)**]

The Haley Bell Blesséd Chair Foundation

The Haley Bell Blesséd Chair Foundation was established in memory of Haley Bell, the granddaughter of country superstar Collin Raye. Haley died in April of 2010 after a life-long battle with an undiagnosed neurological disease. She was ten years old when she died and was a constant source of light and hope to her family. Her family took her everywhere they could, a task that was only possible because of the wheelchair that was specially measured for her size, weight, and fragile frame. Haley's "Poppy", Collin, wrote the song, "She's With Me", about his beloved granddaughter, and in that beautiful tribute he calls her wheelchair, "her blesséd chair".

Collin and Haley's mother, Britanny, were inspired to begin this foundation because they wanted to provide assistance to others in need so that they will not be prevented from providing the necessities that they were so greatly blessed with while taking care of Haley in her final days. The Foundation seeks to assist families of the cognitively and physically disabled by providing them with much needed resources, particularly with wheelchairs and other necessary equipment, as well as medical help, with the purpose of enhancing their loved one's quality of life. It is the express goal of the Foundation to assist families who are struggling to meet the basic medical needs of their disabled family members due to lack of income or lack of adequate health insurance.

The Haley Bell Blesséd Chair Foundation is a program sponsored by United Charitable Programs and is a 501(c)(3) not-for-profit organization. All donations to The Haley Bell Blesséd Chair Foundation are tax-deductible to the fullest extent of the law. Those wishing to donate to the Foundation may do so through the website, www.blessedchairfoundation .org, or may write directly to the address below:

The Haley Bell Blesséd Chair Foundation
P.O. Box 1067
Lebanon, TN 37088

* * * *

Collin Raye Performances and Speaking Engagements

To book Collin Raye for your next concert or event, access the booking page on his website, www.collinraye.com/book-collin-raye/.